Francis Thayer Russell

The use of the voice in reading and speaking

A manual for clergymen and candidates for holy orders

Francis Thayer Russell

The use of the voice in reading and speaking
A manual for clergymen and candidates for holy orders

ISBN/EAN: 9783337282219

Printed in Europe, USA, Canada, Australia, Japan

Cover: Foto ©Lupo / pixelio.de

More available books at **www.hansebooks.com**

THE
USE OF THE VOICE

IN

READING AND SPEAKING:

A MANUAL
FOR
CLERGYMEN AND CANDIDATES FOR HOLY ORDERS.

BY

THE REV. FRANCIS T. RUSSELL, M. A.,

LECTURER IN ELOCUTION AT THE GENERAL THEOLOGICAL SEMINARY, NEW YORK, AND AT
THE BERKELEY DIVINITY SCHOOL, CONNECTICUT, ETC.

NEW YORK:
D. APPLETON AND COMPANY,
1, 3, AND 5 BOND STREET.
1883.

PREFACE.

The following treatise records the results of some thirty years of study and observation in the expressive uses of the voice. During that time the author has had experience, both as a clergyman and as an instructor in elocution. It has been prepared in the sincere hope that it may be of use to the Clergy and Candidates for Orders in the discharge of Divine Service.

Part I. contains exercises in vocal drill, with the statement of some of the principles of elocution, which will be found serviceable to every clergyman, if reduced to practice. The author is emboldened to make this assertion from the testimonials of many pupils, who have been brought out of imperfections in speech, and have attained to eminence as public speakers by drill of this character.

Part II. treats of the reading of the Service throughout — specifically, to a large extent, with such general directions as will cover the reading of the remainder. It might seem presumptuous, when there is so wide divergence of practice in the manner of celebrating Divine Service, for any single clergyman to attempt to suggest how the Liturgy of the Church should be read. Yet, while recognizing the value of all the musical methods, in their proper place and time, whether by *monotoning*, *intoning*, or making it purely *choral*, there is still much use for the ordinary *speaking voice*. The necessities of the case, indeed, for want of musical skill and appropriate accompaniment, generally compel the Clergy to depend upon this method. It becomes, then, simply a question whether it shall be well or ill used in public worship. The effort has been made, in this part of the work, to secure the expressive and appropriate reading of the various divisions of the Divine Service.

Part III. treats of the subject of manner. The essential elements which constitute an effective delivery are here discussed, in the hope of securing a correct standard of pulpit elocution, adapted to the nature of the sacred office and the character of its theme—free from all mannerism, affectation, and artificiality.

The author has undertaken this work at the solicitation, and with the encouragement, of many friends and pupils, and has been greatly indebted to Mr. Melville K. Bailey in preparing it for the press.

If the treatise shall aid, in any way, in making the Service more effective, and if it shall increase the usefulness of any of his brethren, the author will gratefully esteem it privileged labor that he has done.

F. T. R.

August 1, 1882.

CONTENTS.

PART I.
ELOCUTION.

                                                        PAGE

INTRODUCTION 9

CHAPTER I.

PRIMARY CONDITIONS OF VOCAL POWER . . . 11

    Physical health—Fresh air—Proper protection—Warmth—Rest—Mental quiet—Further considerations—Diet—Cold water—Condiments—Exercise—Walking—Caution against over-exertion.

CHAPTER II.

BREATHING EXERCISES 18

    Preliminary remarks—Tidal breath—First series, with reference to complete airing of the lungs—Second series, with reference to the vocal chords—Third series, with reference to the uvula—Fourth series, muscular exercises combined with breathing—Cautions.

CHAPTER III.

ARTICULATION 25

    How differing from apparently synonymous terms—Will power—Drill exercises—Rate of vibrations—Effects of professional life—Defects in speech—Further drill exercises—Result of neglect—Faults found in reading the exhortation—Further defects—In the sentences—In Scripture—Initial "h"—Difficult combinations—Example—Table of elements.

CHAPTER IV.

DELIVERY OF THE VOICE—MODE OF UTTERANCE . . 36

    Poising, or projecting the voice—Expulsive utterance—Example—Effusive utterance—Example—Explosive utterance—Example.

CONTENTS.

CHAPTER V.

THE VOICE—QUALITY 39

It is a reed instrument—Purity—Examples—Smoothness—Examples—Roundness—Examples—Fullness—Examples—Further drill exercises—The sympathetic voice.

CHAPTER VI.

FORCE 57

Degree requisite—Caution against boisterousness—Transition, to be secured by practice—Exercises—Subdued degrees—Examples—Moderate degrees—Examples—Stronger degrees—Examples—The calling voice.

CHAPTER VII.

PITCH 68

Compass of the voice, two octaves—Flexibility—Exercises—Middle pitch—Examples—Low pitch—Examples—Higher pitch—Examples.

CHAPTER VIII.

STRESS 77

Definition—Divisions of the syllable—Radical stress—Median stress—Vanishing stress—Compound stress—Thorough stress—Examples.

CHAPTER IX.

INFLECTION, OR SLIDE 85

Source of impulse—Slides of emotion—Octave—Fifth—Third—Second—The monotone—The semitone—The circumflex, or wave—Examples—Antithetic passages—Examples.

CHAPTER X.

MOVEMENT 101

Determined by subject—Inconsistency—Sameness—Moderate movement—Difficulty of description—Examples—Slow movement—Examples—Lively Movement—Examples.

CHAPTER XI.

PAUSES 113

Decided by impressiveness—Results of inattention to this element—Pause preceding emphatic word—Following it—Both—Few mechanical rules—Pause at "saying," etc.—Example.

CONTENTS.

CHAPTER XII.

EMPHASIS 117
    More than a change of force—Dependent on activity of thought and will—Examples of distinctive emphasis—Continued emphasis—Examples—Errors in emphasis—Example of various interpretations by means of emphasis—Of doctrines—The Decalogue—Examples—Further suggestions in emphasis, illustrated.

CHAPTER XIII.

MELODY 128
    Musical effect dependent on "time"—Various, at different periods of life—Examples.

PART II.

READING OF THE SERVICE.

INTRODUCTION—EXPRESSION 133
    Its importance in Divine Service—Proper mental attitude—Expression founded on feeling—Standard of expression—Not that of the stage, bar, or rostrum—Further reflections.

CHAPTER I.

ANALYSIS OF THE CHARACTERISTICS CONTAINED IN THE BOOK OF COMMON PRAYER AS A GUIDE TO EXPRESSION . . 136
    1. Sublimity and majesty—2. Simplicity—3. Reverential fervor—These must all be present in just proportion—Defect of neglecting a single principle—Fault of undue prominence of a single characteristic—Further defects: rapidity, undue slowness, business-like air, mincing tone, perfunctory style.

CHAPTER II.

THE OPENING SENTENCES, ETC., OF MORNING AND EVENING PRAYER 138
    Three leading characteristics still preserved—Fourth to last sentence—Their penitential character—The first, second, and third sentences, how differing from the others—The *Exhortation*—Its great simplicity—Different shades of feeling in different services—Personality—Must be made an exhortation—Division 1. Opening phrase—2. Statement—3. Enumeration of parts of Di-

vine worship—4. The bidding—Comparison with other exhortations—The *Confession*—Strong emphasis—Low key—Even movement—No marked individualities—The *Absolution*—It is a declaration—First sentence authoritative—Sympathy of second sentence—Deepened expression of last sentence.

CHAPTER III.

THE ANTHEMS, CREED, ETC. 148

Should be sung if possible—Full expression when read—The *Te Deum*—Divisions: 1, Praise; 2, Confession of Faith; 3, Intercession—Value of reading *Benedicite Omnia Opera Domini*—The *Creed*—Peaceful significance at the present time—Solemnity, earnestness, reverence—Each clause characteristically marked—Faults—The *Versicles* require fervent emphasis—Discussion of each.

CHAPTER IV.

THE PRAYERS 155

Subdued expression—Fitting preparation—Analysis of their structure as an aid to expression—1. Invocation: Purpose—Varied character—Simple, deep, and combined qualities—Especially to be reverent—Doctrine or narrative—Examples of invocations—2. The Petition: Supplicatory character—Expression varied according to subject of prayer—Illustrated references—3. The conclusion—The Mediatorial Name—It should be pronounced impressively and sweetly—The ascription, or *Doxology*—Discussion of individual prayers—The *Lord's Prayer*—The *Collects*—The *Thanksgivings*—Value of discussion—The *Litany*—The intensity of its character—The divisions: 1. The Invocation: appeal to the Blessed Trinity, questions as to emphasis—2. The Deprecations: emphasis and inflection, true manner of offering them—3. The Obsecrations: futile criticisms, deep solemnity—4. The Intercessions: their freedom and sympathetic tenderness, change in punctuation—5. The Supplication—Fervor is to be maintained—Earnestness—Conclusion.

CHAPTER V.

THE LESSONS 177

Suggestiveness of term — Proper manner — True standard — Faults: inexpressiveness, lack of sympathy, impropriety, dramatic effect, plaintiveness, undue refinement, mannerism, monotony—Hooker's Theory—Classification for expression: I. *According to styles of writing:* 1. Narrative and descriptive. Three heads under this division: *a*, Familiar; *b*, Elevated; *c*, Middle —2. Didactic: *a*, Epistolary; *b*, Oral and parabolic—3. Pro-

CONTENTS.

phetic: *a*, Bold; *b*, Subdued—4. Lyric—II. *According to the spirit of Fast or Festival:* Examples—III. *As suggested by the emotion:* a, Solemnity; *b*, Pathos; *c*, Consolation; *d*, Sublimity; *e*, Denunciation—IV. *As suggested by the thought*—V. *Expression by inflection:* a, Falling, for irony; *b*, Circumflex, for irony; *c*, Monotone, for awe; *d*, Falling, for denunciation—Further divisions.

THE DECALOGUE 219
    Character of Commandments—Change of utterance—The scene of giving the Decalogue—Discussion of the Commandments—Character of our Lord's words.

THE OFFERTORY 223
    Purpose of the sentences—Summary of their character; 1. Injunctions: 2. Explanatory declarations; 3. Oratorical interrogation; 4. Comforting promises; 5. Example inciting to duty—The Communion Office not further treated of.

THE BURIAL SERVICE 227
    Its perfection—Pervading solemnity—The sentences—The first anthem—The Lesson—Change of style—The second anthem—The Committal—The third anthem—The closing prayers.

PART III.

MANNER IN THE PULPIT.

INTRODUCTION 236
    Authority—Earnestness—High ideal—Physical qualifications—Moral qualifications—Sympathy—Intellectual qualification.

CHAPTER I.

ESSENTIAL REQUISITES FOR EFFECTIVENESS . . . 239
    1. *Life*—Examples—Variety—Examples—Naturalness—Example. 2. *Force*—Authority—Dignity—Freedom—Boldness—Examples. 3. *Warmth*—Love—Example—Sincerity—Examples—Cordiality—Example—Enthusiasm—Example—Reality—Example—Further considerations. 4. *Grace*—Ease—Example—Serenity—Example—Sympathy—Example—Other thoughts.

CHAPTER II.

GESTURE 274
 Scope of expression—Varied degree of power—Position of the body—Carriage of the head—Expression of the face—The arm—Primary laws of gesture—The hand—Its positions—*a.* Supine; *b.* Prone; *c.* Vertical; *d.* Clinched—Further considerations.

MISCELLANEOUS EXAMPLES 282

THE ORDER FOR DAILY MORNING PRAYER . . . 299

THE ORDER FOR DAILY EVENING PRAYER . . . 313

THE LITANY, OR GENERAL SUPPLICATION . . . 323

THE ORDER FOR THE ADMINISTRATION OF THE LORD'S SUPPER, OR HOLY COMMUNION 330

THE MINISTRATION OF BAPTISM TO SUCH AS ARE OF RIPER YEARS, AND ARE ABLE TO ANSWER FOR THEMSELVES . 341

PART I.

ELOCUTION.

INTRODUCTION.

HE who would enter the sacred ministry of Christ must consider that he will need the most intense energy in every faculty. Those powers which God has given him must all be molded and strengthened until they reach the highest perfection of which they are capable. And the bodily faculties are the medium through which all inherent spiritual power is to be impressed on the minds of the congregation, and thence driven into and implanted in their souls. We take it for granted that the strongest desire, the supreme passion of every messenger of Truth, is to command respect for his message; to strengthen the love of those who already are serving God; to reverse the course of rebellious wills; and to bring every thought of every heart into willing subjection to the great Master of souls.

The clergyman, then, as a good general, must review the whole field of his operations, and so marshal his forces and discipline his powers, that, when the hour of battle comes, he can bear through and overcome all opposing enemies. He must be continually on the alert. His foes are spiritual, the unhealthy or malicious feelings of a perverted nature. The thoughtlessness of the gay, the pride of the strong, the despair of the sorrowful, will meet him, at every hour, in the market-place, in the sick chamber, in the drawing-room, and in the church. It is his duty to meet each of these and turn it gently, but firmly and invincibly, into the way of right.

In this he will find a threefold succession of mental action : First, understanding ; then, feeling ; and, lastly, resolution. In each of these he must precede his flock, that he may lead them by experience. And a further analysis will show that in the majority of cases the resolution to the accomplishing of which all his efforts must tend is the immediate result of the feelings. And, unless he be a writer of rare power, he will find that the voice is the chief instrument in arousing the feelings after which he aims. The beneficial influence of true feeling can not be too highly estimated, and the feeling to which the spirit of the Church is so much opposed is not the tender reverence and love of the true Son of God, nor the intense and fiery energy of the prophet, but the disordered frenzy of the dervishes of Christianity, or the weak effusions of a selfish sentimentalism. It is an absurdity to speak of a religion without feeling. The thing does not exist. Not a thought can rise in the mind, not a sentence can be heard, without producing some feeling, either attractive or repellent. It is the part of the sacred speaker, then, to see that the thoughts of his people are religious, to compel them to be religious by the subtle and inevitable influence of the notes of the human voice—an instrument stringed by its Creator to be the medium of divine harmonics. To bring this instrument to its proper perfection, we must go far back to the underlying causes which are to make it effective, or mar its power. The means of this culture will be fully discussed in the succeeding chapters.

CHAPTER I.

PRIMARY CONDITIONS OF VOCAL POWER.

THE primary conditions of strength and purity of voice rest upon good physical health. The public speaker, therefore, who undertakes his work conscientiously, and with the desire and determination to use his voice naturally and effectively, must give his attention first of all to the laws of health. "We can be useful no longer than we can be well," said Dr. Johnson. The weakening influence of ill-health is most disastrous to the work of any one who is to impress his fellow-creatures through the use of the voice. Neglect of sanitary law is not only stultifying in the extreme to the highest ideal of vocality—it is positively immoral. The clergyman who forms any habits, indulges in any occupations that injure the general health, or neglects needful exercise, by so doing completely destroys his power as a speaker. It is impossible for the writer to be too explicit and emphatic on this point. If the clergyman is not disposed to make the best use of his physical gifts, then he is not aiming at the highest moral effect in the right use of his vocal powers. The faculty of speech has been bestowed, like other gifts and faculties, for use, not for abuse or neglect. We are right, then, in making this a fundamental particular in a treatise on the proper discharge of Divine Service. The directions following will assist in establishing this physical condition.

First, the necessity of securing fresh air, by exercise out of doors, and by especial attention to ventilation in the study and in the church, must be emphasized. It seems hardly worth while to state that there is scarcely a church to be found which, after an hour's use, contains a fit material for the use of the voice. The preacher enters the pulpit half exhausted, and the hearers are half wearied from a vitiated atmosphere, when both should be fresh and inspirited, the one to give and the other to receive wholesome impressions of Divine Truth. But, while securing fresh air in full and inexhaustible supplies, every public speaker should beware of speaking in a draught. The last effort in public of the most polished and cultivated speaker in New England was a fatal one to him on this account. Pure air, it should be remembered, is essential to the clear working of the brain, through the proper clarifying of the blood. And whatever affects the condition of the brain is immediately manifested in the voice. Much of the preparatory hemming and hawing, not to say hawking and spitting, which are the embarrassed orator's natural preface, comes from impurity of air. The beneficial effect of pure air upon the health and spirits, and upon the nervous system, is greater than can be stated.

Although the free use of pure air is demanded, care should be exercised, especially in the colder weather, to secure the air at a genial temperature. It is simply impossible to have the vocal organs in the right condition for work when the body is chilled. To insure the proper physical condition for public speaking, the feet should be kept warm. Thin-soled or damp shoes will impair the power of the best orator. Is it not proverbial that much of the health of the English people, of both sexes, is preserved to them by the use of thick-soled shoes? It is very dangerous for the public speaker to sit in the study when the feet are chilled. So simple a protection as a newspaper thrown over the feet during the hours of study will check the draughts on the floor of the room, and keep the head cool by keeping the feet warm. It is well for the student, who is to use his voice, to form the habit of standing during a part of his study hours, that the blood may descend to the extremities. The lamented poet Longfellow, to the last years of his life, practiced the habit of writing at a standing desk. And this custom of standing erect effects not only an easy and erect carriage of the body, but, by strengthening the abdominal and also the dorsal muscles, lessens greatly the fatigue of rendering the public Service. For the dorsal muscles have a twofold function— that of supporting the spinal column, and that of aiding the expulsory muscular action in speaking. This exercise is much more exhausting when using the voice in the kneeling posture, and hence arises the necessity of some natural strengthening discipline of these muscles. At all events, one should avoid the weakening process of their entire neglect during the week. Sitting hour after hour throughout the days of the week, and then kneeling and vocalizing with full voice in the public Service, is quite enough to tax the strength of the strongest. The nervous condition into which many speakers are thrown, during and after the effort of public speaking, can, undoubtedly, be traced to this neglect of the action and use of the dorsal muscles. This would affect the nerve centers in that vicinity of the spine, and, sympathetically, those all the way up to the brain.

While the essential conditions of warmth are insisted upon as necessary to the health of the public speaker, care should be exercised not to overheat the organs of the throat by the use of a muffler in cold weather. As an extraordinary means of protection, it may be used at times; but the continued habit of wearing a close covering for the throat softens the organs, and renders them more sensitive to the harmful influence of cold. The throat can be inured to such climatic conditions as readily as the face or hands. The rare occurrence, at present, of "clerical sore throat," and the decrease in the death-list of consumption, may be largely attributed to our more rational modern custom of leaving the throat exposed. If it be necessary to ride in the open air for any considerable distance before speaking, a newspaper buttoned under the coat will keep the chest warm, and prevent that deep chill which is so disastrous to the voice. If one is compelled to pass directly into the cold air after speaking in a heated room, then the throat should be covered; but it is much better for the speaker to remain for ten or fifteen minutes in the room where he has been exercising his voice, that the blood may be gradually cooled. We believe our advice on this point is clear. It may be summed up by saying that the throat should be left open as long as this strengthens it. When danger arises that a chill will be caused, then it should be protected.

Another essential condition for the preservation and development of the vocal powers is the recognition of nature's demand for healthful rest. The nervous system of the speaker demands it, because that, especially, is worn by the intense concentration of thought and vivid flashes, or continuous fire, of the feelings which accompany public speaking; the muscular system, because in many parts of the body, and especially in the trunk, there is a continued strain upon the muscles, which becomes the more wearisome because varied by the concussive effect of the expulsion of voice. This waste can be supplied only by the proper amount of sleep during the night, when the nerves find their recreation in rest and torpidity, the muscles theirs in quiet secretion. The speaker who exhausts his power by too little sleep, or an excess of it, is deliberately injuring his voice. Insufficient sleep leaves the nerves disturbed, and imparts a harsh, wiry quality to the voice; the excess of it causes that stupefying and sluggish circulation which renders the action of the organs labored and unwieldy, and effects the roughness of tone attending profound somnolency. A brief nap, caught even in a chair, is often a great restorative to the enfeebled energies of body and voice. Excessive or even the usual amount of labor on the day preceding public effort should be avoided. The best possible preparation for effective Sunday work is a Saturday morning of exercise, an afternoon of quiet meditation, and a night of sleep.

Harmonizing with the rest of body is the rest of spirit,

which should precede the placidity and depth of feeling expressed in Divine Service. This tranquillity should be imparted, in turn, to the voice, that through this medium the sweet influences of the Holy Spirit may be the more perfectly shed into the hearts of the hearers; and few things can be more earnestly condemned than the ill-timed haste with which some clergymen approach their divine ministrations. A rush for the vestry, a hurried and superficial glance at the Lessons, the whisking on of a surplice, the sudden assumption of a calm face over a disturbed heart, and the shepherd is ready to lead his flock into the Holy of Holies! It is impossible. A few moments, surely, of calm should precede the approach to the chancel. It is the custom of at least one effective speaker in the Church to so plan his time as to arrive in his vestry-room several minutes before service, in order that he may be seated quietly for a brief space before his work; and the best preparation for the fit rendering of Divine Service is a quiet hour of private meditation. The voice will tell its unwelcome tale in public if the clergyman neglects his duty in private.

In regard to all other matters relating to preservation of health through needful rest, the speaker should realize that the violation of nature's laws will be retributively visited upon him in spite of all efforts to secure the best culture of voice; and, among others, it should be remembered that there are few things so injurious to the voice as protracted mental exertion until late hours of the night.

Another important matter to be considered is close observation of the natural results of proper dieting. The clergy, as a class, suffer more from indigestion than any other body of men—the inevitable result of their sedentary habits and neglect of exercise. This evil is largely increased by eating indigestible food. No single rule can apply to all cases, but whatever is found to be difficult of digestion should be avoided by every man seeking the best use of his voice. The disturbance of the mucous membrane, caused by a disordered stomach, tells immediately on the vocal quality. Almost any one can satisfy himself of this by eating largely of any fatty matter, or highly spiced salads, pickles, nuts, etc. Whatever may be easily digested, that the speaker should consider sufficient nourishment as his meal before speaking. He can gratify the cravings of appetite at other times. The precise hour for using the voice after eating would depend on the condition of the stomach. Strong vocal effort should be avoided immediately after eating a hearty meal, yet it should be remembered that it will not benefit the voice to speak while fasting.

In this connection the author feels the necessity of cautioning all public speakers against the custom of drinking freely of cold water, especially iced-water, either immediately before or during the hours of speaking. It is well also to avoid, as far as possible, the use of condiments as a habit. A medicated lozenge, or even something as simple as a lump of sugar, or, better still, a taste of an orange, may be helpful at times; but to form such a habit is almost of necessity to destroy the more delicate and natural qualities of the voice, and the play of the organs in producing them. We should so drill the organs to a natural and healthful action as to make them independent of all soporifics and stimulants.

There is still another matter left which is, perhaps, of greater moment to the public speaker than any of the considerations preceding, and that is the absolute necessity of paying attention to physical exercise. No man, desirous of using his voice at the best, can accomplish this purpose without some stated exertion, which shall cause the blood to circulate freely and healthfully, and to give tone and vigor to the body. Whatever pertains to physical health immediately affects the voice. It is simply an impossibility that a clear and healthy resonance and a sustained and reserved vocal power can be secured while the bodily health is neglected. The speaker needs elasticity of spirits and physical energy if he is to acquire the magnetic power in expression. The feeble man may excite the sympathies of his congregation, but does not control or direct their thoughts through the living power of his own utterance. It must be admitted that this is to be secured only at the sacrifice of time and effort; but if the end aimed at is not worthy of this, then let the public use of the voice sink into secondary relations, and the clergyman not be blamed for the neglect of this God-given power.

Walking is said to be the natural exercise for students. Energetic gymnastic exercise with labor apparatus, or with machinery that requires the exertion of the will to secure its benefit, is not, ordinarily, the best exercise for the thinker and speaker on sacred subjects. He must deal philosophically with the profounder and greater realities of life, allure to a brighter world, and lead the way thither, and, therefore, can not be careless of the finer sensibilities. Every clergyman can learn to give his body healthful exercise by the use of the imagination, by lifting imaginary weights, reaching to the utmost height and to the greatest distance, throwing the arms open the full sweep, by clinching the fists, and energetically thrusting them forward, downward, upward, etc. By these and similar exercises he may give his body all the necessary drill required for the preservation of the voice.

A caution must be added against exercising with too much violence. The man of studious habits can not expect every fiber in his frame to have the same toughness natural to the body of a working man. He must, therefore, be careful not to take too much as well as too little exercise.

By observing these directions, a vigorous and healthful tone may be secured to the physical organization.

CHAPTER II.

BREATHING EXERCISES.

THERE can be no natural, effective, and long-sustained speaking, conducted with ease both to the speaker and to the hearer, without the proper management of the breath. And, inasmuch as public speaking exceeds in effort the ordinary colloquial use of the voice, it is necessary to keep the lungs supplied with a greater body of air for the former than for the latter. The more powerful efforts of the orator require the physical pressure of a large volume of air deep in the lungs, behind the vocal organs. The delicate uses require that the organs be well trained to emit it in proper quantities. And no less skill is required in replenishing the exhausted store-house than in emptying it effectively. The whole apparatus, from the lips to the lowest cells of the lungs, must be in vigorous condition and in perfect training, before the speaker can expect his thought to be fitly uttered. It is very seldom that men of sedentary habits have occasion to use more than the slightest supply of breath.

The *tidal breath*, so termed, is sufficient for the study, but not for the public auditorium. The prescribed exercises following will not only give full and free expansion to the lungs, but will also exercise the expulsory muscles healthfully, which are called into play in the stronger uses of the voice.*

First Series: With Reference to the Complete Airing of the Lungs.

1. Stand in the erect posture, with arms akimbo, that the weight of the shoulders may be lifted from the chest. Inhale a full breath, with the mouth closed. Exhale with

---

* In all these exercises pure air must be secured, but not the outer air, if it be cold.

BREATHING EXERCISES. 19

a moderate sigh. Repeat the exercise with regard to the *fullest supply of breath* in the inhalation, filling about five seconds of time each with the inspiration and the expiration.

2. Inhale with especial reference to the filling of the *lowest air-cells* in the lungs, and be conscious of the entering current of air as far as it can possibly reach downward. Then exhale so as to exhaust the supply from the lowest air-cells.

3. Inhale as above, *expanding outwardly* the lower air-cells as much as possible. This will cause an outward projection of the lower ribs. Expel the air as before directed, when the lungs have been filled.

4. By muscular effort raise the shoulders, and fill the lungs *upwardly.* Exhale with the downward pressure of the clavicle.

5. Inhale with especial reference to the *outward* and *forward* expansion of the chest, giving it a rounded projection, and throwing the shoulders well back and down. In the exhalation press the ribs inward and upward, so as to exhaust the supply of air.

6. Let the breath be inhaled as before, with the fullest expansion of the chest, and then *retain* it for ten seconds. In repeating the exercise, from time to time, increase the number of seconds of the retention, as far as the exercise may be carried without inconvenience.

7. Take the same exercise as above, walking a few steps across the room, with the lungs inflated, and then exhale.

8. Fill the lungs completely at one gasp.

9. Inhale as before, and exhale with a firm, voluntary action of the muscles, still employing breath, not sound. The object of this exercise is not merely to strengthen the lungs, but also to secure the proper *abdominal* action of the muscles in exhalation. Let the effort be made to exhaust the lungs by throwing the breath entirely through the nostrils. Repeat the same exercise with the mouth open, as

in the action of hearty laughter, still using the aspirated, not the vocalized, breath.

10. With the same inhalation as above, give abrupt and somewhat violent action to the abdominal muscles, so as to produce explosive breathing in the exhalation, resembling a whispered cough.

The previous exercises have primary reference to the effect of the breath upon the lungs. Other suggestions will be given below, in connection with remarks on muscular action. They will be found particularly serviceable as preliminary to the use of the voice in church. Most of them can be followed during the hours of exercise, or on the way to church, or in the vestry-room. Several pupils have expressed to the author their indebtedness for this form of exercise in warming the blood and heating the organs healthfully before the public use of the voice.

Second Series: With Reference to the Vocal Chords.

1. Inhale as before, with the nostrils, and exhale with the whispered sound of "*ah*," caused by the passage of the air over the tense vocal chords.

2. Prolong this expiration for several seconds. Sufficient practice will enable the student to easily double the number of seconds which he found sufficient for the first attempt. One beginning with fifteen seconds as the time for the first expiration will, after a few days, reach from thirty to forty-five seconds, and in a few weeks a full minute, or even more, will not be found exhausting.

3. Fill the lungs as above, and prolong the whispered "*ah*," with a free opening of the vocal chords—the same position of the organs as in sounding the lowest note of the musical scale. Then proceed from this to change the position of the organs to that employed in the production of the highest notes, graduating the exercise through several varying tones. Let the expiration be moderate in each case.

4. Fill the lungs and give the *expulsive* action to the muscles, the breath escaping through the larynx, instead of the nose, as in Exercise 9, First Series.

5. Inspire as above, making a complete occlusion of the vocal chords, and then let the breath be forced out with an *explosive* effort.

Caution.—The two exercises following must be practiced moderately to avoid injury:

6. Inhale with the mouth open, the breath being drawn across the vocal chords so as to be audible, but not properly vocal, making the same effort to produce different notes on the musical scale, with the sound of "*ah.*"

7. Inhale and exhale rapidly, as in panting.

Third Series: With reference to the Uvula.

1. With the uvula *pendent*, sound the lowest aspirated note of the syllable "*aw.*"

2. *Elevate* the uvula, and give the breath an acute sound on the high pitch, with the syllable "*ah.*"

It is a good custom to open and close the breathing exercises with some moderate inhalations and exhalations, the mouth being closed. This closed position should be observed as a rule in the greater part of the exercises. It should also be remembered as a healthful position of the organs for natural breathing, especially in sleep. Any public speaker can verify this assertion by observing the difference between the effect on the voice succeeding the natural position and that following prolonged and slothful slumber, sleep after great fatigue, or attacks of biliousness or indigestion. In the latter conditions the mouth is frequently thrown open, and the effect upon the voice is very different from that which comes after restful sleep with the mouth tightly closed.

Fourth Series: Muscular Exercises combined with Breathing.

1. Fill the lungs completely, and exhale with a strong expulsive effort, so as to project the stream of breath as far as possible. This is a strong form of delivering the exhalation, in the manner known by the boys as "seeing the breath" on a frosty morning.

2. It is very important that the public speaker should have an an erect carriage of the body. He thus not merely secures the full play of the lungs, and avoids the cramped position of the abdomen, which, in time, affects the organs of digestion, but cultivates, at the same time, that upright bearing of the body which is one of the attractive features in public speaking. An enfeebled look or carriage of the body, especially when aggravated by the stooping posture which stomachic disorders naturally produce, sadly detracts from the manly and commanding effects of the orator. All public speakers should acquire, by every effort of will, and at whatever cost of time and exertion, the power to *stand erect*. One of the best exercises to secure this erect carriage, and one which will certainly so result if persisted in, is the following : Stand against some perpendicular surface, and then inhale and hold a full breath, carrying the chin down and in, and the brow back, the heels, head, and all parts of the body being pressed firmly against this surface. Then walk around the room a few times, with the lungs still inflated, and the body held at the undeviating line directed, and return to the former position to see if there has been any variation from the perpendicular. The head and heels should touch the surface simultaneously on returning, in this test. In order to secure the straightest line for this measurement, a door may be opened, and the edge used for the normal line. If this exercise be persisted in as a daily drill, it will, almost by necessity, straighten the form.

BREATHING EXERCISES. 23

3. Every public speaker inclined to the stooping posture, that he may secure the proper carriage, should take especial pains to see that his *sitting* posture is also erect. If the spinal column is pressed against the back of a chair, it will result as above. Chairs with curved backs and scooping seats, particularly the "American rocking-chair," are very injurious to the habits of the speaker in their effect upon the body. If absolute rest is at any time required, it is better to recline at full length than to sit in a cramped position. Chairs with stuffed backs heat the spine, and must, therefore, be avoided.

4. Fill the lungs, and hold the chest full, *tapping* it gently all over with the tips of the fingers.

5. Then, inflating and holding the lungs full as before, *slap* the chest gently with the open hand.

6. Expand as above, and *beat* gently with the fists, with light, elastic blows, so as to make the chest resound.

7. Inflate the lungs, and *press firmly* upon the chest at different parts, as if to break down the muscular resistance of the expansion.

8. Inhale a full breath, set the abdominal muscles on tension, and press against them firmly with the tips of the fingers, so as to feel strongly the resistance.

9. Inflating as before, slap with a light blow of the open hand all the surface of the chest, and as far down as the abdomen.

10. Repeat as above, using the fist gently, and increasing the strength of the blow as the power of resistance increases.

11. Inflate the lungs fully, while extending and moving the arms up gradually from the sides to the highest reach, keeping them perfectly straight.

12. Exhaust the supply of breath, throw the arms up as before, and inhale as they gradually descend to the sides, keeping them open.

13. Exhale, extend the arms in front, with the palms

of the hands together, and inhale while extending the arms on an horizontal line as far back as they can be thrown.

14. Having placed the palms together, as before, inhale while throwing the arms outward and downward.

15. Clinch the fists, raise them to the sides of the chest, and exhale while thrusting the arms forward, at the full length.

16. Inhale with the arms *forward*. Inhale with a gasp while throwing the arms *backward* energetically.

17. With the arms akimbo, fill the lungs, and throw the chest forward and downward as far as possible, retaining the breath. Exhaust the air in the same posture. Inhale while recovering the erect posture.

18. Inflate fully, with the arms akimbo and the heels together, and, retaining the breath, throw the head as far backward as possible.

19. Exhaust the lungs, throw the head back as before, and inhale during the recovery to the erect posture.

20. Stand in the erect posture, with the hands at the sides, lean far to the right while inhaling, and recover posture with the lungs full.

21. Repeat the same exercise, inclining the body to the left.

The above movements should, in every case, be moderately and deliberately practiced until there is sufficient reserved force to increase the violence of the exercise. In all vocal drill, and in all muscular exercise affecting it, no violence should be done at the beginning or at the ending of the discipline by sudden efforts of any kind. Great injury may result from a disregard of this simple direction.

The same care should be used in regard to the number of the exercises. It is not well to indulge in an excessive amount at one time. It may be thought that unnecessary attention is given to the breathing exercises, and those accompanying them; but it should be remembered that the lungs are the bellows to supply the air, and that, when the chest is flexible, and the muscles moving it strong and pliable, the voice will be accordingly benefited by it.

CHAPTER III.

ARTICULATION.

After securing the proper management of the breath, *distinct articulation* is the next excellence to be sought by the public speaker. This has reference, first, to the simple action of the muscles in the articulating process. Like a well-formed joint, the syllable fits into its place in the word, and so moves without hindrance to the ear. Imperfect or unfinished articulation might be termed disjointed. The syllables do not fit into their sockets. And it should be observed that, inasmuch as this relates purely to the muscular action, it is distinct from *enunciation*, which has reference to the sound of the syllable, or *pronunciation*, which decides the correct accent, etc., according to established usage.

Faulty articulation is the result of an imperfect action of the will-power, through inadvertence or inattention, for, in almost every instance, it is a possible thing to articulate, if the speaker wills to do so. Too much care given to this matter becomes quite apparent as a defect. The schoolmaster's pedantic and labored style is plainly the result of paying too close attention to the mechanical action in speech. The following exercises are set down as valuable in this connection:

1. A useful drill-exercise is to give the action of the organs in the articulation of the letters of the alphabet by forming the syllables silently as they occur in a word, but uttering no sound. Articulate the alphabet in this way,

not whispering the elements, nor naming them, but giving them simply the function of silent formation. Let this be repeated with varying degrees of force, from moderate to strongest, and with different rates of movement, from slow to quickest. Practice also with the vocal chords set in the different positions required for varied pitch.

2. Then name the letters of the alphabet, with the varying degrees of force, movement, and pitch, as above.

3. Articulate vocally the separate syllables of a word in succession, e. g., those of the word "*elocution*," giving the successive syllables "*ĕl*," "*ō*," "*cū*," "*tion*." Practice any other words in the same way.

4. Articulate the sounds formed by varying position of the mouth. The following brief table will illustrate the author's meaning, and describe the position of the mouth referred to:

"*Ah*," formed by the widest opening; "*aw*," formed by sinking of the larynx and projection of the lips; "*ă*," formed by drawing the corners of the mouth back; "*ē*," formed with the mouth nearly closed, and the tongue raised in the mouth.

The same study in the position of the organs may be followed with other sounds.

It has been demonstrated by the distinguished scientist Helmholtz, with the aid of ingenious apparatus, that the vowel sounds are each formed by a certain number of vibrations per second of the air propelled in breath. Madame Seiler, his former assistant, now resident in this country, in her work entitled "The Voice in Speaking," has carried this theory still further, and applied it to the consonants. This is testified to by the natural key of the sound of each letter. Imperfections in the sound of elements and syllables is, therefore, the result of an insufficient or excessive number of vibrations employed in forming them, together with the position of the vocal organs. It is not our purpose to enter into any discussion of this matter, but simply to suggest to those who are scientifically or musically interested how the different tones may be formed or their accuracy verified. The references should fix our attention, however, on the fact that the delivery of the correct sound of a syllable requires very delicate action and exact position of the organs. The slightest departure from the standard impairs the accuracy of the sound. When the will of the speaker is inert, and the ear dull, indistinctness results by necessity. This is well illustrated when a person, speaking carelessly, fails to convey a single intelligible word in an entire sentence. The attention of the speaker having been called to this by a request for repetition, he exerts more will, pays closer attention to his utterance, and every syllable becomes distinctly audible. The custom of speaking distinctly, whether in public or in private, may be acquired, as other habits are, by repetition. If the student will but drill himself on the utterance of a single word, giving it clearly and distinctly, he will find the effect quite apparent, after practicing a short time, whenever he has occasion to use the word. The effect of any given mental occupation, or style of delivering thought, upon the manner of speaking, is quite evident in the professions. A schoolmaster, who, for a series of years, has given himself to explicit directions and explanations, and the lawyer, whose custom it is to be emphatically exact in imparting his thought, both show the effect of such professional life.

Defects in speech, if serious, require professional aid to overcome them; but ordinary indistinctness and the slighter impediments may be easily remedied by obeying the directions following:

1. Fasten the attention upon the syllable or word, and utter it with the determined purpose to make it clear and distinct.

2. A preliminary pause will often untwist the chains that tie the tongue, or enable them to untwist themselves.

3. Draw a deep inspiration, to relax the contraction of the nerves and muscles.

4. Mark the time rhythmically for the delivery, somewhat in the style of recitative in music.

5. Form the words in the front of the mouth, rather than in the back of it or the throat, if the elements admit of it.

No speaker should willingly content himself with anything less than such clear articulation as would render every word distinctly audible to every listener.

And yet, while every one would be willing to admit the value and the necessity of this distinctness, probably not one in twenty is heard in every word of the Service by the entire congregation. This is unpardonable negligence on the part of the speaker, and, in many cases, an intolerable annoyance to the hearer. It is not surprising that many in a congregation will not distress themselves to make the special effort to catch the words, when the clergyman himself will not make the necessary exertion to distinctly articulate them.

The acquisition of a distinct articulation lies within the power of every speaker, and he is voluntarily and culpably diminishing his effectiveness by tolerating anything less than a clear and emphatic delivery of every sound in every syllable. Any one can test the matter for himself, by questioning his sexton, or other church officer at the rear of the building, as to whether every word penetrates to the farthest corner. If he will read aloud to himself some such familiar passage as the Exhortation of the Daily Service, he will probably observe a tendency to slight some of the minor syllables, and especially such little words as *and*, *of*, *the*, etc.

That we do not over-state the charges against imperfect articulation will be apparent to any one who will examine a not uncommon reading of the Exhortation. The *a* in *acknowledge* is often given with the short sound of *e* or *i*— *ecknowledge* or *icknowledge*. The *d* in *and* following, and, in a majority of its uses throughout the Service, is commonly dropped altogether, making *an'*. The *a* in the same word is very commonly supplanted by a short *u*, resulting in *und;* and, even still more commonly, both the *a* and the *d* being elided, gives the mere suggestion of the word in the single letter '*n*'. The next word suffers in the first syllable, *o* being elided. The two *ands* following suffer as the first; *nor* becomes *nur*, and, by a change in the first syllable, *Almighty* becomes *Ul*-mighty, or *Ol*-mighty for *All*-mighty. The provincialisms of New England incline us, by using the short *a* in *Father*, to pronounce it *Fäther*, and, in some of the western and southern States, *Fawther*, in place of the beautiful Italian *ä* of Fäther. Continuing, we find *c'nfess* again for *confess, an' obedient* for *and obedient, ubtain* for *obtain, furgiveness an' mercy*, instead of *forgiveness and mercy. Acknowledge*, as above; *an' meet, an' necessary, an' beseech, unt' th' throne*, for *and meet, and necessary, and beseech, unto the throne*, follow in order. In remedying these defects, the student should guard against the fault of producing emphasis by force or labored articulation, and distorting a syllable thus: *A*cknowledge, *a*nd, *c*onfess, *n*or, *All*-mighty, *o*btain, *for*giveness. Read the Exhortation with reference to distinctness of articulation:

"Dearly beloved brethren, the Scripture moveth us, in sundry places, to acknowledge and confess our manifold sins and wickedness; and that we should not dissemble nor cloak them before the face of Almighty God, our heavenly Father; but confess them with an humble, lowly, penitent, and obedient heart; to the end that we may obtain forgiveness of the same, by his infinite goodness and mercy. And although we ought, at all times, humbly to acknowledge our sins before God; yet ought we chiefly so to do, when we assemble and meet together to render thanks for the great benefits that we have received at his hands, to set forth his most worthy praise, to hear his most holy Word, and to ask those things which are requisite and necessary, as well for the body as the soul. Wherefore I pray and beseech you, as many as are here present, to accompany me with a pure heart, and humble voice, unto the throne of the heavenly grace, saying—"

Further defects in Articulation to be avoided. — Observe the tendency to slur *of the* and *unto the* in the second of the Opening Sentences. The sublimity and majesty, in the expression of this Sentence, are seriously impaired by the imperfect utterance of any of the unemphatic syllables. It imparts the effect of the cessation of the authoritative utterance for the moment. In the fourth Sentence say *com*mitted, not *cum*mitted; lawful *and* right, not lawful *an'* right. In the eighth Sentence, *and* repenteth, not *an'* repenteth. In the tenth Sentence *corr*ect, not *curr*ect. In the twelfth, all the *ands* should be carefully observed in their distinctness, though not rendered with emphasis. In the last Sentence, *con*fess and *for*give, in place of the same words with the short sound of *u*. Review the Sentences with this in mind:

Second Sentence: "From the rising *of the* sun even *unto the* going down *of the* same, my Name shall be great among the Gentiles; and in every place incense shall be offered unto my Name, and a pure offering: for my Name shall be great among the heathen, saith the LORD of hosts."

Fourth Sentence: "When the wicked man turneth away from his wickedness that he hath *committed*, and doeth that which is lawful *and* right, he shall save his soul alive."

Eighth Sentence: "Rend your heart, and not your garments, and turn unto the LORD your God; for he is gracious and merciful, slow to anger, and of great kindness, *and* repenteth him of the evil."

Tenth Sentence: "O LORD, *correct* me, but with judgment; not in thine anger, lest thou bring me to nothing."

Twelfth Sentence: "I will arise, *and* go to my father,

and I will say unto him, Father, I have sinned against heaven, *and* before thee, *and* am no more worthy to be called thy son."

Fourteenth Sentence: " If we say that we have no sin, we deceive ourselves, and the truth is not in us; but if we *confess* our sins, God is faithful and just to *forgive* us our sins, and to cleanse us from all unrighteousness."

It is not necessary to repeat the many instances in which the same syllables given above are repeated throughout the Service. The same care should, of course, be observed wherever they may occur.

The omission of the initial *h* of the pronouns in the Gospel narrative is another fault: " Then took *h*e *H*im up in *h*is arms, and blessed *H*im."

Read the following narrative with reference to the pronunciation of the *h* in every pronoun:

" And he cometh to Bethsaida; and they bring a blind man unto him, and besought him to touch him. And he took the blind man by the hand, and led him out of the town; and when he had spit on his eyes, and put his hands upon him, he asked him if he saw aught. And he looked up, and said, I see men as trees, walking. After that he put his hands again upon his eyes, and made him look up; and he was restored, and saw every man clearly. And he sent him away to his house, saying, Neither go into the town, nor tell it to any in the town."—St. Mark, viii, 22–26.

Difficult Combinations.—" Who hast kept with Thy servant David my father, that Thou promisedst him: Thou spakest also with Thy mouth, and hast fulfilled it with Thine hand, as it is this day. Therefore, now, Lord God of Israel, keep with thy servant David my father, that Thou promisedst him, saying, There shall not fail thee a man in My sight to sit on the throne of Israel."—1 Kings, viii, 24, 25.

"The smith with the tongs both worketh in the coals,

and fashioneth it with hammers, and worketh it with the strength of his arms: yea, he is hungry, and his strength faileth; he drinketh no water, and is faint. The carpenter stretcheth out his rule, he marketh it out with a line, he fitteth it with planes, and he marketh it out with the compass, and maketh it after the figure of a man, according to the beauty of a man; that it may remain in the house."—Isaiah, xliv, 12, 13.

" Thou art the Lord the God, who didst choose Abram, and broughtest him forth out of Ur of the Chaldees, and gavest him the name of Abraham; and foundest his heart faithful before Thee, and madest a covenant with him, . . . and didst see the affliction of our fathers in Egypt, and heardest their cry by the Red Sea, and shewedst signs and wonders upon Pharaoh and on all his servants, . . . so didst Thou get Thee a name, as it is this day. And Thou didst divide the sea before them, so that they went through the midst of the sea on dry land. . . . Thou camest down also upon Mount Sinai, and spakest with them from heaven, and gavest them right judgments, . . . and madest known unto them Thy holy Sabbath, and commandedst them precepts, . . . and gavest them bread from heaven, . . . and broughtest forth water for them out of the rock for their thirst, and promisedst them that they should go in to possess the land. . . . Their children also multipliedst Thou as the stars of heaven, and broughtest them into the land concerning which Thou hadst promised to their fathers. . . . Nevertheless they were disobedient, . . . therefore Thou deliveredst them into the hand of their enemies, and in the time of their trouble when they cried unto Thee Thou heardest them, . . . and gavest them saviours, who saved them out of the hand of their enemies. Yet many years didst Thou forbear them, and testifiedst against them by Thy Spirit in Thy prophets: yet would they not give ear: therefore gavest Thou them into the hand of the people of the lands."—Nehemiah, ix, 7–30.

"The mirth of tabret ceaseth, the noise of them that rejoice endeth, the joy of the harp ceaseth."

"This man ceaseth not to speak blasphemous words against this holy place and the law."

"What advantageth it me?"

"Lord, show us the Father, and it sufficeth us."

"So soon passeth it away, and we are gone."

"When thou wast young, thou girdedst thyself, and walkedst whither thou wouldest, but when thou shalt be old, thou shalt stretch forth thine hands, and another shall gird thee, and carry thee whither thou wouldest not."

"Inestimable benefit," "inestimable love," "all our sins, negligences, and ignorances," "innumerable benefits," "and that we may obtain our petitions, make us to ask such things as shall please Thee."

The above and similar passages, and especially all those combinations of the elements of the language which, on account of the structure of the vocal organs, or from careless habit, each individual may have found difficult to utter with ease and distinctness, should be resolutely corrected by frequent repetition, and with varied uses of the voice, until the desired power of execution is acquired. Steady practice will in time overcome all such difficulties, while protracted neglect may result in confirming nervous and muscular impediments, which, in the course of years of inattention, will be likely to become ineradicable.

As a drill exercise, the tables of elements, syllables, and words in "Vocal Culture" will be found of the greatest value. As an exercise in the formation of the vowel sounds, the repetition of the sounds beginning with $\bar{e}$, which requires the closest position, continuing with $\bar{a}$, which directs the breath about midway in the mouth, followed by *ah*, *awe*, *ōh*, and *oo*, we shall find all the spaces filled in succession from the front of the mouth to the larynx. The repetition with vocal effect, beginning with $\bar{e}$, as suggested, and closing with *oo*, and then repeating inversely, will train the ear to detect the changes in sound and the voice in producing them.

The forcible articulation with rapid repetitions of the sound of *b*, *g* hard, and *d*, has a tendency to strengthen the organs for articulation.

Another useful drill for securing distinctness in the articulation is to separate the words from their meaning by repeating them in inverse order in the sentences in which they occur. The attention is thus drawn to the sound of each word, so that the syllables are not liable to suffer from the divided attention which is given to the meaning, as they stand in connected order

These and similar exercises, if persisted in, will produce marked results in the course of a few weeks of practice.

The passage from the Acts, containing so many repetitions of the word *and*, is a useful study for distinctness in articulating this word. The author recalls the reading of this portion of Scripture where the reader failed to articulate a single *and* distinctly :

"And certain men which came down from Judea taught the brethren, and said, Except ye be circumcised after the manner of Moses, ye cannot be saved. When therefore Paul and Barnabas had no small dissension and disputation with them, they determined that Paul and Barnabas, and certain other of them, should go up to Jerusalem unto the apostles and elders about this question. And being brought on their way by the church, they passed through Phenice and Samaria, declaring the conversion of the Gentiles : and they caused great joy unto all the brethren.

"And when they were come to Jerusalem, they were received of the church, and of the apostles and elders, and they declared all things that God had done with them. But there rose up certain of the sect of the Pharisees which believed, saying, That it was needful to circumcise them, and to command them to keep the law of Moses. And the apostles and elders came together for to consider of this matter. And when there had been much disputing, Peter rose up, and said unto them, Men and brethren, ye know how that a good while ago God made choice among us, that the Gentiles by my mouth should hear the word of the gospel, and believe. And God, which knoweth the hearts, bare them witness, giving them the Holy Ghost, even as he did unto us ; and put no difference between us and them, purifying their hearts by faith."—Acts, xv, 1–9.

Great benefit may be derived from drill upon the elements of the language, classified for practice with reference to vocal exercise, in the following table :

Tonics.		Subtonics.		Atonic.	
A,	*A*ll.	*L*,	*L*ull.	*P*,	*P*ipe.
A,	*A*rm.	*M*,	*M*aim.	*T*,	*T*ent.
A,	*A*n.	*N*,	*N*un.	*C* and *K*,	*C*ake.
E,	*E*ve.	*R*,	*R*ap.	*F*,	*F*ife.
OO,	*O*oze.	*R*,	*F*ar.	*C* and *S*,	*C*ease.
OO,	*L*ook.	*Ng*,	Si*ng*.	*H*,	*H*e.
E,	*E*rr.	*B*,	*B*abe.	*Th*,	*Th*in.
E,	*E*nd.	*D*,	*D*id.	*Sh*,	Pu*sh*.
I,	*I*n.	*G*,	*G*ag.	*Ch*,	*Ch*urch.
Ai,	*Ai*r.	*V*,	*V*alve.		
U,	*U*p.	*Z*,	*Z*one.		
O,	*O*r.	*Z*,	*A*zure.		
O,	*O*n.	*Y*,	*Y*e.		
A,	*A*le.	*W*,	*W*oe.		
I,	*I*ce.	*Th*,	*Th*en.		
O,	*O*ld.	*J*,	*J*oy.		
Ou,	*Ou*r.				

CHAPTER IV.

DELIVERY OF THE VOICE.—MODE OF UTTERANCE.

IF the speaker were to deliver his sentences with the intention of making them heard by the most distant person in the house, as though he were addressing him personally, and very much as he would do if he were requesting such a hearer to open the window, close the door, call the sexton, or the like, he would secure the right idea of the proper poising or projecting of the voice. In the strongest form of such a delivery we should find the sustained force of the calling voice. This is useful as a drill exercise; but the speaker is not a "caller," in the use of his vocal organs. It is simply referred to here as the natural direction for the suggestive ideal of the delivery which is to fill the building. It is to give the power of throwing out or projecting the voice into the house, remembering that, if we make the most distant person hear, our words will be audible to all others in the room. The empty-voiced, inaudible speaker is not necessarily one of weak organization, for the weak voice of a child will often fill a large auditorium with most unwelcome clearness. But he fails to throw out the voice, like that of the classical hero, or Macbeth's "Amen," which stuck in his throat. The sound seems to be caught, and unable to get forth from the speaker's lips. It is not the retention of the breath, but its delivery; it is not suppression, but literally *ex*-pression of the voice, at which the speaker aims. This is the ideal of all heraldic effect, to lift up the voice without fear, and boldly to deliver the message of the King. And it is the function of public speaking, as distinguished from the retention of the breath in conversation. This effort of throwing out the voice requires a strong action of the expulsory muscles, and is properly termed expulsive utterance. The exercises given below are for expulsive delivery of the breath in the expression.

Morning Hymn to Mont Blanc.—Coleridge.
"Thou too, hoar Mount! with thy sky-pointing peaks,
Oft from whose feet the avalanche, unheard,
Shoots downward, glittering through the pure serene
Into the depth of clouds that veil thy breast—
Thou too, again, stupendous Mountain! thou
That as I raise my head, awhile bowed low
In adoration, upward from thy base
Slow traveling with dim eyes suffused with tears,
Solemnly seemest, like a vapory cloud,
To rise before me—Rise, O ever rise,
Rise like a cloud of incense, from the Earth!
Thou kingly Spirit throned among the hills,
Thou dread ambassador from Earth to Heaven,
Great hierarch! tell thou the silent sky,
And tell the stars, and tell yon rising sun,
Earth, with her thousand voices, praises God!"

In contrast with this energetic delivery we find that more tranquil expression which befits the unimpassioned, profound depths of quiet feeling, the serenity of composed states of heart and mind, or the gentler and more tender emotions. This is the chastened utterance appropriate to the expression of prayer. The delivery of the breath is a gentle effusion, without impulsive energy, and flows as evenly as the undisturbed current of a stream. In all cases where this mode of utterance is naturally required, the preceding style of expulsion will be utterly destructive to the vocal expression of the feeling. All the charm of this style depends upon the equable flow and even pressure of the sound.

Evening in the Grave-yard.
"I've seen the moon climb the mountain's brow,
  I've watched the mists o'er the river stealing,
But ne'er did I feel in my breast, till now,
  So deep, so calm, and so holy a feeling:

'Tis soft as the thrill which memory throws
Athwart the soul in the hour of repose.

"Thou Father of all ! in the worlds of light,
  Fain would my soul aspire to Thee ;
And, through the scenes of this gentle night,
  Behold the dawn of Eternity :
For this is the path which Thou hast given—
The only path to the bliss of heaven."

The more violent and excited states of feeling call for explosive utterance of the syllables. It is the clear, abrupt shock given to the sound which results from the strongest muscular pressure brought to bear upon the organs, and through which occlusions the impetuosity of the feeling bursts its way. The percussion which is produced by this muscular action strengthens the vocal delivery, and summons the full power of expression to instantaneous action. It bursts upon the ear with a startling, electric effect, and is one of the results to be secured by patient practice. The student, while avoiding gentle effusion, should also pass beyond the more energetic expulsion to the abruptness and percussion of this bolder style of explosive expression. It is a power very seldom called into play in the pulpit, but, when required by the emergency of some excited feeling, or some terse, pointed emphasis of thought, should be prepared to respond to the demands of the speaker and his theme.

"On, ye brave,
Who rush to glory and the grave !
Wave, Munich, all thy banners wave,
And charge with all thy cavalry !

"Strike till the last armed foe expires,
Strike for your altars and your fires,
Strike for the green graves of your sires,
    God, and your native land !"

CHAPTER V.

THE VOICE.—QUALITY.

It is a well-established theory that the organs of the voice form a reed instrument, the trachea and larynx corresponding to the tube, and the vocal chords to the reeds. The air, already vibrating by its movement from the distant air-cells, and gathering volume in its course, becomes compressed at the vocal chords. It is at this moment that the column of breath, passing over the vibrating chords, set in motion by the pressure, has intensity added to its motion, and produces sound. By the combined tension or relaxation of the vocal chords it is modified as acute or grave, and is furthermore rendered high or low in pitch, soft or loud in force, full or attenuated, according to the nature of the feeling expressed, or the will of the speaker. The sound is mechanically produced by the position of the larynx, moved by its controlling muscles, the depression or elevation of the tongue, or uvula, or both, and by the direction of the breath upward into the head or roof of the mouth, into the cheeks, or against the tip of the tongue. The quality of a good, manly voice is naturally pure, smooth, round, and full. It is morally expressive and sympathetic, and physically flexible and varied in sound. A defective voice is aspirated, harsh, sharp, or wiry, and in some voices all these faults are combined. It is, furthermore, unsympathetic and monotonous in delivery. The speaker should test the quality of his voice so as to satisfy himself that it possesses no defect which he can remedy. It is well, therefore, to drill the voice with reference to the various elements of excellence. The following exercises will serve both to establish a standard of comparison and to shape the voice in agreement with it.

I. In order to cultivate purity of sound, deep and free breathing is almost a necessity. In reading the extracts below, let the greatest effort be made to produce a voice absolutely clear and pure in sound. Any particle of breath which is not vocalized injures the effect, and, when excessive, fairly smothers the voice. Practice upon the words "*pure*" and "*clear*," on various keys, and with varying degrees of force, until they suggest to the mind what they name. The reading of poetry, where there is no strongly excited feeling, is a help to the development of purity of tone. The gentleness of feeling contained in the extract following suggests the lighter and purer uses of the voice:

1. *The Sleep.*—Mrs. *Browning.*

"Of all the thoughts of God that are
 Borne inward unto souls afar,
 Along the Psalmist's music deep—
 Now tell me if there any is,
 For gift or grace, surpassing this—
 'He giveth His beloved sleep'?

"What would we give to our beloved?
 The hero's heart, to be unmoved—
 The poet's star-tuned harp, to sweep—
 The senate's shout to patriot vows—
 The monarch's crown, to light the brows?
 'He giveth His beloved sleep.'

"What do we give to our beloved?
 A little faith, all undisproved—
 A little dust, to overweep—
 And bitter memories, to make
 The whole earth blasted for our sake!
 'He giveth His beloved sleep.'

"'Sleep soft, beloved!' we sometimes say,
 But have no tune to charm away
 Sad dreams that through the eyelids creep;
 But never doleful dream again
 Shall break the happy slumber, when
 'He giveth His beloved sleep.'"

In the example below, as the expression is that of mere intellectual communication, the light voice of the head, or pure tone, is the natural quality for the reading of the extract:

2. *Of Studies.—Bacon.*

"Read not to contradict and confute, nor to believe and take for granted, nor to find talk and discourse, but to weigh and consider. Some books are to be tasted, others to be swallowed, and some few to be chewed and digested; that is, some books are to be read only in parts; others to be read, but not curiously; and some few to be read wholly, and with diligence and attention. Some books also may be read by deputy, and extracts made of them by others; but that would be only in the less important arguments and the meaner sort of books; else distilled books are, like common distilled waters, flashy things. Reading maketh a full man; conference a ready man; and writing an exact man; and, therefore, if a man write little, he had need have a great memory; if he confer little, he had need have a present wit; and if he read little, he had need have much cunning, to seem to know that he doth not."

The following sentences from the Daily Service, being explanatory, and therefore intellectual rather than emotional, require the use of the head tone:

3. "When the wicked man turneth away from his wickedness that he hath committed, and doeth that which is lawful and right, he shall save his soul alive."

4. "If we say that we have no sin, we deceive ourselves, and the truth is not in us; but if we confess our sins, God is faithful and just to forgive us our sins, and to cleanse us from all unrighteousness."

The Preface to Confirmation being a simple statement (originally a rubric), is sufficiently expressed with purity of tone.

Preface to Confirmation.

5. "To the end that Confirmation may be administered to the more edifying of such as shall receive it, the Church hath thought good to order, That none shall be confirmed but such as can say the Creed, the Lord's Prayer, and the Ten Commandments; and can also answer to such other Questions as in the Short Catechism are contained: which order is very convenient to be observed; to the end, that children, being now come to the years of discretion, and having learned what their Godfathers and Godmothers promised for them in Baptism, may themselves, with their own mouth and consent, openly before the Church, ratify and confirm the same; and also promise, that, by the grace of God, they will evermore endeavor themselves faithfully to observe such things as they, by their own confession, have assented unto."

The tranquillity and simplicity of the feeling expressed in the twenty-third Psalm find their natural expression through the medium of pure tone.

6. "The Lord is my shepherd; therefore can I lack nothing. He shall feed me in a green pasture, and lead me forth beside the waters of comfort. He shall convert my soul, and bring me forth in the paths of righteousness for his Name's sake. Yea, though I walk through the valley of the shadow of death, I will fear no evil; for thou art with me; thy rod and thy staff comfort me. Thou shalt prepare a table before me against them that trouble me; thou hast anointed my head with oil, and my cup shall be full. But thy loving kindness and mercy shall follow me all the days of my life; and I will dwell in the house of the Lord for ever."—Psalm xxiii.

The tenderness of the reverential feeling and the expressive sympathy of the three opening verses of the sixty-first chapter of the Prophecy of Isaiah, find expression naturally through the head-voice, as fullness and weight of sound would be destructive to the tenderness and sympathy of the entire passage.

7. "The Spirit of the Lord God is upon me; because the Lord hath anointed me to preach good tidings unto the meek; he hath sent me to bind up the broken-hearted, to proclaim liberty to the captives, and the opening of the prison to them that are bound; to proclaim the acceptable year of the Lord, and the day of vengeance of our God; to comfort all that mourn; to appoint unto them that mourn in Zion, to give unto them beauty for ashes, the oil of joy for mourning, the garment of praise for the spirit of heaviness; that they might be called trees of righteousness, the planting of the Lord, that he might be glorified."

The simplicity and familiarity of the style of the Scriptural narrative in the ninth chapter of St. John's Gospel, demand pure tone.

8. "And as Jesus passed by, he saw a man which was blind from his birth. And his disciples asked him, saying, Master, who did sin, this man, or his parents, that he was born blind? Jesus answered, Neither hath this man sinned, nor his parents: but that the works of God should be made manifest in him. I must work the works of him that sent me, while it is day: the night cometh, when no man can work. As long as I am in the world, I am the light of the world. When he had thus spoken, he spat on the ground, and made clay of the spittle, and he anointed the eyes of the blind man with the clay, and said unto him, Go, wash in the pool of Siloam, (which is by interpretation, Sent). He went his way therefore, and washed, and came seeing. The neighbors therefore, and they which before had seen him that he was blind, said, Is not this he that sat and begged? Some said, This is he: others said, He is like him: but he said, I am he. Therefore said they unto him, How were thine eyes opened? He answered and said, A man that is called Jesus made clay, and anointed mine eyes, and said unto me, Go to the pool of Siloam, and wash:

and I went and washed, and I received sight. Then said they unto him, Where is he? He said, I know not."—St. John, ix., 1–12.

The pathetic pleading of Judah before Joseph finds its emotional expression in the same tendency to head-voice, or pure tone.

9. "And Judah said, What shall we say unto my lord? what shall we speak? or how shall we clear ourselves? God hath found out the iniquity of thy servants: behold, we are my lord's servants, both we, and he also with whom the cup is found. And he said, God forbid that I should do so: but the man in whose hand the cup is found, he shall be my servant; and as for you, get you up in peace unto your father. Then Judah came near unto him, and said, O my lord, let thy servant, I pray thee, speak a word in my lord's ears, and let not thine anger burn against thy servant: for thou art even as Pharaoh. My lord asked his servants, saying, Have ye a father, or a brother? And we said unto my lord, We have a father, an old man, and a child of his old age, a little one; and his brother is dead, and he alone is left of his mother, and his father loveth him. And thou saidst unto thy servants, Bring him down unto me, that I may set mine eyes upon him. And we said unto my lord, The lad can not leave his father: for if he should leave his father, his father would die. And thou saidst unto thy servants, Except your youngest brother come down with you, ye shall see my face no more. And it came to pass when we came up unto thy servant my father, we told him the words of my lord. And our father said, Go again, and buy us a little food. And we said, We can not go down: if our youngest brother be with us, then will we go down: for we may not see the man's face, except our youngest brother be with us. And thy servant my father said unto us, Ye know that my wife bare me two sons: and the one went out from me, and I said, Surely he is torn in pieces; and I saw him not since: and if ye take

this also from me, and mischief befall him, ye shall bring down my gray hairs with sorrow to the grave. Now therefore when I come to thy servant my father, and the lad be not with us; seeing that his life is bound up in the lad's life; it shall come to pass, when he seeth that the lad is not with us, that he will die: and thy servants shall bring down the gray hairs of thy servant our father with sorrow to the grave. For thy servant became surety for the lad unto my father, saying, If I bring him not unto thee, then I shall bear the blame to my father for ever. Now therefore, I pray thee, let thy servant abide instead of the lad a bondman to my lord; and let the lad go up with his brethren. For how shall I go up to my father, and the lad be not with me? lest peradventure I see the evil that shall come on my father."—Gen. xliv., 16-34.

II. The directions for breathing correctly given under "purity" should be repeated here, and in practice the ear should be satisfied that the voice flows out as an undisturbed stream, with no throbbing or vibration, no broken fragments of sound, but all merged in a tone flowing smoothly as oil. Practice or repeat the word "smooth" until it sounds with the quality which it names. Repeat several times the sound of "*oo*" with varied key and force, as above.

Any degree of harshness or roughness of the voice in this extract would destroy the subdued tranquillity of the composure of the feeling. Hence its use for practice in smoothness of tone.

1. *Invocation to Evening.—Cowper.*

"Come, Evening, once again, season of peace;
Return, sweet Evening, and continue long!
Methinks I see thee in the streaky west,
With matron step slow moving, while the night
Treads on thy sweeping train; one hand employed
In letting fall the curtain of repose

On bird and beast ; the other, charged for man
With sweet oblivion of the cares of day ;
Not sumptuously adorned, nor needing aid,
Like homely-featured Night, of clustering gems ;
A star or two just twinkling on thy brow
Suffices thee ; save that the moon is thine
Not less than hers, not worn, indeed, on high,
With ostentatious pageantry, but set
With modest grandeur in thy purple zone,
Resplendent less, but of an ampler round—
Come, then ; and thou shalt find thy votary calm,
Or make me so. Composure is thy gift."

The tenderness and solemnity expressed in the next passage require smoothness to give it its best expression.

2. *From The New Priest in Conception Bay.—Robert T. S. Lowell.*

"Mrs. Barré lived on nobly, where the noblest part of her life had been. Once, on a pleasant summer's day, after no wasting or weakening or dependence, when her time came, her life went out, as a star is lost in the day.

"She laid herself down at evening ; bid her maids stay with her a little while ;—by and by sent quietly for the minister ; joined with her voice in the Church prayers, lay still, with soft breathing ;—and the other Christians, priestly and lay, gentle and simple, breathed softly by her bedside, while the sound of waves breaking upon the far-off sand came in, and moonlight and shade lay calmly side by side out of doors. Once she opened her eyes upward, saying through the stillness, 'Yes,' as if in answer ; turned partly with a bright smile to her friends ; then shut the lids down softly for the last time, and so, with a fair veil of smile hung over the dead features, left her body there to be put away, until it shall be raised in new beauty, to walk upon the new earth."

The sympathy and the benedictory character of the

twentieth Psalm call naturally for the same smoothness in sound as above.

3. "The Lord hear thee in the day of trouble ; the Name of the God of Jacob defend thee: send thee help from the sanctuary, and strengthen thee out of Sion : remember all thy offerings, and accept thy burnt-sacrifice : grant thee thy heart's desire, and fulfill all thy mind. We will rejoice in thy salvation, and triumph in the Name of the Lord our God : the Lord perform all thy petitions."— Psalm xx., 1–5.

All benedictory expression requires smoothness for its effective utterance, hence the illustration of the Beatitudes.

4. "And he opened his mouth, and taught them, saying, Blessed are the poor in spirit : for theirs is the kingdom of heaven. Blessed are they that mourn : for they shall be comforted. Blessed are the meek : for they shall inherit the earth. Blessed are they which do hunger and thirst after righteousness : for they shall be filled. Blessed are the merciful : for they shall obtain mercy. Blessed are the pure in heart : for they shall see God. Blessed are the peacemakers : for they shall be called the children of God. Blessed are they which are persecuted for righteousness' sake : for theirs is the kingdom of heaven. Blessed are ye, when men shall revile you, and persecute you, and shall say all manner of evil against you falsely, for my sake. Rejoice, and be exceeding glad : for great is your reward in heaven : for so persecuted they the prophets which were before you."—St. Matt. v., 2–12.

The Exhortation following the Gospel in the Baptismal Service furnishes a marked use of the expressive smoothness of voice.

5. "Beloved, ye hear in this Gospel the words of our Saviour Christ, that he commanded the children to be brought unto him ; how he blamed those who would have kept them from him ; how he exhorteth all men to follow their innocency. Ye perceive how, by his outward gesture

and deed, he declared his good will toward them; for he embraced them in his arms, he laid his hands upon them, and blessed them. Doubt ye not therefore, but earnestly believe, that he will likewise favorably receive this present Infant; that he will embrace him with the arms of his mercy; that he will give unto him the blessing of eternal life, and make him partaker of his everlasting kingdom."

Further Examples.

Third Sentence: " Let the words of my mouth, and the meditation of my heart, be alway acceptable in thy sight, O Lord, my strength and my redeemer."

Ninth Sentence: "To the Lord our God belong mercies and forgivenesses, though we have rebelled against him; neither have we obeyed the voice of the Lord our God, to walk in his laws which he set before us."

III. By uttering the word "round," and contrasting its tone with that of the delicate, descriptive utterance of the word "pure," we note that there is a fullness of resonance in the throat, mouth, and pharynx, in pronouncing the former; that in the word "pure," uttered as suggested, would be more confined to the mouth. The fullest vibration in the chest, the throat, and the head-sounds, which produces the round voice, is termed technically the *orotund* quality. This is the highest excellence of the cultivated voice. It is the natural utterance of the stronger, deeper, and more energetic feelings. Sublimity, grandeur, majesty, praise, and similar ideas, find their expression through this voice. Practice upon the word "round," so as to give it the greatest vibration and resonance.

Let the utterance convey the fullest degree of sublimity in Byron's description of the ocean.

1. *The Sea.—Lord Byron.*

" Roll on, thou deep and dark blue Ocean—roll!
Ten thousand fleets sweep over thee in vain;

Man marks the earth with ruin—his control
Stops with the shore; upon the watery plain
The wrecks are all thy deed, nor doth remain
A shadow of man's ravage, save his own,
When, for a moment, like a drop of rain,
He sinks into thy depths with bubbling groan,
Without a grave, unknelled, uncoffined, and unknown.

. . . .

Thou glorious mirror, where the Almighty's form
Glasses itself in tempests; in all time—
Calm or convulsed, in breeze, or gale, or storm,
Icing the pole, or in the torrid clime
Dark-heaving—boundless, endless, and sublime,
The image of eternity, the throne
Of the invisible; even from out thy slime
The monsters of the deep are made ; each zone
Obeys thee ; thou goest forth, dread, fathomless, alone."

The reading of the passage following with a sharp, thin, wiry voice, will destroy the depth and majesty of the feeling in the utterance. Let the voice be well rounded out, and no such defective result follows :

2. *The Falls of Niagara.—Brainerd.*

"The thoughts are strange that crowd into my brain,
While I look upward to thee. It would seem
As if God poured thee from His 'hollow hand,'
And hung His bow upon thine awful front;
And spoke in that loud voice, which seemed to him
Who dwelt in Patmos for his Saviour's sake.
'The sound of many waters'; and had bade
Thy flood to chronicle the ages back,
And notch His cent'ries in the eternal rocks.

"Deep calleth unto deep. And what are we
That hear the question of that voice sublime ?

O ! what are all the notes that ever rung
From war's vain trumpet, by thy thundering side ?
Yea, what is all the riot man can make
In his short life, to thy unceasing roar ?
And yet, bold babbler, what art thou to Him,
Who drowned the world, and heaped the waters far
Above its loftiest mountains ?—a light wave,
That breaks, and whispers of its Maker's might."

In grateful and joyous exultation "the abundance of the heart" speaks in well-rounded utterance.

3. *Benedicite, omnia opera Domini.*

"O all ye Works of the Lord, bless ye the Lord ; praise him, and magnify him for ever.

"O ye Angels of the Lord, bless ye the Lord ; praise him, and magnify him for ever.

"O ye Heavens, bless ye the Lord ; praise him, and magnify him for ever.

"O ye Waters that be above the firmament, bless ye the Lord ; praise him, and magnify him for ever.

"O all ye Powers of the Lord, bless ye the Lord ; praise him, and magnify him for ever.

"O ye Sun and Moon, bless ye the Lord ; praise him, and magnify him for ever.

"O ye Stars of Heaven, bless ye the Lord ; praise him, and magnify him for ever.

. . . .

"O ye Mountains and Hills, bless ye the Lord ; praise him, and magnify him for ever.

. . . .

"O ye Seas and Floods, bless ye the Lord ; praise him, and magnify him for ever.

. . . .

"O let Israel bless the Lord ; praise him, and magnify him for ever.

"O ye Priests of the Lord, bless ye the Lord ; praise him, and magnify him for ever.

"O ye Servants of the Lord, bless ye the Lord ; praise him, and magnify him for ever."

The heraldic effect of the prophetic passage following is given expressively with the same quality of voice as above :

4. "Ho, every one that thirsteth, come ye to the waters, and he that hath no money ; come ye, buy, and eat ; yea, come, buy wine and milk without money and without price. Wherefore do ye spend money for that which is not bread ? and your labor for that which satisfieth not ? hearken diligently unto me, and eat ye that which is good, and let your soul delight itself in fatness. Incline your ear, and come unto me : hear, and your soul shall live ; and I will make an everlasting covenant with you, even the sure mercies of David. Behold, I have given him for a witness to the people, a leader and commander to the people. Behold, thou shalt call a nation that thou knowest not, and nations that knew not thee shall run unto thee, because of the Lord thy God, and for the Holy One of Israel ; for he hath glorified thee. . . . For ye shall go out with joy, and be led forth with peace : the mountains and the hills shall break forth before you into singing, and all the trees of the field shall clap their hands. Instead of the thorn shall come up the fir tree, and instead of the brier shall come up the myrtle tree : and it shall be to the Lord for a name, for an everlasting sign that shall not be cut off."—Isaiah, lv., 1–13.

IV. To produce "fullness" in perfection, every particle of the breath must be vocalized, and, in practicing, the speaker should aim at a deep resonance in the chest as one quality. Clearness and fullness in the ringing effects of pharyngeal and nasal tones are more apparent at other times, and the voice is further modified by the mellowness and softness of the notes in the throat, or rendered pungent and grasping to the ear by the guttural tones, or, again, swelling with full volume into the cheeks, as in the sound of "*oo.*" To these different qualities, for one or more of which the uncultivated voice is generally noticeable, may be added the delicate finish of the sounds formed in the front part of the mouth by the tip of the tongue and lips, which, when excessive, become the affected simpering of the exquisite. But, in the well-developed and flexible voice, each may be called forth at will—the gravity and base of the manly chest-notes, the healthful resonance, the agreeable mellowing, the incisive pungency, the fullness and finish, which are each fitly demanded in public speaking. Various directions might be added to accurately test the different qualities, but the ear of the speaker will soon determine them naturally and easily. It may be noted, however, that in the chest-tones the vibrations should be perceptibly felt. These elements, rightly balanced and perfected, will compose the good, expressive voice.

Natural transitions from one quality to another, in close contrast, are often very appropriate and expressive—e. g., in St. Paul's statements, in I. Cor. xv., relating to the perishable body, we have the simple declarations in the head-voice; the contrasted clauses following, suggestive of the might and the glory of the triumph over the mortal and the corruptible, would be read naturally with a round and full voice, which suggests the change in the nature of the two passages.

1. "It is sown in corruption; it is raised in incorruption: it is sown in dishonor; it is raised in glory: it is sown in weakness; it is raised in power: it is sown a natural body; it is raised a spiritual body."—I. Cor. xv., 43, 44.

The sublimity of the feeling in the passage below will only be expressed by suggestive fullness of voice:

2. *Angelic Worship.—Milton.*

"No sooner had the Almighty ceased, but all
　The multitude of angels with a shout,
　Loud as from numbers without number, sweet,

As from blest voices uttering joy ;—heaven rung
With jubilee, and loud hosannas filled
The eternal regions ;—lowly reverent,
Toward either throne they bow ; and to the ground,
With solemn adoration, down they cast
Their crowns, inwove with amaranth and gold.
Then crowned again, their golden harps they took—
Harps ever tuned—that, glittering by their side,
Like quivers hung, and with preamble sweet
Of charming symphony, they introduce
Their sacred song, and waken raptures high."

The glorious and triumphant vision of the prophet Isaiah, recorded in the sixtieth chapter, prompts the greatest fullness of voice, in order to suggest the majesty and glory of the spiritual conquest of the Gentile world.

3. "Arise, shine ; for thy light is come, and the glory of the Lord is risen upon thee. For, behold, the darkness shall cover the earth, and gross darkness the people : but the Lord shall arise upon thee, and his glory shall be seen upon thee. And the Gentiles shall come to thy light, and kings to the brightness of thy rising. Lift up thine eyes round about, and see : all they gather themselves together, they come to thee : thy sons shall come from far, and thy daughters shall be nursed at thy side. Then thou shalt see, and flow together, and thine heart shall fear, and be enlarged ; because the abundance of the sea shall be converted unto thee, the forces of the Gentiles shall come unto thee. The multitude of camels shall cover thee, the dromedaries of Midian and Ephah ; all they from Sheba shall come : they shall bring gold and incense ; and they shall shew forth the praises of the Lord. All the flocks of Kedar shall be gathered together unto thee, the rams of Nebaioth shall minister unto thee : they shall come up with acceptance on mine altar, and I will glorify the house of my glory. Who are these that fly as a cloud, and as the

doves to their windows? Surely the isles shall wait for me, and the ships of Tarshish first, to bring thy sons from far, their silver and their gold with them, unto the name of the Lord thy God, and to the Holy One of Israel, because he hath glorified thee. And the sons of strangers shall build up thy walls, and their kings shall minister unto thee: for in my wrath I smote thee, but in my favor have I had mercy on thee. Therefore thy gates shall be open continually; they shall not be shut day nor night; that men may bring unto thee the forces of the Gentiles, and that their kings may be brought. For the nation and kingdom that will not serve thee shall perish; yea, those nations shall be utterly wasted. The glory of Lebanon shall come unto thee, the fir-tree, the pine-tree, and the box together, to beautify the place of my sanctuary; and I will make the place of my feet glorious. The sons also of them that afflicted thee shall come bending unto thee; and all they that despised thee shall bow themselves down at the soles of thy feet; and they shall call thee, The city of the Lord, The Zion of the Holy One of Israel."—Isaiah, lx., 1–14.

The authority and majesty contained in the second "Sentence" require fullness of voice, any insufficiency of the volume being suggestive of weakness and unreality.

4. "From the rising of the sun even unto the going down of the same, my Name shall be great among the Gentiles; and in every place incense shall be offered unto my Name, and a pure offering: for my Name shall be great among the heathen, saith the Lord of hosts."

The fullest outpouring of heartfelt praise and thanksgiving, in recognition of the majesty and glory of the Almighty, as in the "Te Deum," is best suggested vocally by the completed effect of fullness of sound in the utterance.

5. *Te Deum laudamus.*

"We praise thee, O God; we acknowledge thee to be the Lord.

"All the earth doth worship thee, the Father everlasting.

"To thee all Angels cry aloud ; the Heavens, and all the Powers therein.

"To thee Cherubim and Seraphim continually do cry,

"Holy, Holy, Holy, Lord God of Sabaoth ;

"Heaven and earth are full of the Majesty of thy Glory.

"The glorious company of the Apostles praise thee.

"The goodly fellowship of the Prophets praise thee.

"The noble army of Martyrs praise thee."

The exercises following will also prove of service, it is believed, in the mechanical discipline.

1. A very useful drill is to yawn out the utterance of vowel sounds and syllables. The purpose of this is to secure the widest opening of the organs.

2. The practice of hearty, yet controlled, laughter will effect certain desirable results. Laugh out the syllables "ha, ha, ha," "haw, haw, haw," "ho, ho, ho," "hoo, hoo, hoo." This exercise gives a certain freedom from restraint, so desirable for ease, and also, by the laws of suggestion, enlivens the spirits.

The *sympathetic* voice is used when the speaker would ingratiate himself and inspire confidence, as in addressing a child. Let one observe how he would speak to a timid or frightened little girl, in the words, "Dear child, come to me ; I won't hurt you ; don't be afraid." Just as a harsh voice would repel or alarm the child, and therefore we are driven to modify the ruder or more careless utterance, so, in addressing an adult singly or a congregation. When the earnest purpose is to secure a hearing, inspire confidence, and produce conviction, we find the same instinctive adaptation of the sound to the purpose. No one can argue earnestly in private, in the effort to dissuade a youth from ways of wrong-doing, in a voice that is harsh and unsympathetic, and still hope to accomplish his purpose. The laws of sympathetic communication are fixed, and can not be violated without stultifying the very object in view. Let the speaker realize, as the diplomatic messenger in court circles might, that the address, the manner, the whole style of the man, imprint themselves upon his message, and thereby assist in success or failure, and he will have the necessary idea of such uses of the voice as will naturally secure and not repel a hearing. Boorishness must be avoided, even in tones of voice, in the pulpit as well as in the court. A useful exercise for the voice is to frame sentences for such imaginary scenes as are described or suggested above. No speaker has a right to impose disagreeable or unsympathetic tones upon his congregation, when by thoughtful care and practice he may remedy such a vocal defect.

It should be remembered, however, that it is not always the purpose to seek the expression of sympathy. In treating upon topics where indignation or, it may be, execration is demanded, the very reverse of the above style would be the natural expression. If the ear is accustomed to these effects in sound, it will soon become easy to remedy faults. It is largely inattention which causes inexpressive and offensive uses of the voice.

The instinctive adaptation of the voice to occasions and circumstances becomes interesting and profitable matter for study. "To order myself reverently and lowly to all my betters" has in it a value for speech as well as morals. Let the speaker imagine himself in the presence of his superiors, and that he is addressing dignitaries. He will find that the courtly phrases of address, "Your Excellency," "Your Grace," "Your Majesty," are delivered with a circumspect and deferential utterance, indicative of the respect due to the superior. And, as in deportment under such circumstances every man would be on his "best behavior," he would find the same forming influences affecting his voice. In the presence of the Supreme Ruler, the King of Kings, how much more should the best uses of the voice show the reverent homage of the heart!

CHAPTER VI.

FORCE.

It is important that all the degrees of force, from the gentlest to the loudest, should be completely under the control of the speaker. Few things are more enervating to an audience, and for which toleration is less exercised by the critical hearer, than feebleness of voice. While it may excite the sympathy of some, it is also liable to rouse the contempt of others. This want of force displays not only lack of manly vigor, but the deficiency of responsive power to the demands of the stronger degrees of feeling. By the harmony of the human system, when the emotional nature is deeply and energetically excited, a kindred effect is produced on the nerves and muscles which compose the frame. This induces, by necessity, a corresponding action of the vocal organs. And if by any misfortune the known fitness of feeling is not properly expressed in the voice, its use fails. If the feeling of sublimity arises, for instance, an insufficient supply of voice will not convey it to the ear; and as there can be no such thing as enfeebled indignation, neither can we utter that feeling without its peculiar character of force in the sound. Exultation, joy, praise, triumph, without that full degree of force which they require, do not reach the sympathies nor lift the heart with genuine impulse of feeling. The attempt to express these and similar feelings with insufficient force is like the futile effort of the child or woman to assume the full and commanding effect of the male voice.

Though we insist upon an ample degree of force as the characteristic attribute of the effective expression of manly and noble sentiment, a caution is requisite to those who are inclined to anything like boisterous vociferation. The same warning applies to the unsympathetic effects of coarseness and loudness, where gentle feeling demands subdued shades of force in either reading or speaking. An undue degree of force is peculiarly shocking and offensive to the ear when applied to delicacy of sentiment. It is like boorishness in the social circle, pardonable only on the score of some superior, redeeming characteristic, but still productive of anything but genuine and pleasing impressions. Tenderness, delicacy, reverence, serenity, and similar states of feeling, in the force of voice which they require, are, of course, in strongest contrast with the bolder emotions named above.

The occasional transition from the vocal effort requisite to fill a large house to the subdued and quieting effects of unimpassioned thought is agreeable and expressive, and a great relief to the ear. This same use, if it be the natural offspring of feeling expressed in the hushed utterance, as when the heart is tenderly moved, is a further power to be cultivated by the speaker. It is not implied that the transition in any case should be mechanical or unmeaning—it is not anything "put on." It is simply the natural vigor and pliancy of the voice, ready to respond to all changes of emotion, from the grandest, noblest, boldest, and most inspiriting, to the gentlest, tenderest, and most subdued. Monotony in the voice, when there ought to be the varied shades of force, is entirely unimpressive, and vitiates the proper effect in the use of that particular degree of loudness which might be expressive but for its constant repetition. The speaker should remember that loudness is not of itself eloquence, neither is the too frequent and undue repetition of the subdued tones. Every feeling has its own peculiar measure of force, and we are simply at variance with nature when we disregard its appropriate and expressive emphasis.

In all the qualities of voice, persistent practice with reference to the necessary points will secure the desired object. Daily drill upon all the degrees of force for fifteen or twenty minutes will, in the course of a few weeks, develop to a marked extent the power of utterance. Care should be taken to avoid beginning any vocal exercise with extreme uses of the voice. A sudden burst from silence or unimpassioned force to the loudest shout or cry of terror is too violent an exercise for unpracticed organs. But it will prove beneficial to begin with the lighter shades and gradually increase to the extreme of loudness. The repetition of the vowel sounds, or the table of atonic elements (see page 35), should be followed out, with the degrees of force indicated in the paragraph below. Repeat also, with characteristic degrees of force, each of the words following: Whisper, effusive whisper, expulsive whisper, explosive whisper.

The succeeding words should also be repeated upon the same principle, in a half whisper, with the voice just between a pure whisper and vocality: Effusive half-whisper, expulsive half-whisper, explosive half-whisper.

The words following should also be pronounced descriptively: Very soft, soft, subdued, unimpassioned, moderate, energetic, declamatory, impassioned, shouting, calling.

Explanations of these terms in full, and complete illustrations of them arranged for practice, will be found in the "Vocal Culture."

Subdued Degrees of Force.—To be destitute of this power in expression is to render the style of the gentler feelings harsh and forbidding in the expression. It is the natural means of uttering all tender, sympathetic, and chastened emotion.

The delicacy of the sentiment in the passage from Hood is a good exercise for the voice and ear:

1. *We watched her Breathing.—Thomas Hood.*

"We watched her breathing through the night,
  Her breathing soft and low,
As in her breast the wave of life
  Kept heaving to and fro.

"So silently we seemed to speak,
  So slowly moved about,
As we lent her half her powers
  To eke her living out.

"Our very hopes belied our fears,
  Our fears our hopes belied—
We thought her dying when she slept,
  And sleeping when she died.

"For when the morn came dim and sad,
  And chill with early showers,
Her quiet eyelids closed—she had
  Another morn than ours."

The tenderness and sympathy in the description of the virtues of one beloved, and now departed, instinctively prompt the subdued degree of force in the delivery.

2. "It is right that she should not pass from her place among us without a few words of loving comment—very few, however, for the pen dipped in tears does not flow readily. She was born and bred in the Church, and all through her pure, sweet life she never departed from its teachings. Her faith was simple and strong—never severely tried, perhaps, but of the kind that, in the day of trial, would have gone forth in the strength of the Lord and endured unto the end. As she matured from girlhood into womanhood, the extreme loveliness of her person and manners, the refined culture of her tastes, and the very high order of her intellect, attracted toward her an unusu-

ally large circle of admiring friends. The outgoings and incomings of her life were love; she gave out freely from her generous heart, only to receive back again the Gospel's 'good measure' of love 'pressed down and shaken together and running over,' and yet her youth, her beauty, her time and talents, and loving heart, were ever a living sacrifice to God. Home's sweetest ties never fully engrossed her soul. Beyond and above them all, up on the mountain-tops, disengaged and free, she walked in white and lived with God. It was blessed to know and love her, and now, through tears, it is more blessed to look up, and say, in our Saviour's words: 'Blessed are the pure in heart, for they shall see God.'"

The awe-inspiring mystery in the passage from the Book of Job requires, with low pitch and slow movement, a softened degree of force, to be expressive.

3. "In thoughts from the visions of the night, when deep sleep falleth on men, fear came upon me, and trembling, which made all my bones to shake. Then a spirit passed before my face; the hair of my flesh stood up: it stood still, but I could not discern the form thereof: an image was before mine eyes, there was silence, and I heard a voice, saying, Shall mortal man be more just than God? shall a man be more pure than his Maker?"—Job, iv, 13–17.

In the Exhortation to the Holy Communion, it is the solemnity of the duty and its momentous consequences which subdue the voice in force.

4. "Dearly beloved in the Lord, ye who mind to come to the holy Communion of the Body and Blood of our Saviour Christ, must consider how St. Paul exhorteth all persons diligently to try and examine themselves, before they presume to eat of that Bread, and drink of that Cup. For as the benefit is great, if with a true penitent heart and lively faith we receive that holy Sacrament; so is the danger great, if we receive the same unworthily. Judge therefore yourselves, brethren, that ye be not judged of the

Lord ; repent ye truly for your sins past ; have a lively and steadfast faith in Christ our Saviour ; amend your lives, and be in perfect charity with all men ; so shall ye be meet partakers of those holy mysteries."

The Benedictions, both Major and Minor, are uttered most expressively with the subdued degree of force.

5. "The peace of God, which passeth all understanding, keep your hearts and minds in the knowledge and love of God, and of his Son Jesus Christ our Lord : and the Blessing of God Almighty, the Father, the Son, and the Holy Ghost, be amongst you, and remain with you always."

"The grace of our Lord Jesus Christ, and the love of God, and the fellowship of the Holy Ghost, be with us all evermore."—II. Cor., xiii, 14.

Moderate Degrees of Force.—The passages following, not being characterized by the stronger and bolder, nor by the solemn, the sympathetic, or subdued characteristics of feeling, find sufficient expression in moderate degrees of force :

    1. *Abou Ben-Adhem.—Leigh Hunt.*

"Abou Ben-Adhem (may his tribe increase !)
  Awoke one night from a deep dream of peace,
  And saw within the moonlight in his room,
  Making it rich and like a lily in bloom,
  An angel writing in a book of gold :
  Exceeding peace had made Ben-Adhem bold,
  And to the presence in the room he said,
  'What writest thou ?'—The vision raised its head,
  And, with a look made of all sweet accord,
  Answered—'The names of those who love the Lord.'
  'And is mine one ?' said Abou ; 'Nay, not so,'
  Replied the angel.—Abou spoke more low,
  But cheerly still ; and said, 'I pray thee, then,
  Write me as one that loves his fellow-men.'
    The angel wrote, and vanished. The next night
  It came again, with a great wakening light,

And showed the names whom love of God had blessed—
And, lo ! Ben-Adhem's name led all the rest !"

2. *Milton.—Prof. Reed.*

" The first part of Milton's literary life is full of a beautiful reflection of the age that had gone before ; his genius is then glowing with tints of glory cast upon it by the Elizabethan poetry : the meridian of it is in close correspondence with the season of the power of the Parliament and the Protector, when Milton stood side by side with Cromwell ; and the latter period of it was that of sublime and solitary contrast with the times of Charles II. The first was the genial season of youth—studious, pure, and happy ; the second was of mature manhood—strenuous in civil strife, and the dubious dynasty of the Protectorate ; the third was old age —darkened, disappointed, but indomitable."

After the full, authoritative voice in the reading of the Commandments, the words of our Lord, expressive of the gentler law—the law of love—would be heard naturally with that degree of force which enjoins imperative duties, impelled, not by the rigorous exactions of the law of works, but by the gentler demands of love. This feeling would chasten the voice to the subdued degree were it not for the authoritative character of the injunctions. The two effects blended find expression through moderate force.

3. " Hear also what our Lord Jesus Christ saith. Thou shalt love the Lord thy God with all thy heart, and with all thy soul, and with all thy mind. This is the first and great commandment. And the second is like unto it ; Thou shalt love thy neighbor as thyself. On these two commandments hang all the Law and the Prophets."

Most of the Exhortations, in whatever Service, with the exception of that for the Holy Communion, are sufficiently expressed with a moderate degree of force.

4. " Dearly beloved, forasmuch as all men are conceived and born in sin, (and that which is born of the flesh

is flesh,) and they who are in the flesh can not please God, but live in sin, committing many actual transgressions; and our Saviour Christ saith, None can enter into the kingdom of God except he be regenerate and born anew of Water and of the Holy Ghost; I beseech you to call upon God the Father, through our Lord Jesus Christ, that of his bounteous goodness he will grant to these persons that which by nature they can not have; that they may be baptized with Water and the Holy Ghost, and received into Christ's holy Church, and be made lively members of the same."—*Baptism of Adults.*

All didactic passages demand naturally the moderate degrees of force.

5. "Then said Jesus unto them again, Verily, verily, I say unto you, I am the door of the sheep. All that ever came before me are thieves and robbers; but the sheep did not hear them. I am the door: by me if any man enter in, he shall be saved, and shall go in and out, and find pasture. The thief cometh not, but for to steal, and to kill, and to destroy: I am come that they might have life, and that they might have it more abundantly. I am the good shepherd: the good shepherd giveth his life for the sheep. But he that is an hireling, and not the shepherd, whose own the sheep are not, seeth the wolf coming, and leaveth the sheep, and fleeth; and the wolf catcheth them, and scattereth the sheep. The hireling fleeth, because he is an hireling, and careth not for the sheep. I am the good shepherd, and know my sheep, and am known of mine. As the Father knoweth me, even so know I the Father: and I lay down my life for the sheep. And other sheep I have, which are not of this fold: them also I must bring, and they shall hear my voice; and there shall be one fold, and one shepherd. Therefore doth my Father love me, because I lay down my life, that I might take it again. No man taketh it from me, but I lay it down of myself. I have power to lay it down, and I have power to take it

again. This commandment have I received of my Father."
—St. John, x., 7–18.

The Stronger Degrees of Force.—To give the commanding effect of the authoritative reading of the Law of God, as contained in the Ten Commandments, the voice must necessarily be strong and full. Any degree of pathetic expression (by no means an uncommon defect in reading) destroys the character of the expression of authority. Light, deprecating, pleading tones in the reading of the Decalogue are puerile and not commanding. The language is positive and emphatic; the utterance should imply nothing less than this. Majesty and dignity alike demand a just degree of force. Any familiarity or triviality in the vocal utterance would, therefore, destroy the gravity and character given to the voice in proclaiming those laws of God which, by their very utterance, challenge man's obedience. The effort to secure the just degree of authority in the expression should, however, lead the reader carefully to avoid that personality of tone in the utterance which would imply that he was exacting of his hearers absolute obedience to his own laws.

1. I. "God spake these words, and said; I am the Lord thy God: Thou shalt have none other gods but me.

II. "Thou shalt not make to thyself any graven image, nor the likeness of anything that is in heaven above, or in the earth beneath, or in the water under the earth. Thou shalt not bow down to them, nor worship them: for I the Lord thy God am a jealous God, and visit the sins of the fathers upon the children, unto the third and fourth generation of them that hate me; and show mercy unto thousands in them that love me, and keep my commandments.

III. "Thou shalt not take the Name of the Lord thy God in vain: for the Lord will not hold him guiltless, that taketh his Name in vain.

IV. "Remember that thou keep holy the Sabbath-day.

Six days shalt thou labour, and do all that thou hast to do: but the seventh day is the Sabbath of the Lord thy God. In it thou shalt do no manner of work; thou, and thy son, and thy daughter, thy man-servant, and thy maid-servant, thy cattle, and the stranger that is within thy gates. For in six days the Lord made heaven and earth, the sea, and all that in them is, and rested the seventh day: wherefore the Lord blessed the seventh day, and hallowed it.

V. "Honor thy father and thy mother; that thy days may be long in the land which the Lord thy God giveth thee.

VI. "Thou shalt do no murder.

VII. "Thou shalt not commit adultery.

VIII. "Thou shalt not steal.

IX. "Thou shalt not bear false witness against thy neighbor.

X. "Thou shalt not covet thy neighbor's house, thou shalt not covet thy neighbor's wife, nor his servant, nor his maid, nor his ox, nor his ass, nor anything that is his."

All the bolder and more authoritative passages of Scripture demand the louder degrees of force in their expressive rendering.

2. "Hear the word of the Lord, ye rulers of Sodom; give ear unto the law of our God, ye people of Gomorrah. To what purpose is the multitude of your sacrifices unto me? saith the Lord: I am full of the burnt offerings of rams, and the fat of fed beasts; and I delight not in the blood of bullocks, or of lambs, or of he goats. When ye come to appear before me, who hath required this at your hand, to tread my courts? Bring no more vain oblations: incense is an abomination unto me; the new moons and sabbaths, the calling of assemblies, I can not away with; it is iniquity, even the solemn meeting. Your new moons and your appointed feasts my soul hateth: they are a trouble unto me; I am weary to bear them. And when ye spread forth your hands, I will hide mine eyes

from you; yea, when ye make many prayers, I will not hear: your hands are full of blood."—Isaiah, i., 10-15.

Frequent use of the voice in sustained exercise on the louder degrees will give that firmness and body of tone requisite for commanding effects, and which can be acquired in no other way.

Practice upon such passages as the following, with full declamatory effect, will strengthen and improve the voice:

3. *Eloquence of John Adams.*—*Webster.*

"The war must go on. We must fight it through. And, if the war must go on, why put off longer the Declaration of Independence? That measure will strengthen us. It will give us character abroad.

"Why then, sir, do we not, as soon as possible, change this from a civil to a national war? And, since we must fight it through, why not put ourselves in a state to enjoy all the benefits of victory, if we gain the victory?

"Read this declaration at the head of the army; every sword will be drawn from its scabbard, and the solemn vow uttered, to maintain it, or to perish on the bed of honor. Publish it from the pulpit; religion will approve it, and the love of religious liberty will cling round it, resolved to stand with it or fall with it. Send it to the public halls; proclaim it there; let them hear it who heard the first roar of the enemy's cannon; let them see it who saw their brothers and their sons fall on the field of Bunker Hill, and in the streets of Lexington and Concord, and the very walls will cry out in its support.

"Sir, I know the uncertainty of human affairs, but I see, I see clearly, through this day's business. You and I, indeed, may rue it. We may not live to the time when this Declaration shall be made good. We may die; die, colonists; die, slaves; die, it may be, ignominiously and on the scaffold. Be it so. Be it so. If it be the pleasure of Heaven that my country shall require the poor offering of my life, the victim shall be ready, at the appointed hour of sacrifice, come when that hour may. But, while I do live, let me have a country, or at least the hope of a country, and that a free country.

"Sir, before God, I believe the hour is come. My judgment approves this measure, and my whole heart is in it. All that I have, and all that I am, and all that I hope, in this life, I am now ready here to stake upon it; and I leave off, as I began, that, live or die, survive or perish, I am for the declaration. It is my living sentiment, and by the blessing of God it shall be my dying sentiment: independence *now;* and INDEPENDENCE FOREVER."

Sustained vociferation, taking care at the same time to guard against impurity of sound or over-tasking of the organs, is an invigorating drill for the voice. Atonic elements may be called out with the fullest supply of breath and voice, as in the effort to send the sound to a listener half a mile distant. Especial attention should be paid to the production of the voice in the calling exercise, without exhausting effort. The degree of force should be no louder than the vocal and physical powers of the student would warrant.

CHAPTER VII.

PITCH.

THE ordinary compass of the human voice is about two octaves, and the command of all the intervals between the two extremes of highest and lowest is a great power in public speaking. Under the impulse of excitable feelings, in contrast with those which are deep and profound, we naturally find the full scope of pitch above indicated. If, for instance, we express the profoundest horror, and contrast its utterance with that of a loud cry of terror, we shall find the greatest extremes of pitch. Even in colloquial intercourse, the gleeful expression of mirth and impulsive laughter would rise through the compass of several notes above the utterance of deep solemnity. And, in emphatic and earnest communication of thought, intense eagerness and vehement indignation would mark very wide transitions. This, we say, is the prompting of nature, when there are no repressing or distracting influences to divert the attention, impede the expression, or render the speaker unnatural. It would seem as if the office of reading even the sacred volume in public, and proclaiming the truth from the pulpit, necessitated something artificial and unmeaning in the delivery of the voice. For we find clergymen, as a class, in the effort of communication under these circumstances, limiting the range of pitch, on most occasions, to a very narrow compass, and ordinarily making use of less than a third of the power which nature has given them. Where we hear one speaker employing the notes of an octave, we shall find nearly twenty who use no more than three notes.

The cultivation of flexibility of the vocal organs, and the ready perception of the ear, thus become a necessary part of the training process of the voice, in order that the notes, as high or low, may be ready at call to respond to the demands of feeling.

Drill exercises will, if persisted in, secure in time the required flexibility and the desired compass. Practice upon the notes in pitch with the words below, which name the various degrees:

Middle pitch, low, lower, lowest. High, higher, highest. Then vary the exercise by passing from lowest to highest, middle to low, etc.

Middle Pitch.—The proper key for this pitch is a little below that of animated conversation. It is the voice of unimpassioned thought, and is peculiarly expressive and appropriate when properly applied. There are many speakers, who, from the depressing and constraining influences of speaking in public, give, in place of this middle pitch, a dispirited low key, which solemnizes and renders very oppressive the ordinary degree of unimpassioned communication. Others, from undue excitement, form the opposite habit of invariably using the voice on a high key. Both of these faults are equally destructive of the desired effect, for, as there is nothing in unimpassioned thought to depress the voice to a low key, so there is no excitement to lift it to high notes. The proper command of the middle key implies conscious possession of the thought, and conscious purpose to communicate it, as opposed to involuntary impulse in the delivery.

1. *Of Studies.—Bacon.*

"Studies serve for delight, for ornament, and for ability. Their chief use for delight, is in privateness and retiring; for ornament, is in discourse; and for ability, is in the judgment and disposition of business; for expert men can execute, and perhaps judge of particulars one by one; but the general counsels, and the plots and marshalling of affairs, come best from those that are learned. To spend too much time in studies, is sloth; to use them too much for ornament, is affectation; to make judgment wholly by their rules, is the humor of a scholar. They perfect nature, and are perfected by experience; for natural abilities are like natural plants, that need pruning by study; and studies themselves do give forth directions too much at large, except they be bounded in by experience. Crafty men contemn studies, simple men admire them, and wise men use them; for they teach not their own use; but that is a wisdom without them and above them, won by observation."

In the closing address to the sponsors at Baptism, the instructions relating more to binding duties, and in the form of injunction, would naturally throw the voice a little lower than in the preceding extract, but still within the limits of "middle pitch."

2. "Forasmuch as this Child hath promised by you his sureties to renounce the devil and all his works, to believe in God, and to serve him ; ye must remember, that it is your parts and duties to see that this Infant be taught, so soon as he shall be able to learn, what a solemn vow, promise, and profession, he hath here made by you. And that he may know these things the better, ye shall call upon him to hear Sermons ; and chiefly ye shall provide, that he may learn the Creed, the Lord's Prayer, and the Ten Commandments, and all other things which a Christian ought to know and believe to his soul's health ; and that this Child may be virtuously brought up to lead a godly and a Christian life ; remembering always, that Baptism doth represent unto us our profession ; which is, to follow the example of our Saviour Christ, and to be made like unto him ; that as he died, and rose again for us, so should we, who are baptized, die from sin, and rise again unto righteousness ; continually mortifying all our evil and corrupt affections, and daily proceeding in all virtue and godliness of living."

Unimpassioned narrative requires middle pitch. The calm description of the Garden of Eden, therefore, is to be read in that key.

3. "And the Lord God planted a garden eastward in Eden ; and there he put the man whom he had formed. And out of the ground made the Lord God to grow every tree that is pleasant to the sight, and good for food ; the tree of life also in the midst of the garden, and the tree of knowledge of good and evil. And a river went out of Eden to water the garden ; and from thence it was parted, and became into four heads. The name of the first is Pison : that is it which compasseth the whole land of Havilah, where there is gold ; and the gold of that land is good : there is bdellium and the onyx stone. And the name of the second river is Gihon : the same is it that compasseth

the whole land of Ethiopia. And the name of the third river is Hiddekel: that is it which goeth toward the east of Assyria. And the fourth river is Euphrates."—Gen. ii., 8–14.

Low Pitch.—When feeling is chastened by a solemnizing theme, when vivacity and animation are repressed by depth of feeling, then the low notes increase the expressive means of communication. Weight and gravity of thought, seriousness, and moral effect are conveyed through this medium. If the speaker is to impress by the gravity of his theme, if he is to set the minds of his hearers deliberately and thoughtfully at work, he will find the low notes the leading agent in producing this gravity of effect. The absence of power to make the voice resonant on the lower keys is so much loss of impressive and commanding effect. While the higher notes may inspirit, the lower will chasten and subdue in their influence and feeling. And if the speaker who is conscious of having delivered his voice for several minutes on an undeviating high key will but pause, inhale a full breath, in order to change the action of the muscles, and then deliberately pass to a low note, he will himself experience the relief which will gratify his hearer.

The solemnity of the thought of death casts the voice low in pitch; to this should be added the slow movement, with frequent pauses.

1. *In Memoriam.—Tennyson.*

"There sat the Shadow feared of man;

" Who broke our fair companionship,
    And spread his mantle dark and cold;
    And wrapped thee formless in the fold,
And dulled the murmur on thy lip;

" And bore thee where I could not see
    Nor follow, though I walk in haste;
    And think that, somewhere in the waste,
The Shadow sits and waits for me."

In the Service for the Burial of the Dead, the solemnity of the event and the sympathetic sorrow which touches the heart in the presence of death and the bereaved living suppress the voice to the lower notes. The sentences below, to be in harmony with this Service, must, therefore, be on a low key. A high pitch would make the entire Service flippant, unfeeling, or jubilant.

2. "I am the resurrection and the life, saith the Lord : he that believeth in me, though he were dead, yet shall he live : and whosoever liveth and believeth in me, shall never die."—St. John, xi., 25, 26.

"I know that my Redeemer liveth, and that he shall stand at the latter day upon the earth. And though after my skin worms destroy this body, yet in my flesh shall I see God : whom I shall see for myself, and mine eyes shall behold, and not another."—Job, xix., 25–27.

"We brought nothing into this world, and it is certain we can carry nothing out. The Lord gave, and the Lord hath taken away ; blessed be the name of the Lord."—I. Tim., vi., 7. Job, i., 21.

The Committal, in the Burial Service, being an act of the greatest solemnity and significance, requires a still lower key than the foregoing :

3. "Forasmuch as it hath pleased Almighty God, in his wise providence, to take out of this world the soul of our deceased brother, we therefore commit his body to the ground ; earth to earth, ashes to ashes, dust to dust ; looking for the general Resurrection in the last day, and the life of the world to come, through our Lord Jesus Christ ; at whose second coming in glorious majesty to judge the world, the earth and the sea shall give up their dead ; and the corruptible bodies of those who sleep in him shall be changed, and made like unto his own glorious body ; according to the mighty working whereby he is able to subdue all things unto himself."

The description of the Judgment scene, to be portentous

and solemn in effect, would keep the descriptive voice low in pitch:

4. "And I beheld when he had opened the sixth seal, and, lo, there was a great earthquake; and the sun became black as sackcloth of hair, and the moon became as blood; and the stars of heaven fell unto the earth, even as a fig-tree casteth her untimely figs, when she is shaken of a mighty wind. And the heaven departed as a scroll when it is rolled together; and every mountain and island were moved out of their places. And the kings of the earth, and the great men, and the rich men, and the chief captains, and the mighty men, and every bond man, and every free man, hid themselves in the dens and in the rocks of the mountains; and said to the mountains and rocks, Fall on us, and hide us from the face of him that sitteth on the throne, and from the wrath of the Lamb: for the great day of his wrath is come; and who shall be able to stand?"—Rev., vi., 12–17.

Higher Pitch.—The enlivening and inspiriting effects of excited feeling are properly conveyed on a key higher than that designated by "middle" or "low" pitch. There is but little use for the upper notes in the reading of the Service. Occasionally in the pulpit the higher notes are heard, indicative of the earnestness and excitability of the emotion which produces them.

The animated description in the passage following naturally lifts the voice above the middle key. A just degree of rapidity must accompany the expression, to account for the high key.

1. *Human Machinery.—Sewell.*

"Look at that infant at its mother's breast; and then collect from the streets of London all your great artificers and mechanics, painters and sculptors, architects and engineers; and he will surpass them all. He is performing at this moment every one of their operations with a dexterity and accuracy and perfection which baffle even the conception of the highest intellects. He is building himself a house, in which his soul is to reside—a house, not fixed to one spot, but capable of moving about to any place, and adapting itself to every climate. He not only fits together the masonry of his bones, but he makes the masonry itself; a hard, solid, but light concrete of artificial stone. He spins cordage, to thatch his head. He weaves a most delicate tissue for his skin, at once impervious to wet from without and pervious to it from within: no manufacturer has yet been able to solve this necessary problem. He constructs a telescope to see with; an ear-trumpet to hear with; a carriage to ride on; a pantechnicon of mechanical instruments in the hand; a self-repairing mill in his teeth; a most curious system of water-works—pipes, pumps, fountains, and drains—by which he distributes the blood to every part of his mansion, on the most correct principles of hydraulics. He will make an air-pump to ventilate it in his reservoir of the lungs; a vast kitchen filled with stoves, ovens, bake-houses, to concoct his food, besides larders and presses to receive it. He will defy any chemist to equal the menstruum which he invents and employs for the purpose of analyzing and recombining it. At the same time that helpless infant is creating a series of engines of all kinds for raising weights, pulling cords, propelling bodies; branching out into innumerable springs, pulleys, levers, wheels, and valves—all worked, like Mr. Brunel's block-machinery, by one motive power, which no one can see. He is constructing drains and cloacæ to carry off all that is superfluous or noxious. He is ready, if he breaks a bone, instantly to set to work and make a new concrete, or marmoratum, to consolidate it again. And he is also molding a statue; hiding all this machinery under an exquisite figure of grace, beauty, and proportion, which it is the highest aim of modern art to study and repeat. He will paint himself with the delicacy of a Raphael and the richness of a

Titian. He will touch every line of his face with a minute and exquisite feeling, so that his mind may be seen through it as through a transparent veil. He will construct a whole language of signs, in the telegraphic play of the muscles, and the flexibility of the features, with which he will speak to his fellow-men with a most perspicuous and moving and intelligible eloquence. And he will fit up in his throat an orchestra of musical instruments, capable of awakening every pulse of sound, full of life, expression, and feeling, without which all other instruments are cold and insipid. And when all this has been done, he will transmit to others the same wonderful art, the same mysterious powers, and multiply and preserve them through an infinite series of generations. All this he begins to do the moment the breath of life is infused into him."

Quiet humor, of which some of the older divines especially furnish occasional passages, and of which the modern pulpit is not entirely destitute, would, of course, require that flexibility and ready play of voice which harmonize with the quaint play of the conceit, the fitting expression, or the harmless yet expressive play of the imagination. The extract from Walton is introduced as a relief to the ear and voice from more somber passages.

2. *Richard Hooker.*—*Walton.*

"But the justifying of this doctrine did not prove of so bad consequence, as the kindness of Mrs. Churchman's curing of his late distemper and cold; for that was so gratefully apprehended by Mr. Hooker, that he thought himself bound in conscience to believe all that she said; so that the good man came to be persuaded by her, 'that he was a man of a tender constitution; and that it was best for him to have a wife, that might prove a nurse to him; such a one as might both prolong his life, and make it more comfortable; and such a one she could and would provide for him, if he thought fit to marry.' And he, not considering that 'the children of this world are wiser in their generation than the children of light,' but, like a true Nathaniel, fearing no guile, because he meant none, did give her such a power as Eleazar was trusted with—you may read it in the Book of Genesis—when he was sent to choose a wife for Isaac; for even so he trusted her to choose for him, promising upon a fair summons to return to London, and accept of her choice; and he did so in that or about the year following. Now, the wife provided for him was her daughter Joan, who brought him neither beauty nor portion: and for her conditions, they were too like that wife's, which is by Solomon compared to a dripping house: so that the good man had no reason to 'rejoice in the wife of his youth,' but too just cause to say with the holy prophet, 'Woe is me, that I am constrained to have my habitation in the tents of Kedar!'"

CHAPTER VIII.

STRESS.

THE proper definition of this term is not the one in popular use, but is more technical. Dr. Rush, in his "Philosophy of the Human Voice," uses the term to denote the character, degree, or mode of force, as it touches different parts of a syllable. It is most distinctly marked to the ear on those syllables which are emphatic. Being characteristic of the feeling which in every case instinctively secures its own form of stress in expression, we can not depart from the appointed mode without changing the impression of feeling. If that of reverence, for instance, is to be expressed, the "high tide" of force culminates on the middle of each syllable, and the opening and close of the sound are barely perceptible, as in the musical "swell." Now, if we give the percussive opening, which will be natural for the utterance of animation, in the milder degrees of force, or with louder degrees, for the expression of anger, the reverential feeling is entirely dissipated. Or, again, the tremor of timidity would entirely destroy the bold and abrupt utterance necessary to commanding and authoritative expression. The same principle holds good in all the forms of stress.

To discriminate more closely: The three marked divisions of a syllable will furnish us with matter for study. The force may be greatest at the beginning, middle, or close of a sound, and the stress will then be termed *radical, median,* or *vanishing.* There are, besides, combinations of these forms, the *radical* and *vanishing* in the *compound*, and all three in the *thorough* stress. They may be arranged in tabular form, with examples, as below with the single exclamation "oh!"

Opening—Radical—o-o-oh!
Middle—Median—o-o-oh!
Close—Vanishing—o-o-OH!
Opening and Close—Compound—o-o-OH!
Opening, Middle, and Close—Thorough—o-o-OH!

By this table it is intended to represent to the eye, as clearly as possible, the method of pronouncing this exclamation "*oh!*" so as to illustrate each of the five methods of stress. It is to be applied to every syllable of a given passage, or clause, as suggested by the thought or feeling.

The *radical* stress is used, in the louder degrees of force, for excited and impassioned feeling, and with moderate force for all animated and inspiriting expression. It is important that the public speaker should fix his attention definitely and accurately on discerning the sparkling and life-giving effect of the *percussive radical* in all clearly enunciated thought. We say thought, as distinguished from feeling, or even the slight degree of the moral effect which proceeds from some very subdued emotion. By the aid of this element, abstract thought becomes enlightened and sympathetically quickening, while, without it, lifeless and unmeaning dullness would result. If moral reflections, however, be included in the thought, especially when tinged with any feeling akin to regret or anything related to pathos, then the percussive radical gives way to more softened and gentler modes of expression.

The *median* stress is the natural vehicle for conveying solemn, reverential, sublime, and similar emotions. Solemnity, whatever may be its form in language, ceases to be solemn under the use of any other form than that of median stress. Reverential language, deprived of this, will arouse irreverent emotions. Sublimity loses its sustained grandeur and dignity, and becomes brusque in sound. All the other feelings which naturally require this form of stress are subject to the same laws.

The *vanishing* stress expresses the strongest determination and resolution, with full voice and deliberate movement. The same stress, with lighter voice and quicker movement, expresses impatience or petulance. The intermediate or moderate degree of this mode of stress gives utterance to complaint. It is ruinous to the preacher, who seeks to influence souls by every legitimate method possible, to fall into any single, unvarying habit in the use of stress. Yet the tone of complaint is sometimes carried to absolute petulance, through the incessant use of the vanishing stress. This is no better than the harshness of the *radical* or the weakness of the *median* when continually used. Every such fault prevents the sympathetic response to the demands of varied feeling, which the minister of the Divine Word is constantly striving to evoke in the delivery of his message.

In the *compound* stress we find the expression of surprise and contempt, for which there is, of course, very little use in the pulpit. There is, however, an occasional demand in the utterance of indignant astonishment, and then, to make it truly expressive of this complex feeling, the opening and close of each syllable must receive a strongly marked stress. Let the student utter the exclamations, "Indeed!" "What!" with these feelings, and the two distinct movements on the emphatic syllable may be clearly perceived.

The *thorough* stress differs from the *radical* in being sustained to the end of the sound with the same degree of force used at the opening, somewhat augmented toward the middle of the syllable. Bold, commanding, and authoritative utterances are thus marked. The reading of the Decalogue, to be authoritative and commanding, naturally requires this form of stress. If this portion of the Service is to convey the thought of unyielding *law*, then the thorough stress must be its exponent. If displaced by the *radical* stress, the effect is harsh or animating, but not authoritative; if by the *median*, it is gentle and persuasive, but not commanding.

To these may be added the *tremulous* stress, where the voice quivers along the whole sound. This may occur in times of great religious excitement, but is seldom used in the ordinary course of the Service.

RADICAL STRESS.

1. *American Freedom.—Hudson.*

"The great strength and worth of our American freedom lies in the fact of its being strictly historical; that is, a matter of inheritance and prescription. It has come to us, not as a piece of theoretical joinery, devised in the closet of speculation, but as a slow growth and development in the domain of experience and fact; for which cause it vitally coheres and interworks with all the habits, customs, institutes, and circumstances of our national life and character. The frame and model of it were not drafted by any Philosophy of the Rights of Man. The forces of Christian Civilization have been working together for ages in the production of it. It is by their practical, not their logical consequences, that the principles of our liberty have been tested and established. The several parts and organs of it have been adopted and settled, not as they gratified the speculative understanding, but as they have been put to work, and found to bear the actual fruits of order, security, justice, and peace."

2. *Spring.*—*Thomson.*

"The thrush,
And woodlark, o'er the kind-contending throng
Superior heard, run through the sweetest length
Of notes; when listening Philomela deigns
To let them joy, and purposes, in thought
Elate, to make her night excel their day.
The blackbird whistles from the thorny brake;
The mellow bullfinch answers from the grove;
Nor are the linnets, o'er the flowering furze
Poured out profusely, silent; joined to these
Innumerous songsters, in the freshening shade
Of new-sprung leaves, their modulation mix
Mellifluous. The jay, the rook, the daw,
And each harsh pipe, discordant heard alone,
Aid the full concert; while the stockdove breathes
A melancholy murmur through the whole."

MEDIAN STRESS.

1. *Burial of Moses.*—*C. F. Alexander.*

. . . . .

"O lonely tomb in Moab's land!
 O dark Beth-peor's hill!
 Speak to these curious hearts of ours,
 And teach them to be still:
 God hath his mysteries of grace,
 Ways that we can not tell;
 He hides them deep like the secret sleep
 Of him he loved so well."

2. *Friar Lawrence.—Shakespeare.*

"Heaven and yourself
Had part in this fair maid; now Heaven hath all,
And all the better is it for the maid.
Your part in her you could not keep from death;
But Heaven keeps his part in eternal life.
The most you sought was—her promotion;
For 'twas your heaven, she should be advanced;
And weep ye now, seeing she is advanced,
Above the clouds, as high as heaven itself?
O, in this love, you love your child so ill,
That you run mad seeing that she is well.
She's not well married, that lives married long;
But she's best married, that dies married young.
Dry up your tears, and stick your rosemary
On this fair corse; and, as the custom is,
In all her best array bear her to church.
For though fond nature bids us all lament,
Yet nature's tears are reason's merriment."

3. *Little Nell.—Dickens.*

"It was long before the child closed the window and approached her bed. Again something of the same sensation as before—an involuntary chill—a momentary feeling akin to fear—but vanishing directly, and leaving no alarm behind. Again, too, dreams of the little scholar, of the roof opening, and a column of bright faces, rising far away into the sky, as she had seen in some old scriptural picture once, and looking down on her, asleep. It was a sweet and happy dream. The quiet spot, outside, seemed to remain the same, save that there was music in the air, and a sound of angels' wings. After a time the sisters came there, hand n hand, and stood among the graves. And then the dream grew dim, and faded."

COMPOUND STRESS.

Indignation.—Shakespeare.

" Shall one of us that struck the foremost man
Of all this world, but for supporting robbers,
Contaminate our fingers with base bribes,
And sell the mighty space of our large honors
For so much trash as may be graspèd thus?
I'd rather be a dog, and bay the moon,
Than such a Roman!"—*Julius Cæsar.*

VANISHING STRESS.

" How doth the city sit solitary, that was full of people! how is she become as a widow! she that was great among the nations, and princess among the provinces, how has she become tributary! She weepeth sore in the night, and her tears are on her cheeks: among all her lovers she hath none to comfort her: all her friends have dealt treacherously with her, they are become her enemies. Judah is gone into captivity because of affliction, and because of great servitude: she dwelleth among the heathen, she findeth no rest: all her persecutors overtook her between the straits. The ways of Zion do mourn, because none come to the solemn feasts: all her gates are desolate: her priests sigh, her virgins are afflicted, and she is in bitterness. Her adversaries are the chief, her enemies prosper; for the Lord hath afflicted her for the multitude of her transgressions: her children are gone into captivity before the enemy. And from the daughter of Zion all her beauty is departed: her princes are become like harts that find no pasture, and they are gone without strength before the pursuer. Jerusalem remembered in the days of her affliction and of her miseries all her pleasant things that she had in the days of old, when her people fell into the hand of the enemy, and none did help her: the adversaries saw her, and did mock at her sabbaths. Jerusalem hath grievously sinned ; therefore she is removed : all that honored her despise her, because they have seen her nakedness : yea, she sigheth, and turneth backward."—Lam. i., 1–8.

THOROUGH STRESS.

What Constitutes a State?—Sir William Jones.

" What constitutes a state ?
  Not high-raised battlements or labored mound,
Thick wall or moated gate ;
  Not cities proud with spires and turrets crowned ;
Not bays and broad-armed ports,
  Where, laughing at the storms, rich navies ride ;
Not starred and spangled courts,
  Where low-browed baseness wafts perfume to pride.

" No ; men, high-minded men,
  With powers as far above dull brutes endued,
In forest, brake, or den,
  As beasts excel cold rocks and brambles rude—
Men who their duties know,
  But know their rights, and knowing, dare maintain—
Prevent the long-aimed blow,
  And crush the tyrant while they rend the chain.

" These constitute a state ;
  And sovereign law, that state's collected will,
O'er thrones and globes elate
  Sits empress, crowning good, repressing ill.
Smit by her sacred frown,
  The fiend, dissension, like a vapor sinks ;
And e'en the all-dazzling crown
  Hides its faint rays, and at her bidding shrinks."

CHAPTER IX.

INFLECTION OR SLIDE.

THE impulse for expression proceeds chiefly from feeling, rather than from thought. Even passages which appear to be altogether unimpassioned are delivered with a desire to make them known, so that the impelling power is more than purely intellectual. The study of the use of the slides of the voice will lead us naturally to the emotional expression which they convey.

Slides of Emotion.—In the strongest degrees of feeling these are very distinctly marked as compassing a full *octave* in their scope. It is only, however, in highly wrought feeling that this occurs. *Indignant astonishment*, which would induce the upward slide, represents such a compass of the voice on an emphatic syllable. For an illustration, we will imagine that the preacher is expostulating with the apathetic and the wavering in regard to religious duty. He has occasion, we will say, to repeat the excuse of the procrastinator not yet prepared. He rehearses the opportunities, the blessings, the years that have passed, the office of Christ, the love of God, and in view of all these considerations repeats the question with indignant astonishment: "Not *yet* prepared?" And as surely as he has the feeling in full degree, just so certainly will his voice slide through the compass of the rising octave.

We pass from such a slide to one much more frequently used, that of the musical *fifth*, both upward and downward. This is characteristic of heart-felt earnestness. Energetic feeling of all kinds requires this interval to make it truly expressive. Feeble and plaintive uses of the voice will be altogether lacking in the "earnest" slide of the fifth. It is the language of strong and emphatic assertion, and the leading element in manly decision of expression. "Rhetorical inquiry" becomes impressive and forcible under such delivery, while strength of language, and even energy of feeling, are completely hindered if it be lacking. The student who is seeking to develop all utterance of manly properties of delivery must give much time and attention to this natural and expressive element. It is like the bold action impelled by bodily vigor—striking, full of meaning, and appropriate. No speaker can be commanding in his vocal effects without the use of this interval in the slides of his voice. He may be otherwise pleasing, attractive, and expressive, as a speaker, but without it he can not produce the first manly element of energetic expression.

There is an unimpassioned delivery, where the thought is not quickened into energy, which finds utterance through the rise and fall of the musical third. The purpose of this seems to be the expression of quiet and unemphatic communication. Proper mastery of this slide imparts agreeable variety to reading and speaking. If it be excessive in its interval, the expression becomes too emotional, and if it be insufficient, a suppressed or monotonous effect is produced. It belongs to all spirited communication, and the absence of it is a very serious defect.

From a consideration of the general drift of the slide we may pass to its use in clauses and phrases. In all cheerful, animated, and agreeable expression, if these are the dominant elements, the voice, through whatever interval, slides upward. If, on the other hand, gravity, solemnity, emphatic and commanding expression be aimed at, the falling slide becomes the chief medium. Earnest supplication naturally throws the voice downward, in its general course, as unemphatic communication lifts the voice on the upward slide. But the varieties are as great as the changes of thought and its grammatical forms of expression, so that every sentence becomes properly a separate study.

Rise and Fall of the Second.—As the more marked intervals of the third, fifth, and octave are especially characterized at the pauses of the voice, so the still more contracted drift of unimpassioned sentences limits the passages between the pauses and the emphatic words by the rise and fall of the second, as from *do* to *re*, *re* to *do*, on the musical scale. Where this varied and natural play of the voice is wanting we have dull and monotonous expression as the result.

The four preceding divisions give the voice an emotional and intellectual expressiveness, to which it is ever a pleasure to listen. Carried to excess they beget a mechanical and unnatural vivacity, which has no place in natural discourse. They are then in oratory what excessive sprightliness would be to manner in the social circle. While avoiding the fault of unmeaning sameness, therefore, we must also escape an equally meaningless variety in the use of the slides.

The Monotone. — Like the *recitative* music, this sustained effort in the delivery of the voice is, at times, the only mode appropriate. Wherever majesty, dignity, sublimity, mystery, or awe, separately or combined, find utterance, there the superior weight of the feeling tends to more or less repetition of the same note. In the grandeur, sublimity, and awe of several of the descriptive passages of the Revelation, the ordinary varieties of inflection destroy all the mystery and the vision-like effect of the narrative. The cause of this sustained effort is, unquestionably, the unusual weight and depth of feeling, which prevents the elastic play of the muscles and confines the voice to its simplest intervals. It should be observed, however, that the monotone, a legitimate mode of utterance in its place, is vastly different from the inexpressive and inappropriate effect of monotony.

The Semitone.—This slide is produced by carrying the voice half a note short of the ordinary intervals by which the previously described degrees of feeling are expressed. It is the medium of pathos, with all its kindred shades of feeling, and the natural expression of marked degrees of tenderness. When used in excess it is characterized as the whine, and the reader of quick susceptibility and extreme sensitiveness should be on his guard, lest that which is naturally expressive of tenderest feeling become the habitual accompaniment of the voice in all forms of expression. It is simply pitiable to hear the plaintive effect of the minor intervals sounding through some majestic passages of the Church Service, and the lachrymose style of some speakers suggests merely a weakness and effeminacy which are out of character with manly and forcible expression of thought or feeling. The clergyman who reported that his friends assured him that he was "happy at funerals" must have been one of the many who are addicted to the unduly pathetic effect of the minor intervals.

There is still another use of slide called the *circumflex* or *wave*. This is used in a train of thought which involves close and distinctive reasoning. It is employed also in irony and sarcasm. When a deeper meaning is given to a word than is found in its ordinary significance, the circumflex serves the same purpose in vocalizing that italicizing does in printing—e. g., "Let any man resolve to do right *now*, leaving *then* to do as it can, and he will never do wrong." The taunting cry of Elijah to the priests of Baal, "Cry aloud, for he is a god," etc., would be a good example of the circumflex of irony.

It should be observed that much of the vivacity and effectiveness of speech comes from variety in the slides. We have in every clause slight variations of slide, giving musical and rhythmical effect to the ear. To read or speak without this natural play of the voice deprives it of flexibility and of all animation. In antithetical clauses and sentences, the answering of the melody in the contrasted slides is very marked, and, to give both members of the antithesis the same slide will almost assuredly destroy the contrast in the meaning. The inexpressive reader or speak-

or delivers his thought with humdrum sameness in all the slides. To form the incessant habit of using the upward or downward slide only is destructive to expressive variety in meaning, and produces disagreeable monotony. If, for instance, the speaker gives the downward inflections constantly, it will render his style unsympathetic, severe, and dogmatic. If he inclines to the rising inflection, as a habit, he loses all the emphatic effects which belong to the falling slide. The variety here suggested is what makes it so agreeable to listen to the conversation of some people, and the absence of it what renders the vocal effect of the conversation of others so intolerable.

There are natural laws governing the use of slides which are almost universally established. The expressive and melodious delivery of a thought in a complete sentence has one expressive method above all others. If we agree in the interpretation of the meaning of the language, there will be found the same harmony in its vocal expression in the slides of the voice. The author once had occasion to satisfy his own ear in the intonations of a sentence, and, arranging the test-exercise in such a way that his class of twenty theological students could not be imitating one another, he found that they all agreed in the meaning, and nineteen out of twenty gave precisely the same inflections. If we should take the well-known sentence from Patrick Henry, "It is natural for man to indulge in the illusions of hope," and deliver it with the intention of emphasizing the thought that it is native to man to hope, and that hope is delusive, we should find the falling slide upon "natural," a slight lifting of the voice on "man" and "indulge," on the word "illusions" the rising circumflex, a rising upon "of," and the descending slide of completed sense upon "hope." Nineteen out of every twenty readers would give the inflections above indicated, provided they accepted precisely the same meaning. This is simply referred to as one of countless instances where the sentence has a fixed law in its expression. But, as the law must be adapted to the meaning in every case, it would multiply rules too numerously to attempt any detailed arrangement of them. In every case let the reader satisfy himself that he is in full possession of the meaning, and that he is primarily striving to convey that meaning, then, in all probability, the slides will be correct, natural, and expressive. But there is matter enough for years of profitable study and close observation for any public speaker who will give attention to the subject.

Oftentimes the inflection is the leading effect in the interpretation of the language vocally.

The falling inflection through the "earnest" slide—that is to say, the fifth—is essential to the expression of scorn and irony contained in the forty-fourth chapter of Isaiah. The prophet describes the futility and the folly of making a god of a graven image, and falling down unto it and worshipping it. He shows that the molten image is made by human hands, the smith fashioning it with hammers, and that the graven image is from the stock of a tree, which the carpenter makes after the figure of a man. The same fuel is used for the fire, and to this the idolater prays: "Deliver me, for thou art my god." It is of this that the prophet is intolerant, and scornfully and ironically exposes the unreasonableness and wickedness of the deceived heart of the idolater. To read it with the ordinary unimpassioned slide is to make the statements as though they were accepted truth, instead of the emphatic irony which is implied in the constant downward slide of the "earnest" fifth.

1. *Irony and Scorn.*

"They that make a graven image are all of them vànity; and their delectable things shall not pròfit; and they are their own witnesses; they sèe not, nor knòw, that they may be ashàmed. Who hath formed a gòd, or molten a graven image, that is profitable for nòthing? Behold, all his fel-

INFLECTION OR SLIDE. 91

lows shall be ashāmed: and the workmen, they are of mèn: let them all be gathered togèther, let them stand ùp; yet they shall fèar, and they shall be ashāmed togèther. The smith with the tongs both worketh in the coals, and fashioneth it with hàmmers, and worketh it with the strength of his àrms: yea, he is hùngry, and his strength fàileth: he drinketh no water, and is fàint. The carpenter stretcheth out his rùle: he marketh it out with a lìne; he fitteth it out with plànes, and he marketh it out with the còmpass, and maketh it after the figure of a màn, according to the bèauty of a man, that it may remain in the house. He heweth him down cèdars, and taketh the cypress and the òak, which he strengtheneth for himself among the trees of the fòrest: he planteth an òak, and the rain doth nourish it. Then shall it be for a man to bùrn: for he will take thereof, and wàrm himself; yea, he kindleth it, and baketh brèad; yea, he maketh a gòd, and wòrshipeth it; he maketh it a graven ìmage, and falleth dòwn thereto. He burneth part thereof in the fire; with part thereof he eateth flèsh; he roasteth roast, and is sàtisfied; yea, he wàrmeth himself, and saith, Ahà! I am wàrm, I have seen the fìre: and the residue thereof he maketh a gòd, even his graven ìmage: he falleth down unto it, and wòrshipeth it, and pràyeth unto it, and saith, Deliver me, for thou art my gòd. They have not known nor understòod: for he hath shùt their eyes that they can not see; and their hèarts, that they can not understànd. And none considereth in his hèart, neither is there knowledge nor understànding to say, I have bùrned part of it in the fìre; yea, also, I have baked bread upon the còals thereof; I have roasted flèsh, and èaten it: and shall I make the residue thereof an abominàtion? shall I fall down to the stock of a trèe? He feedeth on àshes: a deceived heart hath turned him aside, that he can not deliver his soul, nor say, Is there not a lìe in my right hand?"—Isaiah, xliv., 9-20.

Indignant expostulation and authoritative proclamation of the law require in their expression the "earnest" *downward* slide.

2. "Yet ye say, The way of the Lord is not equal. Heàr now, O house of Israel; is not my way eqúal? Are not your ways unéqual? When a righteous man turneth away from his righteousness, and committeth iniquity, and dieth in them; for his iniquity that he hath done shall he die. Again, when the wicked man turneth away from his wickedness that he hath committed, and doeth that which is lawful and right, he shall sàve his soul alive. Because he considereth, and turneth away from all his transgressions that he hath committed, he shall surely lìve, he shall not die. Yet saith the house of Israel, The way of the Lord is not équal. O house of Israel, are not my ways equal? are not your ways unequal? Therefore I will jùdge you, O house of Israel, every one according to his wàys, saith the Lord God. Repènt, and tùrn yourselves from all your transgrèssions; so iniquity shall not be your rùin. Cast away from you all your transgrèssions, whereby ye have transgrèssed; and make you a nèw heart and a nèw spirit: for why' will ye diè, O house of Israel? For I have no pleasure in the death of him that dieth, saith the Lord God : wherefore túrn yourselves, and livé ye."— Ez. xviii., 25–32.

In the Third Commandment, the downward slide with emphasis upon "vain" and "guiltless" renders these words expressive.

3. "Thou shalt not take the name of the Lord thy God in vaìn; for the Lord will not hold him guìltless that taketh His name in vaìn."

Tender expostulation finds perfect exemplification in the second Warning to the Holy Communion. The pathos of the appeal, the rebuke, expostulation, and affectionate command, all take the downward drift of the voice.

Emphatic Falling Slide of Enumeration.—"For behold

this selfsame thing, that ye sorrowed after a godly sort, what cárefulness it wrought in you, yea, what cleáring of yourselves, yea, what indignàtion, yea, what feár, yea, what vehement desìre, yea, what zeál, yea, what revènge! In all things ye have approved yourselves to be clear in this matter.—II. Cor. vii., 11.

4. —" The Lord's Supper: unto which, in God's behalf, I bid you all who are here present, and beseech you, for the Lord Jesus Christ's sake, that ye will not refuse to come thereto, being so lovingly called and bidden by God himself. Ye know how grievous and unkind a thing it is, when a man hath prepared a rich feast, decked his table with all kind of provision, so that there lacketh nothing but the guests to sit down; and yet they who are called (without any cause) most unthankfully refuse to come. Which of you in such a case would not be moved? Who would not think a great injury and wrong done unto him?

. . . .

Wherefore, according to mine office, I bid you, in the name of God, I call you in Christ's behalf, I exhort you, as ye love your own salvation, that ye will be partakers of this holy Communion."

The earnest interrogation in the following passage from Jeremiah, vii., 9–11, is expressed by the upward slide:

5. "Will ye steál, múrder, and commit adúltery, and swear falsely, and burn incense unto Báal, and walk after other gods whom ye know not; and come and stand before me in this house, which is called by My Name, and say, We are delivered to dó all these abominátions? Is this house, which is called by My Name, become a den of róbbers in your eyes? Behold, even I have seen it, saith the Lord."

Argumentative interrogation has the same *rising* slide:

6. "Are áll apostles? are áll prophets? are áll teachers? are áll workers of miracles? Have áll the gifts of

healing? do áll speak with tongues? do áll interpret?"—II. Cor. xii., 29, 30.

Indignant address, whether in the declarative or interrogative form, has both the rising and falling slide, through the interval of the fifth.

7. "Is it súch a fast that I have chosen? a day for a man to afflict his sóul? Is it to bow down his head as a búlrush, and to spread sackcloth and áshes under him? wilt thou call thís a fast and an acceptable day unto the Lord? Is not this the fast that I have chosen? to loose the bands of wickedness, to undo the heavy búrdens, and to let the oppressed go frèe, and that ye break every yòke? Is it not to deal thy bread to the hùngry, and that thou bring the poor that are cast out to thy hòuse? when thou seest the naked, that thou còver him; and that thou hide not thyself from thine own flèsh?"—Isaiah, lviii., 5–7.

The unimpassioned slides of the voice are chiefly for argumentative declaration and hortatory effect, where thought is aroused and enforced, rather than the impulses of feeling.

8. "I say then, Have they stúmbled that they should fáll? God forbìd: but rather through their fàll salvátion is come unto the Gèntiles, for to provoke them to jealousy. Now, if the fàll of them be the riches of the world, and the diminishing of them the riches of the Gentiles; how much mòre their fullness? For I speak to you Gentiles, inasmuch as I am the apostle of the Gentiles, I magnify mine office: if by any means I may provoke to emulation them which are my flesh, and might save some of them. For if the casting away of them be the reconconciling of the wórld, what shall the recerving of them be but lífe from the dèad? For if the first fruit be hóly, the lùmp is also hòly: and if the root be hóly, só are the brànches. And if some of the branches be broken òff, and thou, being a wild olive trée, wert graffed in amòng

them, and with them partakest of the root and fatness of the òlive-tree; boast not against the brànches. But if thou bòast, thou bearest not the róot, but the róot thèe. Thou wilt say then, The branches were broken off, that I might be graffed in. Wéll; because of unbelièf they were broken off, and thòu standest by faith. Be not high-minded, but feàr: for if God spared not the nàtural brànches, take heed lest he also spare not thèe. Behold therefore the goódness and sevèrity of God; on them which fèll, sevèrity; but toward thèe, goódness, if thou contìnue in his goódness: otherwise thòu also shalt be cut off. And thèy also, if they abide not still in unbelíef, shall be graffed in: for God is able to graff them in again."—Rom. xi., 11–23.

9. "Are they Hèbrews? so am Ì. Are they Ìsraelites? so am Ì. Are they the seed of Àbraham? so am Ì. Are they ministers of Chríst? (I speak as a fool,) I am mòre; in làbors more abundant, in strìpes abóve mèasure, in prìsons more frèquent, in deàths òft. Of the Jews fíve tìmes received I fórty strìpes save one. Thrìce was I beaten with ròds, oncé was I stòned, thrìce I suffered shìpwreck, a night and a day I have been in the dèep; in joùrneyings often, in perils of wàters, in perils of ròbbers, in perils by mine own coùntrymen, in perils by the hèathen, in perils in the city, in perils in the wilderness, in perils in the séa, in perils among fàlse brethren; in wèariness and painfulness, in wàtchings often, in hùnger and thìrst, in fàstings often, in cóld and nàkedness. Beside those things that are withóut, that which cometh upon me daily, the cáre of all the chùrches. Whò is weák, and Ì am not weak? whò is offénded, and Ì búrn nòt?"—II. Cor. xi., 22–29.

10. "But in all things approving ourselves as the ministers of Gód, in much pàtience, in afflìctions, in necèssities, in distrèsses. In stripes, in imprìsonments, in tùmults, in làbors, in wàtchings, in fàstings; By pùreness, by knòwledge, by long sùffering, by kindness, by the Hóly

Ghòst, by lóve unfeìgned. By the word of trùth, by the pówer of Gòd, by the armor of ríghteousness on the ríght hand and on the lèft, by hónor and dishònor, by évil report and goòd report: as decèivers and yet truè; as unknówn, and yet wèll known; as dyíng, and, behold, we livè; as chástened, and not kìlled; as sórrowful, yet alway rejoìcing; as poòr, yet making many rích; as having nóthing, and yet possessing àll things."—II. Cor. vi., 4–10.

11. "Take heed that ye do not your alms before mèn, to be seèn of them: otherwise ye have no reward of your Father which is in heaven. Therefore when thou doest thine álms, do not sound a trùmpet before thee, as the hypocrites do in the synagogues and in the streèts, that they may have glory of mèn. Verily I say unto you, They have their reward. But when thou doest álms, let not thy lèft hand know what thy right hand dòeth: that thine alms may be in sècret: and thy Father which seèth in secret himself shall rewárd thee òpenly. And when thou pràyest, thou shalt not be as the hypocrites are: for they love to pray standing in the synagogues and in the corners of the strèets, that they may be seen of mèn. Verily I say unto you, They hàve their reward. But thou, when thou pràyest, enter into thy clòset, and when thou has shut thy doòr, pray to thy Father which is in sècret; and thy Father which seeth in sécret shalt rewárd thee òpenly. But when ye prày, use not vain repetitions, as the heàthen do: for they think that they shall be heard for their mùch speaking. Be not yè therefore like unto thèm: for your Father knòweth what things ye have neèd of, before ye àsk him." St. Matt. vi., 1–8.

In antithetical passages the clauses are balanced by answering inflections, the first usually taking the rising inflection and the second the falling—both of the unimpassioned *third*. The sameness of the effect in the repetition of the inflection is relieved by changes in pitch, varieties in movement, and varied length of the pauses. These changes render such a passage as the following expressive, instead of being mechanical, from the effect of the mere repetition of sound :

Alternating Slides.

12. "And besides this, giving all diligence, add to your faith virtue ; and to virtue knowledge ; and to knowledge, temperance ; and to temperance, patience ; and to patience, godliness ; and to godliness, brotherly kindness ; and to brotherly kindness, charity."—II. Pet. i., 5–7.

"For I am persuaded, that neither death, nor life, nor angels, nor principalities, nor powers, nor things present, nor things to come, nor height, nor depth, nor any other creature, shall be able to separate us from the love of God, which is in Christ Jesus our Lord."—Rom. viii., 38, 39.

"'To every thing there is a season, and a time to every purpose under the heaven : a time to be born, and a time to die ; a time to plant, and a time to pluck up that which is planted ; a time to kill, and a time to heal ; a time to break down, and a time to build up ; a time to weep, and a time to laugh ; a time to mourn, and a time to dance ; a time to cast away stones, and a time to gather stones together ; a time to embrace, and a time to refrain from embracing ; a time to get, and a time to lose ; a time to keep, and a time to cast away ; a time to rend, and a time to sew ; a time to keep silence, and a time to speak ; a time to love, and a time to hate ; a time of war, and a time of peace."
—Eccl. iii., 1–8.

The antitheses in the Book of Proverbs conform to the suggestions given above, with the occasional exceptions, where both members of the antithesis are of solemn import, when the falling inflection is used in each of them.

The pathos in the extracts from the Book of Genesis below calls for the plaintive utterance of the *semitone*—a marked defect when misused, but properly employed if sympathetically expressive.

13. "And Reuben returned unto the pit ; and, behold,

Joseph was not in the pit; and he rent his clothes. And he returned unto his brethren, and said, The child is not; and I, whither shall I go? And they took Joseph's coat, and killed a kid of the goats, and dipped the coat in the blood; and they sent the coat of many colors, and they brought it to their father; and said, This have we found: know now whether it be thy son's coat or no. And he knew it, and said, It is my son's coat; an evil beast hath devoured him; Joseph is without doubt rent in pieces. And Jacob rent his clothes, and put sackcloth upon his loins, and mourned for his son many days. And all his sons and all his daughters rose up to comfort him; but he refused to be comforted; and he said, For I will go down into the grave unto my son mourning. Thus his father wept for him."—Gen. xxxvii., 29–35.

14. "And Jacob their father said unto them, Me have ye bereaved of my children: Joseph is not, and Simeon is not, and ye will take Benjamin away: all these things are against me. And Reuben spake unto his father, saying, Slay my two sons, if I bring him not to thee: deliver him into my hand, and I will bring him to thee again. And he said, My son shall not go down with you; for his brother is dead, and he is left alone: if mischief befall him by the way in the which ye go, then shall ye bring down my gray hairs with sorrow to the grave."—Gen. xlii., 36–38.

The feeling of contrition contained in the fifth and twelfth of the opening sentences for Daily Prayer is naturally expressed by the plaintive voice of the semitone. Indeed, most of the penitential expressions, wherever found, require the same minor intervals in the slide. This, of course, would include all but the three opening, the fourth, and last sentences.

15. "I acknowledge my transgressions; and my sin is ever before me."—Psalm li., 3.

"I will arise, and go to my father, and will say unto him, Father, I have sinned against heaven, and before thee, and am no more worthy to be called thy son."—St. Luke, xv., 18, 19.

In the deepest states of feeling, when the weight of the emotion suppresses the ordinary uses of the voice, the sustained level of continued sound known as the monotone takes place. This may occur in feelings strongly contrasted with each other, as in rapture and awe. The monotone is also heard in profound solemnity, reverence, grandeur, and highly wrought poetic passages.

16. "And there shall be signs in the sūn, and in the mōon, and in the stārs; and upon the eārth distress of nations, with perplēxĭty; the sēa and the wāves roaring; men's heārts fāiling them for feār, and for lōoking after thōse things which are cōming on the eārth; for the pōwers of heāven shall be shāken. And thēn shall they sēe the Sōn of mān cōming in a clōud with pōwer and grēat glōry."— St. Luke, xxi., 25-27.

The monotonous effect which might be produced by the constant repetition of this inflection in the reading of the portion of Scripture appointed for the Epistle for All Saints' Day, can be varied by emphasizing both words, "twelve" and "thousand," with full length in each case, and the falling slide upon "thoùsand":

"And I sāw another āngel ascēnding from the ēast, having the sēal of the līving Gōd; and he cried with a lōud voice to the fōur āngels, to whōm it was given to hūrt the eārth and the sēa, saying, Hurt not the eārth, neither the sēa, nor the trēes, till we have sēaled the sērvants of our God in their forèheads. And I heard the number of them which were sealed; and there were sēaled an hūndred and fōrty and fōur thoùsand, of āll the trībes of the children of Israel.

"Of the tribe of Judah were sealed twélve thoùsand.
"Of the tribe of Reuben were sealed twélve thoùsand.
"Of the tribe of Gad were sealed twélve thoùsand.
"Of the tribe of Aser were sealed twélve thoùsand.

"Of the tribe of Nephthalim were sealed twélve thoùsand.

"Of the tribe of Manasses were sealed twélve thoùsand.
"Of the tribe of Simeon were sealed twélve thoùsand.
"Of the tribe of Levi were sealed twélve thoùsand.
"Of the tribe of Issachar were sealed twélve thoùsand.
"Of the tribe of Zabulon were sealed twélve thoùsand.
"Of the tribe of Joseph were sealed twélve thoùsand.

"Of the tribe of Benjamin were sealed twélve thoùsand.

"After this I behēld, and lō, a grēat mūltitude, which nō mān could nūmber, of all nātions, and kĭndreds, and people, and tōngues, stōod befōre the thrōne, and befōre the Lāmb, clōthed with whīte rōbes, and pālms in their hānds; and crīed with a loūd voice, sāying, Salvātion to our Gōd which sĭtteth upon the thrōne, and unto the Lamb! And āll the āngels stood round about the thrōne, and about the ĕlders, and the fōur beasts, and fĕll before the thrōne on their fāces, and worshiped Gōd, sāying, Amēn. Blēssing, and glōry, and wīsdom, and thānksgiving, and hōnour, and pōwer, and mīght, be unto our Gōd for ēver and ĕver! Amĕn."—Rev. vii., 2-12.

The solemnity and awe of the Burial Service, in its proper reading, are due to the frequent recurrence of this slide throughout the greater part. In the Lesson, however, and the prayers, greater variety is demanded.

17. *From the Burial Anthem.*

"Lōrd, let me knōw my ĕnd, and the number of my dāys, that I may be certified hōw lōng I have to līve. Behōld, thou hast made my days as it were a spān long, and mine āge is even as nōthing in respect of thēe; and verily ĕvery mān līving is altogether vănity. For mān wālketh in a vāin shădow, and disquieteth himself in vāin; he hēapeth up rĭches, and căn not tĕll whō shall găther them. And nōw, Lōrd, what is my hōpe? Truly my hōpe is even in thĕe. Deliver me from all mine offĕnces, and make me not a rebūke unto the foŏlish. . . . Thou hast set our mīsdĕeds befōre thēe, and our sĕcret sĭns in the light of thy coŭntenance. For whĕn thou art āngry, all our days are gōne; we bring our yĕars to an ēnd, as it were a tāle that is tōld. The dāys of our āge are thrēescōre yĕars and tĕn; and though mĕn be sō strŏng that they come to foŭrscōre years, yet is their strĕngth then but lābor and sŏrrow, so sŏon passeth it awāy, and we are gŏne. So teach us to nŭmber our dāys, that we may apply our hearts unto wisdŏm."

CHAPTER X.

MOVEMENT.

The rate or movement must, of course, be decided by the character of the thought or feeling to be expressed. Gravity of thought and depth of feeling as certainly require a slow movement as a quickening feeling demands the reverse. This arises from the law of the formation of the feeling. If it be gradual, the utterance is correspondingly slow. If it be instantaneous, the expression is of the same sudden character. Awe, for instance, because it is very slowly developed into its deepest degree, can be properly delivered only at a slow rate. Animation, on the other hand, must be quick, or it will lose its true life. As obvious as this natural law is perceived to be, by its mere statement, it is constantly violated in poor speaking.

A movement of the voice at variance with the feeling is simply destructive to the existence of such feeling. It is not merely inexpressive; it is exhausting to the patience of the hearer, when a movement that is too slow takes the place of the quickened rate, requisite to the proper communication of all animated mental action.

An undeviating sameness in movement, especially if it be slow, or even moderate, very seriously impairs a delivery otherwise natural and effective. It not merely empties the style of the feeling which should be there, but is almost equally destructive of the power to impart connected thought to the hearer. The impetuosity which comes from a highly wrought mental condition, a rapid succession of ideas, or an eager desire to imprint the truth on the hearer's mind, is less objectionable than the sluggish movement of expressing dull and scanty thought, yet, being at variance with nature, it makes a sacrifice where a gain might be had.

1. *The Uses of Knowledge.—Alison.*

"One great end to which all knowledge ought to be employed is the welfare of humanity. Every science is the foundation of some art beneficial to men; and while the study of it leads us to see the beneficence of the laws of nature, it calls upon us also to follow the great end of the Father of nature, in their employment and application.

"I need not say what a field is thus opened to the benevolence of knowledge; I need not tell you that, in every department of learning, there is good to be done to mankind. I need not remind you that the age in which we live has given us the noblest examples in this kind, and that science now finds its highest glory in improving the condition, or in allaying the miseries of humanity."

2. *Admonition.—Anonymous.*

"'Tis not in man
To look unmoved upon that heaving waste,
Which, from horizon to horizon spread,
Meets the o'erarching heavens on every side,
Blending their hues in distant faintness there.

"'Tis wonderful—and yet, my boy, just such
Is life. Life is a sea as fathomless,
As wide, as terrible, and yet sometimes

As calm and beautiful. The light of heaven
Smiles on it; and 'tis decked with every hue
Of glory and of joy. Anon dark clouds
Arise; contending winds of fate go forth;—
And Hope sits weeping o'er a general wreck.
 "And thou must sail upon this sea, a long,
Eventful voyage. The wise *may* suffer wreck—
The *foolish* must. Oh! then be early wise!
Learn from the mariner his skillful art
To ride upon the waves, and catch the breeze,
And dare the threatening storm, and trace a path
'Mid countless dangers, to the destined port
Unerringly secure. Oh! learn from him
To station quick-eyed Prudence at the helm,
To guard thy sail from Passion's sudden blasts,
And make Religion thy magnetic guide,
Which, though it trembles as it lowly lies,
Points to the light that changes not—in heaven."

Moderate Movement.—It is difficult, by description, even to suggest an approach to the precise movement properly termed *moderate*, because, with the same subject-matter, the rate of delivery would vary according to the size of the auditorium where it was to be delivered. A large building requires a proportionally slow movement, as compared with a church of smaller dimensions. Distinctness of articulation and other proprieties require this. But the rate of movement between that which would be recognized as slow or quick, yet slower than that of ordinary communication, would be a safe standard to follow. It implies deliberation and maturity of precomposed thought and a sufficient degree of seriousness in imparting it. It involves far more than would at first sight appear. For it implies clearness of perception in the thought, evident purpose in its delivery, a full degree of self-command, and a respectful recognition of, or deferential regard for, the hearers to whom the discourse is addressed. Precipitate utterance, and irregularity or fitfulness in the movement, or an unnecessary drawl, are all at variance with these considerations. The following extract should be read with moderate movement:

3. *Church Bells.—N. P. Willis.*

"I know of few things more imposing than to walk in the streets of a city when the peal of the early bells is just beginning. The deserted pavements, the closed windows of the places of business, the decent gravity of the solitary passenger, and, over all, the feeling, in your own bosom, that the fear of God is brooding, like a great shadow, over the thousand human beings who are sitting still in their dwellings around you, were enough, if there were no other circumstance, to hush the heart into religious fear. But when the bells peal out suddenly with a summons to the temple of God, and their echoes roll on through the desolate streets, and we are unanswered by the sound of any human voice, or the din of any human occupation, the effect has sometimes seemed to me more solemn than the near thunder."

Slow Movement.—The measured and deliberate movement of profoundest thought and deep feeling is an especial power, to be under the complete control of the speaker. Solemnity and all kindred feelings compel a measured movement, whose rate must be gauged according to the depth of the emotion. In practice, the speaker's ear should be able to mark the precise rate as distinctly as would be implied by the terms used in music. Reverence, to be truly expressed, should retard the movement, at whatever sacrifice of the minutes devoted to Divine Service. The indecent haste and rapidity of some readers of the Liturgy savor more of a desire to reach the sermon than the reverent worship of the God whom we serve. Familiarity with the Service and its frequent repetition are very liable to lead one unconsciously into irreverence in the expression, and should be guarded against as one of the errors in the careless use of a precomposed form. Extemporized prayer has no advantage in this respect, however, if fluency of expression is allowed to degenerate into undue familiarity of manner.

The following extract, being, in its degree of feeling, very near the moderate movement, is placed first as an example of the slow movement. The succeeding illustrations follow each other in natural order, retarding the slow till it reaches the slowest degree:

1. *Manfred (alone).—Byron.*

"The stars are forth, the moon above the tops
Of the snow-shining mountains. Beautiful!
I do remember me that in my youth,
When I was wandering—upon such a night
I stood within the Coliseum's wall,
'Midst the chief relics of almighty Rome;
The trees which grew along the broken arches
Waved dark in the blue midnight, and the stars
Shone through the rents of ruin; from afar
The watch-dog bay'd beyond the Tiber; and
More near from out the Cæsars' palace came
The owl's long cry, and, interruptedly,
Of distant sentinels the fitful song
Begun and died upon the gentle wind.
Some cypresses beyond the time-worn beach
Appear'd to skirt the horizon, yet they stood
Within a bowshot. Where the Cæsars dwelt,
And dwell the tuneless birds of night, amidst
A grove which springs through level'd battlements,
And twines its roots with the imperial hearths,
Ivy usurps the laurel's place of growth;
But the gladiator's bloody Circus stands,
A noble wreck, in ruined perfection!

While Cæsar's chambers, and the Augustan halls,
Grovel on earth in indistinct decay.
And thou didst shine, thou rolling moon, upon
All this, and cast a wide and tender light,
Which soften'd down the hoar austerity
Of rugged desolation, and fill'd up,
As 'twere anew, the gaps of centuries;
Leaving that beautiful which still was so,
And making that which was not, till the place
Became religion, and the heart ran o'er
With silent worship of the great of old!—
The dead, but sceptered sovereigns, who still rule
Our spirits from their urns."

Pathos, being a deeper feeling than that of the tranquillity preceding, naturally calls for slow movement.

2. *The Captive.—Sterne.*

"I looked through the twilight of the captive's grated door, to take his picture.

"I beheld his body half wasted away with long expectation and confinement, and felt what kind of sickness of the heart it is which arises from hope deferred. Upon looking nearer, I saw him pale and feverish: in thirty years the western breeze had not once fanned his blood; he had seen no sun, no moon, in all that time: nor had the voice of friend or kinsman breathed through his lattice: his children—

"But here my heart began to bleed; and I was forced to go on with another part of the portrait.

"He was sitting upon the ground, upon a little straw, in the farthest corner of his dungeon, which was alternately his chair and his bed. A little calendar of small sticks was laid at the head, notched all over with the dismal days and nights he had passed there; he had one of these little sticks in his hand, and with a rusty nail he was etching another day of misery to add to the heap. As I darkened the little light he had, he lifted up a hopeless eye toward the door, then cast it down, shook his head, and went on with his work of affliction. I heard his chains upon his legs, as he turned his body to lay his little stick upon the bundle. He gave a deep sigh; I saw the iron enter into his soul. I burst into tears. I could not sustain the picture of confinement which my fancy had drawn."

3. *Thanatopsis.—Bryant.*

"So live, that when thy summons comes to join
The innumerable caravan, that moves
To that mysterious realm, where each shall take
His chamber in the silent halls of death,
Thou go not, like the quarry slave at night,
Scourged to his dungeon, but, sustained and soothed
By an unfaltering trust, approach thy grave,
Like one who wraps the drapery of his couch
About him, and lies down to pleasant dreams."

4. *Paradise Lost.—Milton.*

"Thee, Father, first they sung, omnipotent,
Immutable, immortal, infinite,
Eternal King: Thee, Author of all being,
Fountain of light, thyself invisible
Amidst the glorious brightness where Thou sitt'st
Throned inaccessible, but when Thou shad'st
The full blaze of thy beams, and, through a cloud
Drawn round about Thee, like a radiant shrine,
Dark with excessive bright, thy skirts appear,
Yet dazzle Heaven that brightest seraphim
Approach not, but with both wings veil their eyes."

The extract from the Baptismal Service calls for the natural transition from the "moderate" movement to the "slow," in passing from the address to the sponsors to the solemn demands of the Questions and the sign of the engrafting into the covenant.

5. "Dearly beloved, ye have brought this Child here to be baptized ; ye have prayed that our Lord Jesus Christ would vouchsafe to receive him, to release him from sin, to sanctify him with the Holy Ghost, to give him the kingdom of heaven, and everlasting life. Ye have heard also that our Lord Jesus Christ hath promised in his Gospel to grant all these things that ye have prayed for : which promise he, for his part, will most surely keep and perform.

"Wherefore, after this promise made by Christ, this Infant must also faithfully, for his part, promise by you that are his sureties (until he come of age to take it upon himself) that he will renounce the devil and all his works, and constantly believe God's holy Word, and obediently keep his commandments.

"I demand therefore,

"Dost thou, in the name of this Child, renounce the devil and all his works, the vain pomp and glory of the world, with all covetous desires of the same, and the sinful desires of the flesh, so that thou wilt not follow nor be led by them ?

"*Answer.* I renounce them all ; and, by God's help, will endeavor not to follow, nor be led by them.

"*Minister.* Dost thou believe all the Articles of the Christian Faith, as contained in the Apostles' Creed ?

"*Answer.* I do.

"*Minister.* Wilt thou be baptized in this Faith ?

"*Answer.* That is my desire.

"*Minister.* Wilt thou then obediently keep God's holy will and commandments, and walk in the same all the days of thy life ?

"*Answer.* I will, by God's help.

. . . .

"We receive this Child into the congregation of Christ's flock ; and do sign him with the sign of the Cross, in token that hereafter he shall not be ashamed to confess the faith of Christ crucified, and manfully to fight under his banner, against sin, the world, and the devil ; and to continue

Christ's faithful soldier and servant unto his life's end. Amen."

In the reading of the first of the "Sentences" of Daily Prayer, if the reader is to utter the words as actually in the Lord's presence, and is to impress his fellow-worshipers that the Lord is with them of a truth, then he must by necessity give that gravity and solemnity to the movement which alone can correspond with the thought.

6. "The Lord is in his holy temple; let all the earth keep silence before him."—Hab. ii., 20.

7. *From the Burial Service.*—"Man, that is born of a woman, hath but a short time to live, and is full of misery. He cometh up, and is cut down, like a flower; he fleeth as it were a shadow, and never continueth in one stay.

"In the midst of life we are in death: of whom may we seek for succor but of thee, O Lord, who for our sins are justly displeased?

"Yet, O Lord God most holy, O Lord most mighty, O holy and most merciful Saviour, deliver us not into the bitter pains of eternal death.

8. "I heard a voice from heaven, saying unto me, Write, From henceforth blessed are the dead who die in the Lord: even so saith the Spirit; for they rest from their labors."— Rev. xiv., 13.

The majesty of the theme in the first chapter of Genesis demands the "slow" movement to fitly give the character of the narrative.

9. "In the beginning God created the heaven and the earth. And the earth was without form, and void; and darkness was upon the face of the deep. And the Spirit of God moved upon the face of the waters. And God said, Let there light: and there was light. And God saw the light, that it was good: and God divided the light from the darkness. And God called the light Day, and the darkness he called Night. And the evening and the morning were

the first day. And God said, Let there be a firmament in the midst of the waters, and let it divide the waters from the waters. And God made the firmament, and divided the waters which were under the firmament from the waters which were above the firmament: and it was so. And God called the firmament Heaven. And the evening and the morning were the second day. And God said, Let the waters under the heaven be gathered together unto one place, and let the dry land appear: and it was so. And God called the dry land Earth; and the gathering together of the waters called he Seas: and God saw that it was good. And God said, Let the earth bring forth grass, the herb yielding seed, and the fruit-tree yielding fruit after his kind, whose seed is in itself, upon the earth: and it was so. And the earth brought forth grass, and herb yielding seed after his kind, and the tree yielding fruit, whose seed was in itself, after his kind: and God saw that it was good. And the evening and the morning were the third day."— Gen. i., 1–13.

An emphatically slow movement, when rightly employed, giving deliberation to the expression of the thought, and weighing the words of solemn import, increases the solemnity of expression to a marked degree, if it be not continued too long. And a still deeper impression is produced in the utterance of awe and similar feelings. Indeed, there can be no proper expression of awe when there is any approach to a quick, or even moderate movement.

"Out of the deep have I called unto thee, O Lord; Lord, hear my voice. O let thine ears consider well the voice of my complaint. If thou, Lord, wilt be extreme to mark what is done amiss, O Lord, who may abide it? For there is mercy with thee; therefore shalt thou be feared. I look for the Lord; my soul doth wait for him; in his word is my trust. My soul fleeth unto the Lord before the morning watch; I say, before the morning watch. O Israel, trust in the Lord; for with the Lord there is mercy, and with him is plenteous redemption. And he shall redeem Israel from all his sins."

Lively Movement.—This element of expression has two distinct uses—one for the natural increase in the rapidity of the movement for enlivened feeling, such as might be classed under the head of animation, and, secondly, that degree of rapidity which energetic and excited feeling in all divisions would require. We may easily mark five natural distinctions of rate or movement of the voice in the divisions for exercise—slowest, slow, moderate, animated, quick. It should be observed that these are natural, not arbitrary, distinctions, and the speaker who confines himself to one undeviating movement, by such use of his voice, impedes his own power in the vocal expression of his thought or feeling. These distinctions, from their simplicity, would appear to be the veriest truisms. Indeed, they are so obvious that they would find no mention here were it not for the fact that many speakers, who admit them in theory, utterly disregard them in practice. They acknowledge the propriety and absolute necessity of adapting the measurement of the voice to the sentiment, in every case, yet hold to a sameness of expression that seriously weakens their power of delivery. As we could not endure the incessant repetition of the same thought in language, so we can not more easily accept the continued use of the same movement. It is dull, soporific, and stupefying to the greatest degree.

Rapid Movement.

1. *How they brought the Good News.—Browning.*

" Behind shut the postern, the lights sank to rest,
And into the midnight we galloped abreast.

" Not a word to each other; we kept the great pace
Neck by neck, stride for stride, never changing our place;

I turned in my saddle and made its girth tight,
Then shortened each stirrup, and set the pique right,
Rebuckled the check-strap, chained slacker the bit,
Nor galloped less steadily Roland, a whit."

The following selection, from its mental vivacity, will serve as an excellent illustration of quick movement:

2. *To a Skylark.—Shelley.*

Hail to thee, blithe spirit,
 Bird thou never wert,
That from heaven, or near it,
 Pourest thy full heart
In profuse strains of unpremeditated art.

Higher still and higher,
 From the earth thou springest
Like a cloud of fire ;
 The deep blue thou wingest,
And singing still dost soar, and soaring ever singest.

3. "Every difficulty, and every trial, that occurs in your path is a fresh opportunity presented by his kindness of improving the happiness after which he hath taught you to aspire. By every hardship which you sustain in the wilderness you secure an additional portion of the promised land. What though the combat be severe ? A kingdom, an everlasting kingdom, is the prize of victory. Look forward to the triumph which awaits you, and your courage will revive. Fight the good fight, finish your course, keep the faith : there is laid up for you a crown of righteousness, which the Lord, the righteous Judge, shall give unto you at that day. What though, in the navigation of life, you have sometimes to encounter the war of elements? What though the winds rage, though the waters roar, and danger threatens around ? Behold at a distance the mountains appear. Your friends are impatient for your arrival;

already the feast is prepared, and the rage of the storm shall serve only to waft you sooner to the haven of rest. No tempests assail those blissful regions which approach to view—all is peaceful and serene; there you shall enjoy eternal comfort, and the recollection of the hardships which you now encounter shall heighten the felicity of better days."

CHAPTER XI.

PAUSES.

ONE means of separating the various divisions of thought in a sentence or paragraph is by proper *rests*, or *pauses*.

Words which express one idea are thus set apart by themselves, and the ear instinctively associates this classification of language with the relations of a single thought. The length of the pause is decided by the impressiveness of the thought we are striving to convey, or the emphasis we would give to one expression over another, by resting in preparation, or pausing after the emphatic idea, in order that it may be duly received.

All impressive and emphatic effect is especially dependent upon this element of expression. This may be seen by observing closely the natural result of pausing when a teacher would impress the memory, or emphasize a thought, or when a parent would give explanatory instruction or administer earnest rebuke to his child. To run the words together, without these natural separations by pausing, is very much like the old style of printing without spacing between the words.

There are few things in utterance which render the effect so puerile and expressionless as the disregard of these natural cessations of voice at the appropriate intervals. For this implies that the mind is not working consciously and intently, and is very much like the unmeaning sameness of a child's voice, in syllabication, while learning to read. But the right use of the pause implies not merely the intelligent appreciation of the thought expressed, but the determination to impress it on others. It pertains to mastery, in the effect of expression, by deliberate self-control, and by the utterance of the clearly defined conception of the idea. A speaker who is impelled by nervousness or excitement omits the rests which should impart an air of deliberation and thoughtfulness to the style, and reveals thereby a weakness, in being controlled by surrounding circumstances, rather than by what he intends to express.

It will be found, by attentive study and observation, that a pause preceding, as well as following, the emphatic word, gives great character to the expression. It implies, in such a case, the deliberate intention of maintaining the truth which is asserted, and assuming all the responsibility which such an assertion may imply—e. g., in the passage : "I maintain that the assertion is willfully and maliciously *false*," to give the word "false" with the strongest emphatic effect necessitates a pause before and after "willfully" and "maliciously," and that a pause preceding "false" be added to the pause following "maliciously," so as to double the time of the rest given after the word "willfully." The same impressive effect is frequently heard where there is solemnity of feeling to be conveyed. As : "There is one sure refuge for the oppressed, one sure resting-place for the weary—*the grave*." To disregard the pause preceding the words "the grave" annuls the sense, but is still more destructive to anything like solemn emotion.

There are few mechanical rules which can avail much to guide the voice in pausing, for it depends largely on every change of thought and feeling. The old-time direction of regarding the points of punctuation, as if primarily arranged for the elocutionary expression of the thought, has, fortunately, given way to something more sensible and reliable. It would undoubtedly be very convenient in reading if some system of punctuation could be devised to guide the rests of the voice in length and frequency, according to the intention of the author. This, however, would be complicated, and is impracticable. The use of the points of punctuation is for the grammatical arrangement of words, and not necessarily for distinctions of thought, or emphasis of feeling. This does not forbid a frequent coincidence of the pauses of the voice with the points of punctuation, but they are used in the text for another purpose, and frequently can not be observed in reading without subverting the sense. Moreover, the pause of the voice at completed sense, and, consequently, at a period, would be varied in its length according to the varieties of feeling. Under the influence of excited feeling, a pause of this sort would be very brief, while the reverse would be true if impressive thought or deep and solemn emotion were to be conveyed. There are also frequent pauses, some of them in the utterance of depth of feeling, and many of them very long, when no grammatical point can be found.

A proper introduction of pauses, to mark the natural divisions of the discourse, rests the ear and assists the memory. Even the pause preceding the discourse has much to do with the commanding effect of delivery. It implies a just regard of the solemnity of the office of declaring spiritual and momentous truth, and mastery of the occasion. Like other effects which are appropriate in their proper places, excessive use of this element of power becomes a defect. For let what might be termed the preparative pauses of a discourse be carried the slightest fraction of a second too far, and the effect not only loses all solemnity, but becomes positively ludicrous.

The Pause at the Introductory Words "saying," "say," and "said."—At the end of the Exhortation for Daily Prayer we have the expression, "Wherefore I pray and beseech you to accompany me with a pure heart and humble voice unto the throne of the heavenly grace, saying—" In the American book the word "saying" is punctuated with a dash after the word, which would seem to imply that the pause belongs properly here, at the end of the exhortation, and that the word should be uttered before kneeling. The opinion is expressed with great deference to those who prefer to utter it as immediately introductory to the Confession. But, if the English book be examined, it will be noted that, in the earlier prayer-books of 1552, 1559, 1604, and 1662, the phrase was originally "saying after me.", printed with a period, which would seem to render it inappropriate as an immediate introduction to the Confession. And, according to the last English standard, the same phrase is used—" saying after me;"—printed with a semicolon. These are the reasons why it seems fitting to use the word "saying" as a part of the Exhortation, and not simply as an introduction to the Confession.

In the Thanksgiving of the Baptismal Service, there being no rubric for change of posture, the expression, "Let us faithfully and devoutly give thanks unto Him, and say," is followed by a comma, which would seem to place it with the Exhortation, rather than with the Thanksgiving after it. In the Preface to the Decalogue, the deliberate emphasis on the word "said," in the expression, "God spake these words and said," with the pause following, gives weight to the thought of the Divine authority in the proclamation of the Law.

The whole moral effect of the extract below depends upon the gradually retarded movement, and the pause preceding and following "His" in the last line.

Pause.

" I smiled to think God's greatness flowed around our in-
    completeness—
Round our restlessness His rest."

CHAPTER XII.

EMPHASIS.

By this term we should understand something more than a change of force on a particular word or syllable. Almost every element of elocution will be called into play in some one or another of the changes of voice implied in "emphasis." A sudden percussion of explosive utterance would render a syllable emphatic—e. g., "It is *base* for a man to suffer when he ought to act." A change in quality may be equally emphatic : "There is one sure refuge for the weary—the grave," where the change from *pure* tone of the opening words to the *pectoral* quality, "the grave," renders the expression emphatic.* An increase of force emphasizes the expression : "Bearing for its motto no such miserable interrogatory as 'What is all this worth?' but everywhere, spread all over, in characters of living light, etc." A change in pitch may render a word or passage emphatic : "He woke (*high*) to die" (*low*). So through all the changes of stress, the sudden change to any feeling requiring a change in the stress would render the passage or syllable emphatic. In movement the change from fast to slow, or the reverse, will produce the effect of emphasis.
"Many ports will exult at the gleam of her mast. (*Fast.*)
Hush! hush! thou vain dreamer, this hour is her { *Very*
last."   { *slow.*

The intervals of the inflections become equally emphatic and expressive by their changes from preceding intervals in pitch. Pauses, in the same way, preceding and following emphatic words, are apt and expressive, according to their length and frequency. So slight a matter as increased distinctness of the utterance of a syllable may produce a

---

* It will be observed that the *pause* preceding "the grave," as described in the previous chapter, is also an element of the emphasis, which is further augmented by the change in *quality*.

marked emphatic effect. Indeed, as we study into the matter, we shall find that any marked change of the voice is a vehicle of emphasis. There is no necessity, therefore, for making the effect of emphasis dependent on force only, or upon any other single element of expression.

The right use of emphasis is primarily dependent on activity of thought, will, and sensibility of emotion, and, judiciously applied, would break up any tendency to unmeaning and undeviating monotony in reading and speaking. It serves the same purpose to the ear that nature presents to the eye in a vari-colored landscape, and which it is the highest aim of the painter's art to reproduce in form and color. The precise coloring of the tone in vocality which makes a word or phrase justly emphatic is the result of ready perception of sound by the ear, and expression and intelligence in its delivery. The humdrum and perfunctory tone of a heartless and, as we might say, thoughtless delivery, is indicated by the absence of all emphasis in the expressive effect. This becomes intolerably tedious in the delivery of thought from the pulpit, and scarcely less than irreverent in the reading of the prayers. It can not be that the speaker has the heart, the determination, to convey and impress his thought, unless there are those cases of emphasis in expression which reveal that purpose and indicate such determination. And, in the reading of the prayers, unless there is something like sympathetic response emotionally, and therefore vocally, the natural distinction implied in confession, in supplication, in gratitude, and thanksgiving, the heart of the reader and of the hearer alike are in danger of remaining unmoved. The same thought in the reading of the prayers would carry us naturally to those finer shades of feeling and those delicate colorings of emotion which are naturally suggested by the significance of the various titles of the Deity, and the subject-matter of the petitions following.

The object to be aimed at in the reading of the following extract is to mark clearly and emphatically the distinction between manly and womanly attributes in the description, and the commingling and interchanging of each, to form the ideal, intellectual, and moral unity of a perfect type. Without pointed emphasis, the thought will not be conveyed, much less enforced.

1. *From " The Princess."—Tennyson.*

"For wóman is not undevelopt mán,
But divèrse : could we make hèr as a mán,
Sweet love were slain, whose dearest bond is this
Not like to thée, but like in difference :
Yet in the long years liker must they gròw :
The mán be more of wóman, shé of mán ;
Hè gain in swéetness and in mòral héight,
Nor lose the wrèstling thèws that throw the world ;
Shè méntal breàdth, nor fail in childward càre :
More as the double natured Pòet each :
Till at the last she set herself to man,
Like perfect music unto noble words ;
And so these twáin, upon the skirts of Time,
Sit síde by síde, fùll-súmm'd in áll their pòwers,
Dispensing harvest, sowing the To-be,
Sélf-rèverent eách and rèverencing eách,
Distínct in individuàlities,
But like eách òther even as those who lòve.
Then comes the statelier Eden back to men ;
Then reigns the world's great bridals, chaste and calm ;
Then springs the crowning race of human kind.
May these things be !"

2. *All Christians Heralds of Divine Truth.—Leighton.*

"What the apòstles were in an extraòrdinary wáy (befitting the first annunciation of a religion for all mankind), this áll téachers of móral trúth (who aim to prepare for its reception by calling the attention of men to the law in their own hearts) máy, without presumption, consider themsélves to bé, under órdinary gifts and círcumstances: námely, ambàssadors for the Gréatest of Kìngs, and upon no mèan emplóyment, the great Treaty of Peáce and Reconcílement betwixt Hím and Mankìnd."

3. "But of those who seémed to be sómewhat, whatsoever they were, it maketh no matter to me: God accepteth no man's person: for they who seémed to be somewhat in cónference added nòthing to me: but còntrariwise, when they saw that the gospel of the ùncircumcision was committed unto mé, as the gospel of the circumcision was unto Péter; (for he that wrought effectually in Pèter to the apostleship of the círcumcision, the same was mighty in mé toward the Gèntiles;) and when Jámes, Céphas, and Jóhn, who seemed to be pillars, perceived the grace that was given unto me, they gave to mé and Bárnabas the right hands of fèllowship; that wè should go unto the héathen, and théy unto the circumcision."—Gal. ii., 6-11.

4. "For ye are not come unto the moùnt that might be toúched, and that bùrned with fíre, nor unto blàckness, and dàrkness, and témpest, and the sound of a trùmpet, and the voice of wòrds; which voice they that heard entreated that the word should not be spoken to them any more: (for they could not endure that which was commanded, And if so much as a beast touch the mountain, it shall be stoned, or thrust through with a dart: and so terrible was the sight, that Moses said, I exceedingly fear and quake:) but ye are come unto mount Sìon and unto the city of the lìving Gòd, the héavenly Jerùsalem, and to an innùmerable cómpany of àngels. To the general assembly and chúrch of the firstborn, which are written in héaven, and to Gòd the Judge of all, and to the spirits of jùst mén made pérfect. And to Jèsus the mediator of the new còvenant, and to the blóod of sprìnkling, that speaketh better things than that of Àbel."—Heb. xii., 18-24.

5. "For Christ also hath ònce súffered for sìns, the jùst

for the unjust, that he might bring us to God, being put to death in the flesh, but quickened by the Spirit: by which also he went and preached unto the spirits in prison; which sometime were disobedient, when once the longsuffering of God waited in the days of Noah, while the ark was a preparing, wherein few, that is, eight souls were saved by water. The like figure whereunto even baptism doth also now save us, (not the putting away of the filth of the flesh, but the answer of a good conscience toward God,) by the resurrection of Jesus Christ: who is gone into heaven, and is on the right hand of God; angels and authorities and powers being made subject unto him."—I. Pet. iii., 18–22.

Sometimes the very life of an entire passage (not necessarily scriptural) is dependent upon the emphasis applied throughout, e. g.:

1. "If Reason, in some of her most successful efforts, has disclosed some truths of great worth and divine import, the best of her productions are, nevertheless, but as the image in Nebuchadnezzar's dream: *though the* HEAD *be of* GOLD, *the* FEET *are of* IRON *and* CLAY."

Cumulative emphasis from repetition:

1. "Are they *Hebrews? So am I.* Are they *Israelites?* So AM I. Are they the seed of *Abraham?* SO AM I.

2. "From these walls a spirit shall go forth that shall survive, when this edifice shall be like an unsubstantial pageant faded. It shall go forth, exulting in, but not abusing, its strength. *It shall go forth*, remembering, in the days of its prosperity, the pledges it gave in the time of its depression. IT SHALL GO FORTH, uniting a disposition to correct abuses, to redress grievances. IT SHALL GO FORTH, uniting the disposition to improve, with the resolution to maintain and defend, by that spirit of unbought affection which is the chief defense of nations."

"What was it, fellow-citizens, which gave to Lafayette his spotless fame? *The love of liberty.* What has consecrated his memory in the hearts of good men? THE LOVE OF LIBERTY. What nerved his youthful arm with strength, and inspired him, in the morning of his days, with sagacity and counsel? THE LIVING LOVE OF LIBERTY. To what did he sacrifice power, and rank, and country, and freedom itself? TO THE LOVE OF LIBERTY PROTECTED BY LAW. . . . Listen, Americans, to the lesson which seems borne to us on the very air we breathe while we perform these dutiful rites. Ye winds, that wafted the pilgrims to the land of promise, fan in their children's hearts the love of freedom! Blood which our fathers shed, cry from the ground—echoing arches of this renowned hall, whisper back the voices of other days— glorious Washington! break the long silence of that votive canvas; speak, speak, marble lips; teach us THE LOVE OF LIBERTY PROTECTED BY LAW!"—*Everett.*

The negative *not* receives no emphasis unless in contradiction or especial contrast by antithesis. The contractions in colloquial use would show this—wouldn't, mustn't, can't, won't, etc. In the Ten Commandments, the emphasis is "shalt not," "ye would not." Also, "Rachel weeping for her children, and would not be comforted, because they are not," "Enoch was not, for God took him." And in the General Confession the emphasis is—"We have left undone the things which we ought to have *done.*" If the emphasis is placed on "ought," the inference is that on the whole we are about right.

In the Litany, avoid the error of saying "and all who are desolate and oppressed." The emphasis upon all would imply that all fatherless children and widows are oppressed. Avoid also the primary emphasis upon the first syllable of "circumcision"—a habit resulting from the frequent contrast of the word with "uncircumcision." There is a tendency, not uncommon, to emphasize the first syllables of "*cre*ation" and "*pre*servation," as if they were in contrast. In the Creed, the emphasis should be "the third day He *rose* again," not "rose *again*"; and the clause following, "according to the Scriptures," should be fully emphasized, to avoid the impression of flippancy. In the first prayer of the Baptismal Service, the pause preceding and the emphasis upon the word "water" are essential to the meaning, "Noah and his family were saved in the ark | by water," and is thus applied in the Baptismal Service. It was not from perishing by water that they were saved, but they were saved by water in the ark. "Suffer *us* not in *our* last hour" (not an uncommon misreading) by inference reflects upon the peace of the departed in *his* last hour. In the Lord's Prayer, "as *we* forgive those who trespass against *us*" is the clear meaning of the antithesis, for, as we have trespassed against God, and our fellow-men have trespassed against us, we pray to be forgiven, as we forgive them.

In reading the Lessons, the instances where false emphasis conveys a wrong meaning are almost numberless. Sometimes one may properly be in doubt as to the precise interpretation to be given to a passage. But whatever emphasis is used, some meaning in contrast with another which might be given is conveyed. This will be the case with all passages in which there is more than one allowable interpretation. Let us take a single passage—the words of Agrippa to St. Paul: "Almost thou persuadest me to be a Christian." In the revised version the phraseology is changed, so as to make a single meaning more obvious. But we will hold to the received version for study. If the primary emphasis is to be given according to the surface-meaning, and King Agrippa is really pondering the force of the apostle's words, and half-inclined to submit himself to the truth and become, like St. Paul, a believer in Christ, then the passage should be read as follows: "Almost thou persuadest me to be a *Christian*.

If, however, the king is thinking of St. Paul's conversion, and, submitting himself to the influences of the hour, thinks that it would be well for him also to become a Christian, then the sincerity of his half-persuasion would give the antithetic emphasis on "me," as if he had said to St. Paul: "*Thou* art a Christian, and thou almost persuadest *me*, also, to be one."

Another of what might be considered as the sincere utterances of the king could be expressed by placing the chief emphasis on "almost" and "persuadest." This would show the profound feeling of Agrippa, and the troubled condition of his mind, under the eloquent appeal of the apostle.

From these we might pass to the study of the passages as expressing irony, whether relating to the manner of conversion, the character of the proud king himself, the time taken in persuading him, or whatever additional thoughts might be involved in the discussion. Each reader must adopt the interpretation which seems most reasonable to him; only let him have some decided opinion, if possible, and express that, or else adopt none, and avoid any accent in reading which would bias the minds of his hearers.

In addition to the principles of interpretation, we find doctrine rightly or wrongly presented by the expression of the emphasis. In the first chapter of St. John's Gospel, if the primary purpose be to declare the divinity of the Word by His co-equality with the Father, then the emphasis is misplaced upon the words "with" and "was." If, however, this is not the chief thought of the Evangelist, then the emphasis may fall upon the little words. The first reading suggested above would give us the emphasis as follows:

"In the beginning was the *Word*, and the *Word* was with *God*, and the *Word* was *God*." By the second interpretation the accent would be as given here:

"In the beginning was the Word, and the Word was *with* God, and the Word *was* God."

These suggestions would apply to several of the verses following the one quoted above. In the words, "The world was made by *Him*," the emphasis would seem to fall properly upon the pronoun rather than upon the preposition.

And in the passage, "Without Him was not anything *made* that was *made*," the emphasis lies with greater force upon "made" than upon "was."

The reading of the Decalogue is emphatic throughout, and any suggestion of feebleness in the utterance implies insufficient authority. If we take the Third Commandment, for example, and read it without emphasis, we shall see how unsuggestive the language becomes, and how easy, not to say natural, a thing it would be for the listener to make light of the Law. How different is the effect when the voice of stern authority emphasizes the words "vain" and "guiltless" with full force and deliberate pausing!

As already suggested, it is apparent that the study of emphasis, to be fully exhaustive, would lead us through almost every passage of the Prayer-Book, the greater part of the sacred Scriptures, and all the utterances of the pulpit. The treatment of the subject in this place can, therefore, be only fragmentary and suggestive.

Passages of Scripture for Study in Emphasis.

The "*Emphatic Tie*," which is the tying of the voice in the connected passages by a return to the same force, pitch, etc., after the interruption of a parenthesis or the like :—

1. "For as many as have sinned without law, shall also perish without law : and as many as have sinned in the law, shall be *judged by the law*, ‖ (for not the hearers of the law are just before God, but the doers of the law shall be justified. ‖ For when the Gentiles, which have not the law, do by nature the things contained in the law, these, having not the law, are a law unto themselves : which showed the work of the law written in their hearts, their conscience also bearing witness, and their thoughts the meanwhile accusing, or else excusing, one another :) ‖ ‖ *in*

the day when God shall judge the secrets of men by Jesus Christ according to my gospel."—Rom. ii., 12-16.

2. "It is not expedient for me doubtless to glory. I will come to visions and revelations of the Lord. *I knew a man in Christ* above fourteen years ago, (whether in the body, I cannot tell; or whether out of the body, I cannot tell: God knoweth;) *such an one caught up to the third heaven. And I knew such a man,* (whether in the body, or out of the body, I cannot tell: God knoweth;) *How that he was caught up into paradise, and heard unspeakable words, which it is not lawful for a man to utter.*"—II. Cor. xii., 1-4.

Further Suggestions in Emphasis.—The fundamental principles of emphasis are so associated with the true rendering of the meaning that it seems almost superfluous to state that, in the critical study of the language for expression, some knowledge of the original Hebrew or Greek is essential. Of course, the profounder and more accurate the scholarship, the more certainly will the true reading rightly represent its labors. But it will be found that such knowledge is not all that is involved. For we have to take as our text the received version, and we are liable, even then, to misrepresent the teaching of a given passage. E. g., in St. Luke, xxiv., 25: "O fools, and slow of heart to believe all that the prophets have spoken!" A false emphasis not only subverts, but contradicts, the meaning, and makes it appear that the disciples were fools for believing what the prophets had spoken. The proper way of pronouncing the words is represented as follows: "O fools, and slow of heart to believe | all that the prophets have spoken!"

Other illustrations may be given to mark the same principle.

"Determined to sail *by* Ephesus"; the emphasis should here be given on "by," not on "Ephesus."—Acts, xx., 16.

"Saw in a vision *evidently*, about the ninth hour of the day;" emphasize "evidently."—Acts, x., 3.

"And there were two other | malefactors led with Him to be put to death"; emphasize "other," and pause.—St. Luke, xxiii., 32.

"They found Mary and Joseph, | and the babe lying in a manger." — St. Luke, ii., 16. A pause is not unfrequently heard after "babe," so as to class it with "Mary and Joseph."

The following may be explained by marks of emphasis:

"Servants, obey in all things your másters according to the flésh."—Col. iii., 22.

"And they that have believing masters, let them not despíse them, because they are brethren."—I. Tim. vi., 2.

"Wherefore, remember that ye being in time past Gentiles in the flesh, who are called Uncircumcision by that which is called the Circumcision | in the flesh | made by hands."—Eph. ii., 11.

"For then would they not have ceased to be óffered?"—Heb. x., 2.

"Because greáter is hé that is in yóu than hé that is in the wórld."—I. John, iv., 4.

"And he spáred not to take of his own flock."—II. Sam. xii., 4.

"They took Him even as He wás in the ship."—St. Mark, iv., 36.

"Take heed to thyself that thou offer not thy burnt offering in *every* place that thou seest: but in the place which the Lord shall *choose* in one of thy tribes, *there* thou shalt offer thy burnt offerings."—Deut. xii., 13, 14.

The following note was given to the author by a former professor of Hebrew at the Berkeley Divinity School:

"In Is. liii., 4, 'Surely *He* hath borne our griefs, and carried our sorrows, etc.,' attention is directed in the Hebrew to the subject 'He,' the pronoun being there expressed for emphasis."

The following are some of the passages that the author has heard read with erroneous emphasis. They are printed as they ought to be pronounced, the error consisting in disregarding the emphatic words:

"But to *this* man will I look."—Is. lxvi., 2.

"He that killeth an ox is *as if he slew a man;* he that sacrificeth a lamb, as if he cut off *a dog's neck;* he that offereth an oblation, as if he offered *swine's blood;* he that burneth incense, as if he blessed an *idol*."—Is. lxvi., 3.

"Therefore I said, Surely these are poor; they are foolish: for they know not the way of the Lord nor the judgment of their God. I will get me unto the great men, and will speak unto them; for they have known the way of the Lord and the judgment of their God; but *these* [i.e., *also*] have altogether broken the yoke and burst the bonds."—Jer. v., 4, 5.

"Now that He ascénded, what is it but that He also descénded first into the lower parts of the earth? He that descénded is the same also that ascénded up far above all heavens, that He might fill all things."—Eph. iv., 9, 10.

There is here no play upon the initial syllables of the words "ascended" and "descended," the antithesis being upon the height and depth.

CHAPTER XIII.

MELODY.

THE *musical* effect in the sustained delivery of some speakers is imparted largely by the rhythmical flow of voice. The pleasing impression of the recurrence of emphatic syllables in graduated successions of "time" is one of the graces of speech. When it is excessive, it is destructive to forcible and manly utterance; and when it is wanting the style is rendered harsh and brusque to the ear.

Practice upon passages of verse where the melody is

strongly marked is a serviceable drill to the ear and to the voice in securing this power of musical expression.

The practiced reader and speaker always has something of this effect of melodious utterance which distinguishes his more mature from his earlier efforts in public speaking, and which displays the mastery, self-possession, and deliberation in delivery which follow almost necessarily from years of practice. The more musical the style without sacrificing force in the effect, the more desirable does it become.

The voice should give the fullest musical and rhythmical flow to this passage:

1. *Drama of Exile. Chorus of Eden Spirits.—Mrs. Browning.*

   Spirits of the Trees.

   "Hark! the Eden trees are stirring,
   Slow and solemn to your hearing!
   Plane and cedar, palm and fir,
   Tamarisk and juniper,
   Each is throbbing in vibration
   Since that crowning of creation,
   When the God-breath spake abroad,
   Pealing down the depths of Godhead
   Let us make man like to God!
   And the pine stood quivering
     In the Eden-gorges wooded,
     As the awful word went by;
   Like a vibrant chorded string
     Stretched from mountain-peak to sky!
   And the cypress did expand,
     Slow and gradual, branch and head;
     And the cedar's strong black shade
   Fluttered brokenly and grand!
   Grove and forest bowed aslant
   In emotion jubilant."

Voice of the same, but softer.
"Which divine impulsion cleaves
  In dim movements to the leaves,
Dropt and lifted, dropt and lifted,
In the sunlight greenly sifted—
In the sunlight and the moonlight
  Greenly sifted through the trees.
Ever wave the Eden trees
  In the nightlight, and the noonlight,
With a ruffling of green branches
Shaded off to resonances;
  Never stirred by rain or breeze!
  Fare ye well, farewell!
The sylvan sounds, no longer audible,
  Expire at Eden's door!
  Each footstep of your treading
Treads out some murmur which ye heard before:
  Farewell! the trees of Eden
  Ye shall hear nevermore."

Flower Spirits.
"We linger, we linger,
  The last of the throng!
Like the tones of a singer
  Who loves his own song.
We are spirit-aromas
  Of blossom and bloom;
We call your thoughts home, as
  Ye breathe our perfume;
To the amaranth's splendor
  Afire on the slopes;
To the lily-bells tender,
  And gray heliotropes!
To the poppy-plains, keeping
  Such dream-breath and blé,
That the angels there stepping
  Grew whiter to see!

To the nook, set with moly,
  Ye jested one day in,
Till your smile waxed too holy
  And left your lips praying!
To the rose in the bower-place,
  That dripped o'er you sleeping;
To the asphodel flower-place,
  Ye walked ankle deep in!
We pluck at your raiment,
  We stroke down your hair—
We faint in our lament,
  And pine into air.
Fare ye well, farewell!
The Eden scents, no longer sensible,
  Expire at Eden's door!
Each footstep of your treading
Treads out some fragrance which ye knew before:
  Farewell! the flowers of Eden
  Ye shall smell nevermore."

Subdued Force.

2. *Tranquillity.—Montgomery.*

"Behold the bed of death—
  This pale and lovely clay!
Heard ye the sob of parting breath?
  Marked ye the eye's last ray?
No;—life so sweetly ceased to be,
  It lapsed in immortality."

Tenderness.

3. *The Death-Bed.—Hood.*

"We watched her breathing through the night,
  Her breathing soft and low,
As in her breast the wave of life
  Kept surging to and fro.

" Our very hopes belied our fears,
  Our fears our hopes belied ;
We thought her dying when she slept,
  And sleeping when she died.

" For when the morn came, dim and sad,
  And chill with early showers,
Her quiet eyelids closed—she had
  Another morn than ours."

SADNESS.

4. *The Dream.*—*Byron.*

"I saw him stand
Before an altar—with a gentle bride ;
Her face was fair, but was not that which made
The star-light of his boyhood ; as he stood
Even at the altar, o'er his brow there came
The selfsame aspect, and the quivering shock
That in the antique oratory shook
His bosom in its solitude ; and then—
As in that hour—a moment o'er his face
The tablet of unutterable thoughts
Was traced—and then it faded as it came,
And he stood calm and quiet, and he spoke
The fitting vows, but heard not his own words,
And all things reel'd around him ; he could see
Not that which was, nor that which should have been—
But the old mansion, and the accustom'd hall,
And the remember'd chambers, and the place,
The day, the hour, the sunshine and the shade,
All things pertaining to that place and hour,
And her who was his destiny, came back,
And thrust themselves between him and the light :
What business had they there at such a time ?"

PART II.

READING OF THE SERVICE.

INTRODUCTION.

EXPRESSION.

It is of unspeakable importance that the reader of Divine Service, and the preacher in the pulpit, should have a full degree of expressive power, the ability to display before the minds of his hearers, and imprint on their hearts, his inner thought. Any deficiency in this faculty is a most deplorable defect, and, if it can possibly be eradicated, is inexcusable in the leader of the devotions of a congregation and the herald of divine truth. If the reader does not convey the impression that his heart and mind are actually engaged in offering prayer to GOD, or in declaring his heavenly message, he misrepresents his sacred office. It is what is *forced out* of a man's mind by the pressure of his devotional feelings and affections which makes his voice the fit instrument of prayer to the Almighty, or of instruction to the people. Necessity is upon him, "yea, woe is unto" him, if he makes the duties of his office a mere lip-service, and that his mouth does not speak out of the abundance of his heart. Expression implies reality, truthfulness, vividness, and inexpressive utterance in the language of prayer, praise, or preaching, is unnatural and unreal. The man whose heart remains unmoved, or whose mind is inert, in addressing GOD with and for His people, or the people for

God, should seriously consider with himself whether he is devoutly fulfilling all that was implied in his ordination vows.

These thoughts are not recorded here for the purpose of discouraging any who may not possess a favored degree of sensibility, or ardor of conviction, but simply with the aim of correcting the neglect to stir up the gift that is in them. In all the criticisms and suggestions which are made it is the ideal standard which is held up to view. And who is not bitterly conscious of the vast difference between the ideal and the actual achievement? Who, that rightly appreciates the solemnity and responsibility of the sacred office, would not shrink from undertaking his unspeakably momentous duties, or fail to appreciate the hesitation of those earlier heralds of the Divine Word—of Moses, who said: "Who am I, that I should go unto Pharaoh, and that I should bring forth the children of Israel out of Egypt? . . . They will not believe me, nor hearken unto my voice: for they will say, The Lord hath not appeared unto thee. . . . O my Lord, I am not eloquent, neither heretofore nor since Thou hast appeared unto Thy servant; but I am slow of speech, and of a slow tongue"; or of Isaiah, who said: "Woe is me! for I am undone; because I am a man of unclean lips, and I dwell in the midst of a people of unclean lips"; or of Jeremiah: "Ah! Lord GOD, behold, I can not speak, for I am a child"; or of Jonah, who rose to flee from the presence of his GOD; or even of the chief speaker of the apostolic college, who recorded against himself that he was in speech contemptible, and prayed that a door of speech might be opened to him, to tell the mystery of Christ, as he besought men, in Christ's stead, to be reconciled to GOD. These passages do not, of course, apply primarily to the art of elocution, but indirectly they certainly do so apply. And in the great Ambassador from GOD to man—Who must have had some peculiarly attractive and expressive grace in His utterances, Who "spake as never man spake," "as one having authority, and not as the scribes," causing the people to wonder at the "gracious words which proceeded out of His mouth"—we find the highest inspiring Model. If we fail in a resemblance to Him, it should strengthen us, if we recall those other instances which show that the voice, as well as power of heart and mind, has been committed to earthen vessels.

If there is to be expression, there must, then, be feeling to found it upon. The study of the character of the Service becomes helpful to this end. The moment, however, that we begin upon interpretation, we encounter different schools of thought and opposing theories, which forbid the closest analysis, and confine us to those particulars in which the majority may be found to agree. Every clergyman would naturally have his preference in using the discretion granted in the rubric, as to whether he will "read, say, or sing" the Service. Our discussion relates simply to its expressive and appropriate *reading*.

There are certain thoughts relating to a standard of expression, which must be obvious to the great majority of readers, yet which are disregarded by some. The standard is not that of the stage, for the purpose of theatrical representations is to reproduce human life and passion by purely mimetic effects. There is simulation, but no originating power in this. Nor is the eloquence of the bar to be taken as the rule, which is chiefly argumentative, not hortatory, nor intercessory. Again, the oratory of the rostrum, being for the display of the theme, and not for the immediate purpose of affecting the lives and souls of men, is no more reliable as a standard of the sacred office. Prayer, praise, and preaching are of a temper and character different from all these, and their impressive effects can not be legitimately engrafted upon the Prayer-Book or the sermon.

Other reflections suggest themselves, relating to the character in which the reader and preacher stands before the people: in the solemn office he bears, in the momentous import and high aim of every public service, in the nature of the Service itself, the place in which it is celebrated, and the twofold purpose which, like the inscription on the high-priest's breast-plate, must be the perpetual motto of all work of the sacred ministry : "For the glory of GOD and the edifying of His people."

CHAPTER I.

ANALYSIS OF THE CHARACTERISTICS CONTAINED IN THE BOOK OF COMMON PRAYER AS A GUIDE TO EXPRESSION.

THE Service has *sublimity* and *majesty*, which give dignity and force in its expression. It has also perfect *simplicity*, which gives the naturalness and directness to the reading. And it has, finally, *reverential fervor*, which imparts warmth to the style.

Now, if the reader will question with himself whether these effects are secured by his reading, and finds that they are, in these respects, at least, the reading is good. But, if any one of the characteristics above described be wanting, the result must fall short of the true standards. For instance, if the style be sufficiently dignified, and properly tempered by its opposite, the due simplicity, yet lack the reverent and fervent effect of the third characteristic, it will still be imperfect. Or if the simplicity and reverential fervor be expressed, without a just degree of dignity, that lack will render the reading defective and unpleasant. Or, again, omitting the natural and direct expression, which interprets the simplicity of the Service, we have only dignity and fervor, without that personality which appeals immediately to the heart.

Defects appear still further in giving undue prominence to a single quality of the Service, as where the style is untempered with simplicity and fervor, and the excessive majesty renders it pompous. Quite as objectionable is the error of making simplicity the prominent effect, so that, unbalanced by the weight of dignity, and unwarmed by chastened fervor, it becomes simply trivial. The intensified manner of fervor, unrestrained by dignity or simplicity, is often unpleasant, through the lack of those elements.

It would seem scarcely necessary to discuss at great length those unfortunate misrepresentations of the Service which are found in addition to those already mentioned, yet they are so frequent as to require notice here. First, undue *rapidity* is to be avoided, since from this it would appear that the reader thought little and felt less in regard to the Service, that he was in haste to be rid of it, that he had a contemptuous disregard for the entire Order of Prayer, and was only hurrying to have it out of the way as soon as possible. To say the least of such reading, it is unpardonably irreverent, and rattles through the august titles of the Supreme God as if they were so many items in the advertisement of an auctioneer. The author once heard a reader give the entire Exhortation with but two catches of his breath, which were barely sufficient to enable the voice to gallop through at his greatest speed.

The opposite of this flippant rapidity is an intolerable and monotonous dullness of the *slow* movement, which is apathetic and soporific in its influence, and, therefore, unendurable. The weariness created by this drawling movement is certainly of no more moral benefit than the fault of rapid flippancy.

Thirdly, we sometimes note a *business-like air*, which is better adapted to the clerk making sales at the counter than to the clergyman in the chancel or the pulpit.

The *mincing tone* of false taste is another serious hindrance to propriety of expression. There can be only words of condemnation for that style of reading which imitates *theatrical effects*, in startling and unexpected varieties of flashing emotion. The *perfunctory* and *heartless* style—another extreme, though less offensive—is still decidedly out of character. Such are a few of the prominent defects in the leaders of public worship. It would be well for every reader of the Service to observe narrowly his own style, to see whether he is representing thus imperfectly the worship of the Church, and to satisfy himself, if possible, that his reading is characterized by the dignity, the simplicity, and the reverential fervor which, when united, give tone and character to the Service.

CHAPTER II.

THE OPENING SENTENCES, ETC., OF MORNING AND EVENING PRAYER.

It should be observed that the three leading characteristics already mentioned are presupposed in advance of all the various discussions of secondary topics.

Leaving, for the time, the three opening Sentences, found only in the American book, we begin with the fourth.

"When the wicked man turneth away from his wickedness that he hath committed, and doeth that which is lawful and right, he shall save his soul alive."—Ezek. xxiii., 27.

The teaching of the Sentence prompts repentance. The voice, therefore, should have the expression of the distinct and emphatic announcement of the conditions of pardon, and the miraculous efficacy of turning from unrighteousness to obedience.

"I acknowledge my transgressions; and my sin is ever before me."—Psalm li., 3.

The fifth Sentence candidly utters the deep sense of our sinfulness. The contrite voice of confession differs slightly from the voice of statement of the express conditions in the fourth Sentence.

"Hide thy face from my sins; and blot out all mine iniquities."—Psalm li., 9.

Earnest entreaty under the deepest conviction of sin is the character of the sixth Sentence.

"The sacrifices of God are a broken spirit: a broken and a contrite heart, O God, thou wilt not despise."— Psalm li., 17.

Instruction to the contrite and confession to Almighty God are the two characteristics of the seventh Sentence.

"Rend your heart, and not your garments, and turn unto the Lord your God; for he is gracious and merciful, slow to anger, and of great kindness, and repenteth him of the evil."—Joel, ii., 13.

Stern command to duty and comforting assurance to the obedient form the expression for the eighth Sentence.

"To the Lord our God belong mercies and forgivenesses, though we have rebelled against him. Neither have we obeyed the voice of the Lord our God, to walk in his laws which he set before us."—Dan. ix., 9, 10.

To inspire confidence in the Divine mercy, with confession of sinfulness, marks the teaching of this, the ninth Sentence.

"O Lord, correct me, but with judgment; not in thine anger, lest thou bring me to nothing."—Jer. x., 24; Psalm vi., 1.

Reverent submission, with contrition, is the spirit of the tenth Sentence.

"Repent ye; for the Kingdom of Heaven is at hand." —St. Matt. iii., 2.

Authoritative exhortation to repentance is the teaching of the eleventh Sentence.

"I will arise, and go to my father, and I will say unto

him, Father, I have sinned against heaven, and before thee, and am no more worthy to be called thy son."—St. Luke, xv., 18, 19.

In the twelfth Sentence we find contrite resolution and self-abasement.

"Enter not into judgment with thy servant, O Lord; for in thy sight shall no man living be justified."—Psalm cxliii., 2.

Earnest entreaty, with penitent pleading, is the language of the thirteenth Sentence.

"If we say that we have no sin, we deceive ourselves, and the truth is not in us; but if we confess our sins, God is faithful and just to forgive us our sins, and to cleanse us from all unrighteousness."—I. John, i., 8, 9.

To admonish and instruct the self-righteous is the teaching of the last Sentence.

All these Sentences have a penitential character. Upon their teaching are founded the words of the General Exhortation. The Confession follows in natural order, and demands the comfort of the Absolution succeeding. These Sentences, then, are harmonious in their general spirit, and tend to a single conclusion. The voice of the reader should, as far as possible, interpret and enforce these various instructions, so that the wicked man may really feel exhorted to turn from his wickedness; that the transgressor of GOD'S laws may feel deeply and truly the acknowledgment of his ever-present sin; that the soul, overwhelmed with a sense of its sinfulness, may feel, in very truth, that the cry goes up to GOD to hide His face from the sin, and blot out all the iniquity; that the contrite heart is not despised by GOD; that the rending of the heart, and not the garments, is the turning to GOD, and secures His favor; that, although we have not obeyed the voice of the Lord our GOD, there still is mercy with Him; that we pray for correction, but with a judgment tempered with mercy; that the kingdom of heaven is at hand, and, therefore, we must repent; that we are, as the profligate prodigal, no longer worthy the name of son; that we deprecate the Divine judgment, according to our deeds, for then none living may be justified; that we are warned against self-righteousness, which pronounces us without sin, and are taught that it is confession to GOD which brings us the needed cleansing.

This, or something akin to this, is the plain language of the penitential sentences. They certainly mean as much as this, they certainly aim to establish such convictions; and to read them in a heartless, perfunctory, unmeaning way would seem to be a deliberate effort to deprive them of their true sense and to nullify their mission to human souls.

While, however, they are so expressive, and are thus to teach their own inspired truth, the reader must bear in mind that there is a harmony to be established in the Service throughout, that the three leading effects of the *dignity*, the *simplicity*, and the *fervor* of the Service are at all times to be preserved; that no one portion of the Service is to be made to stand out in undue prominence above the rest; and that the entire expression aims not to startle the ear, or to produce dramatic effect, but simply to reach the soul, to convince it of its own sinfulness, and of God's readiness to pardon every repentant and contrite heart. The manner of such a reader as the late lamented Rev. Dr. Francis Hawks will better verify the truthfulness of the theories here advanced than any labored argument to this end. We can but sum up all by saying that the utterance of the Sentences should be with expression according to their meaning, with the variety which they naturally suggest, and yet with the harmony of unity in their intelligent use.

The three Sentences remaining to be considered, not being penitential, may be discussed separately.

The first is expressive of the profoundest depth of reverential awe, and enforces the truth, so thrillingly impressive, when it first strikes the mind consciously, that we as a worshiping assembly are actually in the Divine presence. "Wheresoever two or three are gathered together in My name, there am I in the midst of them." All that is trivial or irreverent, hasty or ill-considered, in the expression, is utterly at variance with the profound solemnity of the truth declared. If we are verily persuaded that God is with us of a truth, we can not declare the fact of His presence without being impressed by, and conveying in the utterance, the vocal interpretation of the thought.

"The Lord is in his holy temple; let all the earth keep silence before him."—Hab. ii., 30.

The second Sentence utters a sublime and glowing prophecy of the omnipotent might and majesty of the Name of GOD, before Whom all the nations shall bow; from the east to the west shall GOD be honored and glorified. With such thoughts and such language to guide the utterance, and such a glorifying of the Divine name, how pitiably inexpressive, how puerile and characterless, would seem to be the precipitate haste and the unmeaning mumbling of thoughtless and inefficient expression!

"From the rising of the sun even unto the going down of the same, my Name shall be great among the Gentiles; and in every place incense shall be offered unto my Name, and a pure offering: for my Name shall be great among the heathen, saith the Lord of hosts."—Mal. i., 11.

The simplicity of the third Sentence, being so purely a personal prayer of aspiration, is in marked contrast with the profound awe of the first and the majesty of the second Sentence.

"Let the words of my mouth, and the meditation of my heart, be alway acceptable in thy sight, O Lord, my strength and my redeemer."—Psalm xix., 14, 15.

It would be well if every reader would occasionally catechise himself by the strictest laws of the interpretation of the Sentence, so as to satisfy himself that he is giving, in some degree, penitential expression—that he is actually touching human hearts, and leading them through contrition to pardon, and that he is really, as in the first and second Sentences, impressing the souls of his flock with the direct and immediate influence of God's presence among them, and with the glory of His holy name.

The Exhortation

is characterized by a greater degree of simplicity than the preceding Sentences. The reverential fervor is changed by the pastoral element, which appears in the address to the people, as distinguished from the voice of devotion. It is not an easy thing to balance the just degrees of the dignity and the simplicity in the reading, for the standard of the expression varies considerably, according to the place and time in which the Exhortation is read. For instance, the effect of the reading differs in a large church from the expression appropriate in a country school-house. The solemnity of the Exhortation, on the occasion of an Ash-Wednesday Service, differs entirely from the jubilant expression appropriate to the Consecration Service, etc. But in every event the reader, as pastor, is exhorting the congregation to a solemn duty. The earnestness and directness of the expression, which is partly personal in character, should be strongly marked, as though the reader were actually exhorting and instructing the people to confess their sins, especially at that time. This would prevent anything like perfunctory and mechanical coldness in the style. If, however, the personality of the manner is carried too far, it destroys the dignity and impressiveness, and produces an effect such as was described in the simple language of a child in the words: "He spoke it as though it came right out of his own mind." In reading the Service in the Book of Common Prayer, it must ever be remembered that the reader is using the appointed thought and language of the Church, and, while he is personally in deepest sympathy with every utterance, he is not the originator of the language, so that, in this sense, it lacks one element of personality. We use a Book of *Common* Prayer, which, by necessity, suppresses much of individualism of expression in reading.

The peculiarity of the rhetorical structure of the composition of the Exhortation renders it one of the most difficult portions of the Church Service to read expressively. But the leading thought of the reader should be to make it truly an *exhortation.* How often is this, its leading character, in any way impressed upon the attention of the worshiper? How often do we feel that we are *exhorted* to discharge a duty? If the reader keeps this in mind, it will assist in giving emphasis and reality to this portion of the Service. If, in giving his "notices," the pastor has occasion to exhort his flock, they are left in no doubt as to what he would have them do. Is there any reason why there should not be something of the same clearly defined effect following the reading of the Exhortation?

For expressive reading, the succeeding analysis may prove suggestive:

1. *The phrase of address:* "Dearly beloved brethren." "Brethren" implies one degree of affectionate interest, "beloved" expresses this in increased degree, and "dearly" deepens the feeling still further. It is pastoral in character. If the words mean anything, they express the affectionate interest and solicitude which the minister of Christ must feel in addressing the people, or exhorting them to a duty whose faithful discharge brings peace and pardon to the soul. There is danger, indeed, of making the expression excessive, and therefore ridiculous, which is no better than a business-like style, that has no address to the soul.

2. *The statement:* "The Scripture moveth us, in sundry places, to acknowledge and confess our manifold sins and wickedness; and that we should not dissemble nor cloak them before the face of Almighty God our heavenly

Father; but confess them with an humble, lowly, penitent, and obedient heart; to the end that we may obtain forgiveness of the same, by his infinite goodness and mercy. And although we ought, at all times, humbly to acknowledge our sins before God; yet ought we chiefly so to do, when we assemble and meet together—"

A slight emphasis is to be given on the word "Scripture." The directions as to the manner of confessing our sins should be emphasized explicitly, and with solemnity of deprecation against hypocrisy before GOD. "To the end" should receive full emphasis, as the final aim of the Confession to which we are exhorted—which is the forgiveness of our sins by the infinite mercy of God.

3. *The enumeration of the different parts of Divine worship:* "To render thanks for the great benefits that we have received at his hands, to set forth his most worthy praise, to hear his most holy Word, and to ask those things which are requisite and necessary, as well for the body as the soul." The various particulars here enumerated should be given with *distinctive* emphasis, that the people may be reminded of the various duties and privileges set before them—thanksgiving, praise, instructions from God's Word, and prayer.

4. *The bidding:* "Wherefore I pray and beseech you, as many as are here present, to accompany me with a pure heart, and humble voice, unto the throne of the heavenly grace, saying—" The language now being more personal, the force of voice is more subdued, although the expression loses none of its earnestness, but is rather increased in that respect. "Unto the throne of the heavenly grace" should be given with full voice, the word "saying"* subdued.

As exhortation to duty inclines to solemnity of expression, the falling slides are frequently heard throughout. The inflection in the phrase of address on the word "brethren" may be suspended, or falling, according to the de-

* See Topic "Pause" on the word "saying."

gree of the solemnity of feeling to be expressed at the time.

"Its expressions are adapted to instruct the ignorant, to admonish the negligent, to support the fearful, to comfort the doubtful, to caution the formal, and to check the presumptuous—tempers which are found in every mixed congregation, and which ought to be prepared for the solemn work of confession of sin." *

It will be found suggestive in study to compare the General Exhortation with the addresses and exhortations in the various other services. Some of them, as in the Holy Communion Service, contain far greater solemnity, and others, as in the Baptismal Service, less of it, than that required in the Exhortation for the Daily Prayer.

The Confession.

We pass now from the voice of instruction to the voice of confession and prayer, from speaking to men to speaking unto God. The depth and earnestness of the feeling prompt to that emphasis, stronger than in ordinary prayer, which is characteristic of confession and contrition. The exhortation has already sounded the key, so to speak, in the words "with an humble voice." To give it with loud force is, to say the least, opposed to the manner of utterance as suggested by the exhortation. Sinking the voice entirely to *pianissimo* is not leading the congregation. In all portions, when the congregation accompany the minister, a rhythmical evenness of the movement must be sustained, in order that the congregation may easily follow. What will be said in the discussion of the voice in the reading of the Prayers will apply equally well here, and to that the student is referred. The marked particulars of the expression of the various portion, being lost in the response of the voices of the congregation, require but little discussion.

* Proctor on the Book of Common Prayer.

The Absolution.

The title and the rubric here furnish us with the first suggestions for the reading. It is the *declaration* of Absolution. The article *the* seems by its definiteness to give a certain degree of force and precision to the character of the act to be done; the effect would be softened by the use of the indefinite *a*. The Absolution is *declared*, the Benediction is *pronounced*, the Exhortation is *said*, the Sentences are *read*, the Psalms and Hymns are *announced*, etc. These terms are not used without meaning; they are not synonymous; in each case they suggest something, however slightly, for the expression, in the nature of the act performed.

The Absolution is the only passage which has "declared" attached to it. It is, no doubt, on account of its authoritative character, and is all the stronger for being impersonal in form. The priest declares it, not of himself nor for himself, but for Almighty GOD. "He pardoneth and absolveth." It is a declaration—officially, not personally authoritative—in the name of GOD.

The voice of authority, and of deliberate, emphatic declaration (not crier-like), should be heard, and the declaration is softened by the thought of infinite love and mercy which it sets forth, strengthened also by the "power and commandment" which GOD hath given to His Ministers to declare His terms of pardon to His people. It is a declaration of divine mercy by the voice of official authority.

In the second sentence the expression becomes marked by the sympathetic tones which show the deep and tender interest the Minister takes in the spiritual welfare of those for whom he thus officiates, and yet this is not to overcome the dignity and authority of the expression.

The closing sentence, being hortatory, requires the change which marks the difference between exhortation and declaration. This is the third distinct division for study in expression, to be marked with corresponding changes of voice. The expression naturally deepens and softens, and requires a retarded movement and increasing length of pause at each clause throughout the sentence.

The reader should aim to secure such an expression for the whole passage as to satisfy him that no one present can possibly be ignorant of GOD's terms of forgiveness, as they have been proclaimed; and then if, in addition to this, he can satisfy himself that he has declared the will of GOD so affectionately, earnestly, and authoritatively, that no one present ought to be unmindful of it, he may be assured that his reading befits his sacred office. This implies, without a doubt, a certain degree of sensitiveness both in the ear and conscience.

In review, the natural threefold division of the Absolution should be impressed on the memory, as an aid to its correct reading, the first sentence being the declaration of the authority of the sacred office, the second a declaration of GOD's tender mercies, and the third an exhortation to prayer for spiritual graces and the help of the Holy Spirit.

CHAPTER III.

THE ANTHEMS, CREED, ETC.

THE title implies, of course, that these portions of the Service which are found following the Lessons, and the *Venite*, preceding the Psalter for the day, were designed primarily for singing, and not for reading. But, wherever they are read, it should be understood that they are offerings of the praise and thanksgiving of the heart, as truly in their reading as in the higher art of music. When we are "singing and making melody in our hearts to the Lord," it is the instinct of nature to sing with the voice, and that is described in inspired language as the utterance of the worshipers on high. It is only the restricting necessities of the case which compel us to suppress this natural instinct of the soul when attuned to harmony, and drives us to accept the expedient of the ordinary speaking voice. But even with this impaired power of expression there should be, at least, the impulse to make a "joyful noise" when we "feed on thoughts that voluntary move harmonious numbers," and attune heart and voice to praise the Lord.

The heart and zest of such expressions as "Let us heartily rejoice in the strength of our salvation," "And show ourselves glad in Him with psalms," "Let us worship and fall down . . . before the Lord our maker," "O worship the Lord in the beauty of holiness," "O be joyful in the Lord, all ye lands, . . . come before his presence with a song," "O go your way into His courts with praise," "Show yourselves joyful unto the Lord, all ye lands," "With trumpets also and shawms, O show yourselves joyful before the Lord the King," "Let the sea make a noise," "Let the floods clap their hands, and let the hills be joyful together before the Lord," "I will rejoice in giving praise for the operations of Thy hands," "Praise the Lord, O my soul, and all that is within me, praise His holy Name," imply a suggestive fullness of expression which saves the language from becoming utterly weak and inexpressive through reading. It is not only incongruous, but borders closely upon the absurd, where such lofty expressions of whole-hearted and whole-souled praise and thanksgiving are uttered with the unmeaning flippancy of indifferent colloquial familiarity. The opposite error of an expression offensively pompous is simply another indication of a heart out of tune with the sublimity and the beauty of the jubilant portions of the Service. Any expression in any part of the Service which is mechanical, unnatural, or assumed, grates offensively upon the ear, whether it be in the reading of praise, instruction, or prayer. But the defects to which we are liable should never discourage the reader in the effort to make the words of praise sound through the full-tuned voice of heartfelt gratitude.

The *Te Deum* is, of course, the grandest hymn of praise, and is invaluable as a study for emotional and vocal expression. The art of music has lent its aid to its proper emotional interpretation, and the study of its varied expression may help the reader to fully receive its meaning. The liturgical divisions are of further aid to the vocal expression; they are threefold: First, the act of Praise, or the Doxology; second, the Confession of Faith; and, third, the act of Intercession. These divisions are all alike expressions of praise, but the first has the fullest measure of it. The Confession of Faith, which is jubilant and eucharistic in character, begins at the words, " The Holy Church throughout all the world doth acknowledge Thee," and extends to the words, " We therefore pray Thee, help Thy servants," the remainder being supplicatory, with gratitude sustained throughout.

I. *The Doxology.*—This division should be rendered with the fullest voice of grateful praise. A sufficient degree of slowness, with marked emphasis to interpret the majesty and glory of the theme, should characterize the expression. A light degree of force and rapidity of movement destroy the dignity and grandeur of the thought, and do not awaken the heart to the genuine fervor of gratitude.

" We praise thee, O God ; we acknowledge thee to be the Lord.

" All the earth doth worship thee, the Father everlasting.

" To thee, all Angels cry aloud ; the Heavens, and all the Powers therein.

" To thee, Cherubim and Seraphim continually do cry,
" Holy, Holy, Holy, Lord God of Sabaoth ;
" Heaven and earth are full of the Majesty of thy Glory.

"The glorious company of the Apostles praise thee.
"The goodly fellowship of the Prophets praise thee.
"The noble army of Martyrs praise thee."

II. *The Confession of Faith.*—This portion has the same movement and emphasis as before, but the pitch is naturally on a lower key. The drift of the voice is to the downward slides, to impart the effect of declaration.

"The holy Church throughout all the world doth acknowledge thee;
"The Father, of an infinite Majesty;
"Thine adorable, true, and only Son;
"Also the Holy Ghost, the Comforter.
"Thou art the King of Glory, O Christ.
"Thou art the everlasting Son of the Father.
"When thou tookest upon thee to deliver man, thou didst humble thyself to be born of a Virgin.
"When thou hadst overcome the sharpness of death, thou didst open the Kingdom of Heaven to all believers.
"Thou sittest at the right hand of God, in the Glory of the Father.
"We believe that thou shalt come to be our Judge."

III. *The Intercession.*—The voice of prayer is naturally more subdued than that of praise. Hence the chastened effect in the expression of the third division, which has the same degree of fervor, although a less forcible form of expressing it than before.

"We therefore pray thee, help thy servants, whom thou hast redeemed with thy precious blood.
"Make them to be numbered with thy Saints, in glory everlasting.
"O Lord, save thy people, and bless thine heritage.
"Govern them, and lift them up for ever.
"Day by day we magnify thee;
"And we worship thy Name ever, world without end.
"Vouchsafe, O Lord, to keep us this day without sin.
"O Lord, have mercy upon us, have mercy upon us.

"O Lord, let thy mercy be upon us, as our trust is in thee.

"O Lord, in thee have I trusted; let me never be confounded."

Frequent practice upon the *Benedicite, Omnia Opera*, is of great value in forming the voice and ear in the expression of praise. Its daily use entire would sustain sufficient firmness and fullness of voice for the ordinary uses of public speaking.

To conclude the discussion of the anthems, if the reader is to give the laudatory portions of the service characteristically, they must actually sound as praise to the ear.

The Creed.

We are now brought to consider the expression of the belief of the Church, her articles of faith as expressed in the creed of the centuries. If the act of a public confession of faith may have lost something of its significance in these peaceful times, when the Church is permitted to share the universal liberty of opinion, and to express her belief in the truth of revelation, without persecution or disturbance, yet the importance of a frequent and general declaration of the chief doctrines of our creed is in no respect diminished, whether we regard it as a demonstration against false doctrine and unbelief, or as encouragement to ourselves to hold fast the form of sound words, once delivered to the saints. According to either view, it is a solemn act of professing, in the presence of GOD, our belief in the sublime truths of revelation; and it should be performed with becoming deliberation. Its hurried recital in a medley of voices, and almost in a single breath, destroys the significance of the custom, and suggests the irreverent notion of a rivalry in speed of utterance between the Minister and his choir. Even the plain reading of it is not free from habitual errors, such as, "He rose *again* from the dead," as if we declared our belief in a repetition of the act; the coupling together of the Crucifixion, Death, and Burial in one undiscriminating sentence, instead of making them emphatic and distinct articles of belief.

The true idea of the expression would be to give to the utterance the solemn, earnest, and reverent asseveration of belief, each article delivered emphatically and deliberately, as though uttering the deepest convictions of the soul. The personal form of the expression, "I believe," enforces this, and the thought that it is the essential faith of the Church, and has been so in all time, should forbid any careless, flippant, or indifferent delivery of the "form of sound words."

The clauses should be marked with some degree of their own characteristic expression, as in those especially relating to the humiliation of the Redeemer — "Suffered," "Crucified," "Dead," "Buried" — in contrast with the triumphant thoughts of His Resurrection, Ascension, and Session in glory.

In the clauses of the Nicene Creed — "God of God, Light of Light, very God of very God" — the voice should express the profoundest reverence, with deliberate emphasis, marking the word "of" distinctly, as a strong emphasis of the meaning lies there. It should be observed that the emphasis of the clause, "By Whom all things were made," decides for the ear to which of the sacred persons the clause applies. If it refers to the Father, no preceding pause is used. If it refers primarily to the Son, the introductory pause and the "emphatic tie" carry the voice and expression back to those clauses which relate to Christ personally. The pause preceding "Whose kingdom shall have no end" should be observed, lest the common, careless expression should connect this clause with the preceding, "quick and dead." In the third paragraph the pause should be after "Lord," to disconnect it from the word "life," "Lord" referring to the Holy Ghost, not "life."

The Apostles' Creed.

"I believe in God the Father Almighty, Maker of heaven and earth :

"And in Jesus Christ his only Son our Lord ; Who was conceived by the Holy Ghost, Born of the Virgin Mary ; Suffered under Pontius Pilate, Was crucified, dead, and buried ; He descended into hell, The third day he rose from the dead ; He ascended into heaven, And sitteth on the right hand of God the Father Almighty ; From thence he shall come to judge the quick and the dead.

"I believe in the Holy Ghost; The holy Catholic Church, The Communion of Saints ; The Forgiveness of sins ; The Resurrection of the body; And the Life everlasting. Amen."

The Nicene Creed.

"I believe in one God the Father Almighty, Maker of heaven and earth, And of all things visible and invisible :

"And in one Lord Jesus Christ, the only-begotten Son of God, Begotten of his Father before all worlds ; God of God, Light of Light, very God of very God, Begotten, not made, Being of one substance with the Father ; By whom all things were made ; Who, for us men, and for our salvation, came down from heaven, And was incarnate by the Holy Ghost of the Virgin Mary, And was made man, And was crucified also for us under Pontius Pilate. He suffered and was buried; And the third day he rose again, according to the Scriptures ; And ascended into heaven, And sitteth on the right hand of the Father. And he shall come again with glory to judge both the quick and the dead ; Whose kingdom shall have no end.

"And I believe in the Holy Ghost, the Lord and Giver of Life, Who proceedeth from the Father and the Son, Who with the Father and the Son together is worshipped and glorified, Who spake by the Prophets. And I believe one Catholic and Apostolic Church. I acknowledge one Baptism for the remission of sins, And I look for the

Resurrection of the dead, And the Life of the world to come. Amen."

The Versicles.

These, being condensed and ejaculatory in the form of expression, require fervent emphasis in their delivery.

"O Lord, open *Thou* our lips."

The emphatic word is "Thou," as a moment's reflection would show, although some misreading is very frequently heard.

"Glory be to the *Father*, and to the *Son*, and to the *Holy Ghost*."

The full voice of praise is expressive here.

"Praise ye the Lord."

Hortatory and commanding effect should be given with full force, of heraldic manner.

"The *Lord* be *with* you."

Reverent solemnity would be the natural delivery of this versicle. The emphasis strikes the words "Lord" and "with."

In the bidding for prayer, "Let us *pray*," the emphasis is upon the act in which we are to be engaged, and not upon the word of exhortation.

In the supplication,

"O Lord, show thy *mercy* upon us,"

the emphasis is upon "mercy"; and in

"O God, make *clean* our hearts within us,"

observe that both the "k" and hard "c" are to be clearly enunciated.

CHAPTER IV.

THE PRAYERS.

As we have insisted that praise in Divine Service should have the voice of praise in its utterance, so equally emphatic must be the simple declaration that the prayers should have the voice of prayer. By this we mean that as there is a change in the nature of the feeling, when we pass from exhortation, praise, and declaration of belief, to prayer, so the voice should indicate the nature of the change. It is the leading effect of exhortation that it be explicit; of praise, that it be reverently grateful; of declaration, that it be emphatically distinct; while the very essence of expressive prayer is found in reverential fervor. In exhortation, we stand in the presence of men; in praise, we offer our unrestrained gratitude; in the declaration of the faith, we utter our deepest convictions; but in prayer we are more conscious of our own insignificance and unworthiness, of our urgent needs as suppliants, and of the purity and the omnipotence of our GOD. We seem to be more immediately in His presence, and our hearts are naturally touched with a deeper reverence for the Almighty. We certainly do not address GOD vocally in prayer, as we speak to our fellows in exhortation.

All pious study, devout meditation, and holy communion with God, which assist in developing the profoundest depths of reverential feeling, are a natural and helpful preparation for expression in the true reading of the Prayers. We can not study too deeply into their nature and their meaning. Analytical discussion of the teachings they convey, in such works as Dean Comber's "Companion to the Temple," Dean Goulburn on the Collects, Nicholls' "Paraphrase of the Common Prayer," and similar works, will be found suggestive for the reading of the Prayers. Perhaps the habit of silent reflection upon the teaching of the language, in order to secure freshness and vividness in the expression, may be superior to anything else. In fact, this habit of silent study of the Service throughout, on every occasion, before its rendering, will, of itself, improve the style of every reader.

Analysis of the Structure of the Prayers, as an aid to Expression.—The three liturgical divisions are the Protasis, the Apodasis, and the Conclusion.

THE PRAYERS. 157

For study in expression, we will use the more familiar terms of Invocation, which includes the doctrine or narrative; the Petition, embracing the confession and supplication of the prayer proper; and the Conclusion, the latter comprehending the mediation, or ascription.

Beginning with

1. *The Invocation*, we find this to be in several forms, so expressed for the purpose of expressing the natural emotion of our hearts, in beginning the petitions. They should be examined, not after the manner of a scientific study, but with personal reverence and gratitude, and a desire truly to learn and utter to the ear the varied attributes of our Father in heaven.

And, first, we find the simpler emotions expressed, as reverence, awe, gratitude, majesty, tenderness, and other kindred qualities. These would naturally be aroused in prayers opening with such words as "Lord," "Blessed Lord," "Lord God," "Lord most holy," "Merciful Lord," "Most gracious Lord," "Lord of all power and might," and other titles expressing the rulership of God, and His simpler attributes. The mind is here fixed with the utmost intensity upon the personality of the Divine Ruler.

Besides these there is at times an even deeper feeling, often shaded by other emotions, as we remember the mystery and power of the Divine Essence, named in the word GOD, and deepening into reverential and majestic awe. Such profound emotions are summoned forth and realized by the Minister as he pronounces the titles: "O God," "Lord God," "O Lord God." "Almighty God," and "O Almighty God." The voice of the sincere petitioner should sink in humility with his heart as he utters that august Name which none can understand. So great, indeed, is the natural reverence of God's ministers that many mar the utterance of the word through an excess of feeling. This fault should be avoided for the sake of the congregation. Full and clear, low and submissive, should be the sound of the voice when we address Almighty God in public worship.

But it is not alone His might which has been revealed, but a might tempered with most cherishing love. And thus the heart of the worshiper is softened by emotions of filial reverence, which are colored by tenderness and gratitude, and rendered sublime by majesty. And so the language and voice express such tender, grateful, and majestic reverence in the titles, "Father," "Our Father," "Merciful Father," "O most merciful Father," "Our Father who art in Heaven," "O most gracious Father," "Almighty and most merciful Father."

There are also compounds of these titles which express the intense feeling of mingled emotions. The depth of some passes beyond the compass of perfect expression, yet, if the mind be intently fixed upon the thought, the feeling is almost sure to be aroused in some degree, and to inspire suitable expression in the voice of the Minister, and kindle responsive emotions in the hearts of the hearers. Such are the titles: "O Lord and Heavenly Father," "O Father of mercies, and God of all comfort," "Almighty and most merciful God and Saviour," "O Almighty God, the sovereign commander of all the world," "O God, Whose mercy is everlasting and power infinite," and others of a similar class. To these may be added the *Invocations* of the Litany, and many others which will readily occur to the student.

It should be noted that the suggestive changes of the voice for utterance do not imply all the power of expression, given in every particular. We find even in the chanting of the Creed, while there is perfect harmony in the effect of the monotone, yet that the accompaniment of the organ prompts to natural changes in everything but the key, and which are appropriate and naturally expressive. In like manner we find the general drift of the harmony and unity of the Service, with such variety as the changes of thought and feeling indicated in the preceding analysis instinctively demand.

A fair test of the truthfulness of the foregoing analysis occurs in the style of expression in a discourse where the purpose of the preacher is to explain and impress upon his hearers the significance of the same Divine titles. How vivid and graphic are they made in such a discussion! Should they be less impressively uttered when we use the same titles upon which we base our petitions before GOD? The substitution of other titles less reverent, or less appropriate, would further enforce the same thought by contrast.

Above all things, the introduction to our prayers, in reading—that is, the *Invocation*—should be reverent; not with undue boldness, as in the tone of command, nor yet in that timidity of spirit which led a good critic to say to a young deacon: "You read the Divine titles just like a boy learning to swear."

The subdivision of the *Invocation*, described by some writers as the *doctrine*, or *narrative*, is a further profitable study for correct reading. In *doctrine* it expresses more fully much of that which is involved in the Title. The *Narrative* is a natural continuance of the feeling already expressed, or a fuller introduction to the *petition* following. These clauses are, in part, confession of our faith in the attributes of GOD, or of our faith in His power and mercy, previously manifested, encouraging us to prayer. Ordinarily the Narrative, in precomposed prayer, is very brief, for there can be but little of the spirit of reverential supplication in sustained narration. One of the longest is the passage in the Litany quoted from the Psalter: "O God, we have heard," etc. Several examples from the Services are subjoined.

Morning Prayer.—"Who art the author of peace and lover of concord." *For Peace.*

"Who hast safely brought us to the beginning of this day." *For Grace.*

"The high and mighty Ruler of the Universe, Who dost from Thy throne behold all the dwellers upon earth."
For the President.
"From whom cometh every good and perfect gift."
For Clergy and People.
Evening Prayer.—"From Whom all holy desires, all good counsels, and all just works do proceed."
For Peace.
"By Whose almighty power we have been preserved this day."   *For Aid against Perils.*

Litany.—"Who despisest not the sighing of a contrite heart, nor the desire of such as are sorrowful."

"We have heard with our ears, and our fathers have declared unto us, the noble works that thou didst in their days, and in the old time before them."

Special Prayers.—"Whose gift it is that the rain doth fall, and the earth bring forth her increase."
In Time of Dearth.
"Whose power no creature is able to resist, to whom it belongeth justly to punish sinners, and to be merciful to those who truly repent."   *In Time of War.*

Church Year.—"Who hast caused all Holy Scripture to be written for our learning."   *Second S. Adv.*

"Who knowest us to be set in the midst of so many and great dangers, that by reason of the frailty of our nature we cannot always stand upright."
Fourth S. after Epiph.
"Who hatest nothing that Thou hast made, and dost forgive the sins of all those who are penitent."
Ash Wednesday.
"Who, of Thy tender love toward mankind, hast sent Thy Son, our Saviour Jesus Christ, to take upon him our flesh, and to suffer death upon the cross, that all mankind should follow the example of His great humility."
S. next before Easter.
"Who through thine only begotten Son Jesus Christ

hast overcome death, and opened unto us the gate of everlasting life." *Easter-Day.*

These and many other similar passages should be considered as an aid to expression, the longest forms being found in the Proper Prefaces in the Service for Holy Communion. It is only necessary to state that the expression of the voice should, in each case, correspond with subject-matter.

II. *The Petition.*—The utterance naturally changes from the solemnity of the confession of our faith, as we call upon God by His titles, or as we continue the descriptive form of the same attributes, to the voice of supplication. The Petition is, indeed, only another form of the confession of our faith, but it is absorbed in the fervor of the supplication, which expresses primarily our need. As before we have confessed something, in the Petition we plead for something. In pleading, the voice naturally rises in pitch. The ear should be taught to make this natural transition in pitch from the solemnity of confession to the urgency of supplication. The degree of the change of voice will depend, in every case, upon the slightly varying nature of the feeling found in the Invocation and Petition. In some instances the change is very slight; in others it must be very marked, or lose entirely its expressive character. There are always proprieties to be consulted, which the common sense of the reader, or his musical ear, must teach him to respect. It is always safer in reading to err on the side of defect, rather than excess, in expression, as, in this case, the ear of the listener is less disturbed; but it is better still to aim at giving just character to the thought and expression. While avoiding, therefore, the defect which merges the voice of petition in that of invocation, we should be equally desirous of not interrupting the continuous flow of feeling which has been once awakened by invoking God through his attributes.

The expression of the Petition throughout must depend, in part, upon particulars which are included, and their character. Sometimes these particulars, being closely and naturally related, may properly be read with slight variation in the expression, while in others they are distinct and independent, and consequently demand a marked change in the utterance—e. g., the closing paragraph of the Prayer for all Conditions of Men calls naturally for a sympathetic expression, which the preceding passages do not require: "Finally we commend to thy fatherly goodness all those who are anyways afflicted, or distressed, in mind, body, or estate; that it may please thee to comfort and relieve them, according to their several necessities; giving them patience under their sufferings, and a happy issue out of all their afflictions." In the Prayer for the Church Militant, after the Supplication, including ourselves, the Church, Christian rulers, Bishops, and other Ministers, all people, and especially for the congregation present, our hearts must be tenderly touched in sympathy with the suffering and the wicked. "And we most humbly beseech thee, of thy goodness, O Lord, to comfort and succor all those who, in this transitory life, are in trouble, need, sorrow, sickness, or any other adversity." So, again, is there a change in the same prayer in the clause following, in the devout commemoration of the departed: "And we also bless thy holy Name for all thy servants departed this life in thy faith and fear; beseeching thee to give us grace so to follow their good examples, that with them we may be partakers of thy heavenly kingdom." A similar change occurs in the Prayer for the Sick, where, after the fullest expression of sympathy and tenderness, in the Supplication, we pass to the solemnity of most reverent submission: "Or else give him grace so to take thy visitation, that, after this painful life ended, he may dwell with thee in life everlasting." Several other instances might be adduced, but these are sufficient for illustration, and are, moreover, strongly marked. If any reader doubts the naturalness of these suggested changes, let him observe the difference in the expression of a reader who is immediately and personally concerned with these petitions of sympathy, and contrast the expression with that utterance used when there is no such tenderness of interest. He will see the depth and reality of feeling in the one case, and, too often, a cold and mechanical expression in the other, which reveals only too plainly the fact that the heart is not moved to offer the words of its own petition. May it not be that infrequency of request for the special prayers arises too often from a perfunctory manner of reading them?

What is true of the above strongly contrasted passages, in regard to changes of voice, applies in moderated degree to variations which are less marked. If we are in living sympathy with the subject of each supplication, it will instinctively lead to those shadings of expression which the language demands. If the reader, in a silent analysis of the subject-matter of the prayers, will but trace the changes in thought and feeling, which are suggested by the phraseology, he will find it sufficiently suggestive of variety in the reading.

The Conclusion.—In this we bind our prayers with the might of the Mediatorial Name. There is a rhythmical emphasis with which the form of the close of the prayer is ended. We come boldly to the Throne of Grace, in reverent and confident claim of the fulfillment of the Saviour's promise! "Whatsoever ye ask the Father in My Name, He will give it you." The Mediation of the conclusion should not be carelessly or hurriedly uttered. It should not be weakened in emphasis nor quickened in its movement. It is a deliberate and emphatic claim that the entire prayer be heard through, or for the sake of Jesus Christ our Lord. The utterance of the Saviour's Name should be distinct and reverent. It is related of one of the English worthies that he made the Name in prayer "as honey to the ear." The author was told, a few years since, by a brother clergyman, who was out of sympathy with the theology of an aged bishop, now departed, that he could never withstand the attractive sweetness and impressive power which he gave to every utterance of the Name of the Redeemer. Indistinct articulation and careless utterance of the Name, with perfunctory reverence, can not achieve such results as those referred to.

"Christ's Name hath made it strong."

The alternative form for the conclusion is the Ascription, or Doxology, which, being the utterance of grateful praise, requires greater fullness of voice than in other closing forms. It is important, in all the prayers, that the voice should be kept full and strong to the end ; and a full inhalation at the close of the petition, for this purpose, prevents the effect of weariness and fatigue to both reader and hearer. Every prayer should close with energy unspent and emotion unflagging. This is peculiarly the case with the Doxology, for a feeble utterance there implies a weakened degree of feeling not consonant with the offering of praise. These and similar forms are useful for study: "To Whom, with Thee and the Holy Ghost, be all honor and glory, world without end." "By Whom and with Whom, in the unity of the Holy Ghost, all honor and glory be unto Thee, O Father Almighty, world without end." "Where with Thee, O Father, and Thee, O Holy Ghost, He liveth and reigneth ever one God, world without end."

The following discussion of the petitions in the Order of Morning Prayer may be of service :

"*A Collect for Peace.*

"O God, who art the author of peace and lover of concord, in knowledge of whom standeth our eternal life, whose service is perfect freedom ; Defend us thy humble servants in all assaults of our enemies ; that we, surely trusting in thy defence, may not fear the power of any adversaries, through the might of Jesus Christ our Lord. *Amen.*"

The tranquillity of peace and the harmony of concord will characterize the utterance of the opening clauses. It should be observed that the expression "in knowledge of whom" does not mean "in whose knowledge" our eternal life stands, but "in knowing whom." "Whose service is perfect freedom" should have a spirit in the expression somewhat correspondent with its theme, and differing from the tranquillizing and solemnizing character of the clauses preceding. "Surely trusting" and "might" are emphatic thoughts, and call for the same effect in delivery. A feeble utterance might imply that the faith was weak, and the contest uncertain. Avoid the careless pronunciation of "*congcord*."

"*A Collect for Grace.*"

"O Lord, our heavenly Father, Almighty and everlasting God, who hast safely brought us to the beginning of this day; Defend us in the same with thy mighty power; and grant that this day we fall into no sin, neither run into any kind of danger; but that all our doings, being ordered by thy governance, may be righteous in thy sight; through Jesus Christ our Lord. *Amen.*"

"Defend" is the emphatic word, rather than "in"; and "thy mighty power" should be read with fullness of voice, the invariable descriptive effect of utterance when expressing the thoughts of power, might, majesty, etc. The words "thy governance" are both emphatic.

"*A Prayer for the* President of the United States, *and all in Civil Authority.*

"O Lord, our heavenly Father, the high and mighty Ruler of the Universe, who dost from thy throne behold all the dwellers upon earth; Most heartily we beseech thee with thy favour to behold and bless thy servant THE PRESIDENT OF THE UNITED STATES, and all others in authority; and so replenish them with the grace of thy Holy Spirit, that they may always incline to thy will, and walk in thy way. Endue them plenteously with heavenly gifts; grant them in health and prosperity long to live; and finally, after this life, to attain everlasting joy and felicity; through Jesus Christ our Lord. *Amen.*"

The majesty and loftiness of the expression should have some accompanying utterance which shows the reality of the faith that calls upon the omnipotent Ruler. The logical connections would require a pause after "bless," rather than after "behold," a common fault, for we beseech the Lord to behold and bless all others in authority, as well as the President of the United States.

"*A Prayer for the Clergy and People.*

"Almighty and everlasting God, from whom cometh every good and perfect gift; Send down upon our Bishops, and other Clergy, and upon the Congregations committed to their charge, the healthful Spirit of thy grace; and, that they may truly please thee, pour upon them the continual dew of thy blessing. Grant this, O Lord, for the honour of our Advocate and Mediator, Jesus Christ. *Amen.*"

In this prayer, the Bishops and other Clergy, and their Congregations, should all be distinctly noted in the emphasis, and the beauty of the rhetorical expression should characterize the voice at such passages as "healthful spirit of thy grace," and "continual dew of thy blessing."

"*A Prayer for all Conditions of Men.*

"O God, the Creator and Preserver of all mankind, we humbly beseech thee for all sorts and conditions of men; that thou wouldest be pleased to make thy ways known unto them, thy saving health unto all nations. More especially we pray for thy holy Church universal; that it may be so guided and governed by thy good Spirit, that all who profess and call themselves Christians may be led into the way of truth, and hold the faith in unity of spirit, in the bond of peace, and in righteousness of life. Finally, we commend to thy fatherly goodness all those who are any ways afflicted, or distressed, in mind, body, or estate; that it may please thee to comfort and relieve them, according to their several necessities; giving them patience under their sufferings, and a happy issue out of all their afflictions. And this we beg for Jesus Christ's sake. Amen."

A misapplication of emphasis is sometimes heard in the expression "hold *the* faith" by emphasizing the article. "The *faith*" covers the ground in emphasis. The sympathy in the expression of the closing sentence has been already remarked upon elsewhere. The fervor of the expression should not be allowed to diminish, but urgent supplication should mark the character of the expression on such clauses as "thy ways known," "thy saving health unto all nations," "Christians," "way of truth," "unity of spirit," "bond of peace," "righteousness of life."

"*A General Thanksgiving.*

"Almighty God, Father of all mercies, we, thine unworthy servants, do give thee most humble and hearty thanks for all thy goodness and loving kindness to us, and to all men. We bless thee for our creation, preservation, and all the blessings of this life; but above all, for thine inestimable love in the redemption of the world by our Lord Jesus Christ; for the means of grace, and for the hope of glory. And, we beseech thee, give us that due sense of all thy mercies, that our hearts may be unfeignedly thankful, and that we may show forth thy praise, not only with our lips, but in our lives; by giving up ourselves to thy service, and by walking before thee in holiness and righteousness all our days; through Jesus Christ our Lord, to whom, with thee and the Holy Ghost, be all honour and glory, world without end. *Amen.*"

As already suggested, the voice of genuine, heartfelt gratitude should be heard in this portion of the Service, which culminates with a fullness of expression upon the clauses, "for thine inestimable love in the redemption of the world by our Lord Jesus Christ, for the means of grace, and for the hope of glory."

The personality of the supplication following requires more subdued effect, with gravity and deliberation in the reading, and fullness of expression on the Doxology.

"*A Prayer of* St. Chrysostom.

"Almighty God, who hast given us grace at this time with one accord to make our common supplications unto thee; and dost promise that when two or three are gathered together in thy Name thou wilt grant their requests; Fulfil now, O Lord, the desires and petitions of thy servants, as may be most expedient for them; granting us in this world knowledge of thy truth, and in the world to come life everlasting. *Amen.*"

As this is a general summary of all the foregoing petitions, it should be uttered with a fervor which is intensified, rather than weakened, by the prospect of a conclusion of the duty. Care should be taken to place the marked pause where it belongs, after "time," giving only a secondary pause after "accord," which expression should receive full emphasis, as indicative of the harmony of the hearts offering the Service. Strong emphasis should mark the claim for the fulfillment of the Divine promise, "wheresoever two or three are gathered together," etc. Full emphasis should be given upon "this world," "knowledge," "truth," with a pause after "the world to come," and fervent expression upon "life everlasting."

The expressive reading of the minor Benediction has been previously discussed.

The remarks upon the *General Confession* will apply also to the *Lord's Prayer*, which, being said by both Minister and people, does not require the same study as in individual expression. The same shades of meaning are there, in all their suggestive variety, but the finer uses of the voice would be lost in the general utterance by the congregation. It is sufficient if the even flow and somewhat measured rhythmical utterance of the leader can be easily and naturally followed by the congregation. Very marked changes and fitfulness in the time and frequency of the pausing are at variance with the desired effect.

The Collects, being simply condensed forms of prayer, rest upon the same principles of expression as in the longer and fuller forms of petition. In some instances a single feeling remains unchanged throughout, as in the reverent yearning of the Collect for the Sixth Sunday after Trinity:

"O God, who hast prepared for those who love thee such good things as pass man's understanding; Pour into our hearts such love toward thee, that we, loving thee above all things, may obtain thy promises, which exceed all that we can desire; through Jesus Christ our Lord."

Others, again, contain changes from the above, as in the Collect for the Seventh Sunday after Trinity, and require greater varieties in the expression:

"Lord of all power and might, who art the author and giver of all things; Graft in our hearts the love of thy Name, increase in us true religion, nourish us with all goodness, and of thy great mercy keep us in the same; through Jesus Christ our Lord."

Inasmuch as the language is so brief and condensed in the Collects, a corresponding terseness in the emphasis is appropriate, and is, indeed, necessary to interpret fully the meaning.

The Thanksgivings.—These differ from the Prayers, in analysis for appropriate expression, only in this respect, that the voice of gratitude is heard in place of supplication. The difference between prayer and praise should be marked as distinctly to the ear as the two acts of worship differ emotionally. As, "out of the abundance of the heart the mouth speaketh," there is more of impulsive utterance in gratitude than in supplication. Impulsive feeling takes an expulsive expression. The prayer within a form of praise, as in the General Thanksgiving, certainly differs in tone and character from the opening portion, and, as the voice is to interpret the feeling, full-voiced praise should be heard in the opening in contrast with the more subdued effect of the prayer with which it closes.

The Benedictory Prayer, with which so many Services of the Church are closed, is most appropriately fixed where it stands, possessing a character which differs from that of the prayers preceding, because of its benedictory character. If its full significance is taken into view, and the grace, love, and peace which it suggests are to find interpretative expression, then deliberate movement of the voice, expressive emphasis, and impressive pauses, should be the characteristic utterance. Every one has felt the benedictory force of the passage where it was feelingly read, and has also felt the want of such reverent and chastening effect where the utterance of the language was made almost unmeaning by defective reading. The words which are used appropriately in describing the act or manner of the reader would be serviceable for study here.

It might be thought by some that vocal practice upon the Prayer-Book is irreverent, and likely to encourage irreverence, and produce a mechanical result, as the mind is directed to the manner rather than to the offering of the Prayers.

It may be replied to this objection that a great benefit comes simply from the mental study of the Service. A deepened sense of its meaning is gained, and there can be nothing irreverent in teaching the people the meaning of their forms of worship. It is, on the contrary, a duty. And this practice is found to be only another means of reaching the mind through the ear. The object of practice is to promote the truth by preventing false interpretations and false impressions, to aid in keeping the mind fixed upon the meaning, in order that feeling may be reached and properly conveyed. There need be nothing irreverent, unless it be the purpose of the reader to make it so. But, if the form, and not the spirit, is the result of practice, if it chills devotion and helps to wandering thoughts, by all means let it be cast aside. Untutored voices and inapt reading, however, sacrifice legitimate and reverent effects, which thoughtful and judicious study and practice may secure.

There is nothing more irreverent in the analytical study and tentative practice than there would be in the previous study of the musician, adapting music to the expression of the language; or in the rehearsal of any of the musical portions of the Service for its proper and most expressive rendering.

THE LITANY.

This remarkable liturgical composition, in the dignity of its sublimity, the depth of its solemnity, the tenderness of its pathos, the anguish of its contrition, the intense fervor of its reverence, is the most difficult of all the passages of the Service to render expressively, characteristically, and reverently. Read without emotion, it is the most tedious of all portions of the Service. Read with manifestly assumed expression, the artificiality is more painful and shocking than in any other part of our worship. But, read with propriety, it is the most heart-searching and comforting of all the prayers we offer. If the congregation are led properly and expressively through the Litany, they realize deeply the meaning and application of its fervent petitions, and these vivid and graphic descriptions of their own spiritual condition and their needs.

The liturgical divisions, as they have been classified by the standard writers, are of themselves suggestive of natural changes in expression. These are, first, the Invocations, extending from the opening to "Remember not," etc.; secondly, the Deprecations, to "By the mystery," etc.; thirdly, the Obsecrations, from here to "We sinners do beseech Thee," etc.; fourthly, the Intercessions, from "We sinners," etc., to "That it may please Thee to give and preserve to our use," etc. ; fifthly, the Supplications, from this point to the close.

1. *The Invocations.*

In view of the differing authorities, equally eminent, and, therefore, to be equally respected, the author feels moved to quote from Goddard's " Reading of the Liturgy " : " Upon the question of the proper manner of reading the opening appeal to the three Persons of the Blessed Trinity, it might be presumptuous, after the discussions that have been raised, to pronounce a decisive opinion. But finding myself well supported by the judgment of authorities well qualified to determine such questions, I have no hesitation in advising that there be no pause between the words 'the Father of Heaven,' and that they should be read as if it were, ' O God Heavenly Father.' This indeed is the meaning. It is not the being ' of Heaven ' that constitutes the differential property by which each of the Persons in the Blessed Trinity is appealed to, but the property of being respectively the Father, the Son, and the Holy Ghost ; and therefore the subordination of the other, the being ' of Heaven,' which is not peculiar to the Father, should be maintained by making no comma, and reading it as above directed, ' O God, the Father of Heaven.' "

If the purpose were to single out, so to speak, the personality of each Person of the Holy Trinity, would not the received pointing require the addition of a comma after "Father" ? But no standard book gives this punctuation. It is, therefore, by the descriptive titles, or the offices of each of the Sacred Persons, that they are individually invoked. Hence, the prominence given to " Father of Heaven," " Redeemer of the World," and "proceeding from the Father and the Son." In the musical rendering of this portion of the Service, the rhythm of the movement naturally requires no pause after "the Father."

The question arises as to the proper emphasis in the

clause, "Have mercy upon us miserable sinners." The primary prayer is, unquestionably, for mercy, which would seem to throw the emphasis necessarily on the words "mercy" and "upon." But if we consider the fact that we, while calling for mercy, confess ourselves to be "miserable sinners," then the emphasis would fall upon "mercy" and "us," while omitting the adjective would throw the emphasis on "us," as descriptive of our state. "Have mercy upon *us sinners.*" If in this form we omit the emphasis on "us," it throws the word "sinners," grammatically, into the vocative case, which would, of course, be absurd. And, further, if we test the structure by transposition, which would leave the meaning unchanged, we should be again compelled to render the word "us" emphatic; thus: "upon *us, sinners,*" or "*us, miserable sinners,* have mercy." There can be no difference of opinion here, and the meaning is not essentially changed in this particular of the description of our condition in the confession of it simply by transposing the phrases.

The foregoing are simply intellectual considerations, as the language is marked by the profoundest reverential awe. The voice must be low, slow, and emphatic, with full pauses.

2. *The Deprecations.*

No emphasis should be thrown upon "our" in "*our* sins," for this would imply that the Divine vengeance had been visited upon the sins of our forefathers. The sensitive and reverent heart can not truthfully utter the words, "Thy most precious blood," without some degree of the tenderness and sympathy which the language awakens.

The clauses within the paragraphs or verses of the Deprecations are pointed with a semicolon, except the last clause, in each case, which is followed immediately by the response of the people, and is marked with a comma. This has led to the theory that the voice should not fall at the end of each suffrage, which some readers have distorted into a rising inflection. The natural law of feeling in expression dominates the law of merely intellectual utterance. Earnest supplication takes naturally the falling inflection in enumeration. Hence the clauses take the falling slide, with the exception of the last, which has the suspended slide, sufficiently to connect the words of supplication, in the response, with the enumeration of the particulars of the preceding clauses. This suspended or sustained use of the voice is, however, different from the defined rising slide, which would seem to make the mind more intent upon the grammatical structure of the language than upon the earnestness of the feeling which it describes. In the third of the Deprecations the emphasis falls upon the word "uncharitableness." In the fourth, attention is called to the increasing use of the full sound of the last syllable of "dev*il*." There is as yet, however, no standard authority recognizing its use. It came into vogue, undoubtedly, from the singing of the syllable, which, with the final vowel elided, would make the singing of the word almost impossible. In this division the word "deceits" requires special emphasis, together with "the world, the flesh, and the devil."

In the next, care should be taken to avoid sinking or hurrying the voice on the words "sudden death." In the sixth Deprecation every important word receives marked and distinctive emphasis.

Finally, the passages in this division should be delivered as genuine Deprecations, with a keen sense of being alive to the fatal dangers and the dreaded evils from which we pray to be delivered. The careless and perfunctory reading seems to imply not only indifference to the result, but also imperfect apprehension of the evils which are named, and from which we should urgently pray to be delivered.

3. *The Obsecrations.*

The objection brought against these forms, on the score of their sounding like incantations, seems groundless. These events in the life of our blessed Lord are certainly a part of His mediatorial work, and the enumeration of them can be no unmeaning form; nor the prayers, to be heard because of their efficacy, superstitious incantation. Simplicity and godly sincerity must be the law which guides to reverent expression, where these incidents of the Saviour's life, and the awful mystery of His passion and death, mingled with thoughts of our own last hour, and the solemn reckoning in the Day of Judgment, are made the heart-burdened pleas by which we cry, "Deliver us!" While avoiding excessive emphasis upon "by," the long and not the short sound of the letter should be given. The solemnity of the feeling deepens as the historical recital of the awful mysteries proceeds, culminating in the Death and Burial, succeeded by the expression of the triumph of the Resurrection and Ascension. The deep solemnity and the directness of the personal thought of our own death and judgment should chasten and subdue the utterance.

4. *The Intercessions.*

The heart naturally lifts itself up in greater freedom after the oppressive thought of death and the judgment contained in the preceding passage. It would be natural to raise the voice correspondingly to a higher key, and to quicken the movement. Mark especially, with discriminating emphasis, the different degrees of earnestness which the petitions relatively demand. Mark also the sympathetic tenderness of the three paragraphs immediately preceding the last of this division. Contrast this with the more general intercession for "magistrates," etc., etc. It should be noted that the punctuation changes in this division, and the order is reversed from the last, the separate clauses being chiefly pointed with commas, and the entire suffrage with a semicolon. Irrespective of the points of punctuation, the same law, relating to earnestness of supplication, obtains as above. As the connection is not so immediate with the response as before, a falling slide is heard more frequently than the suspended. The more condensed the expression, the more frequent is the use of the falling inflection, and the use of the semicolon—e. g., "That it may please Thee to strengthen such as do stand ; and to comfort and help the weak-hearted; and to raise up those who fall; and finally to beat down Satan under our feet." Contrast this with the more narrative form of "That it may please Thee to give to all Thy people increase of grace to hear meekly Thy Word, and to receive it with pure affection, and to bring forth the fruits of the Spirit." Observe the sympathy in the suffrages, "That it may please Thee to succor, help, and comfort all who are in danger, necessity, and tribulation", "all sick persons and young children, and to show Thy pity upon all prisoners and captives"; "for fatherless children, and widows, and all who are desolate and oppressed." "*Kindly* fruits of the earth" means, of course, fruits of the earth after their kind. It, therefore, does not require the gentle expression upon "kindly."

5. *The Supplications.*

Care must be exercised to avoid any diminishing of the fervor. This caution is a very necessary one, when we consider the tendency to lessen the ardor of our devotion, through physical fatigue. There are but few whose reading would be characterized as sufficiently sustained in fervor to the close. We are victims of habit in this, as in all other matters pertaining to the reading of the Service. In the supplication, "Son of God, we beseech Thee to hear us," the reverential earnestness should be strongly marked, and a faulty emphasis upon "Thee" should be avoided, which would imply that the Second Person of the Holy Trinity had not before been invoked, whereas the form of Obsecrations would show that the greater part of the Litany was primarily addressed to the eternal Son. And, for this reason, when we pass to the prayer, "We humbly beseech

Thee, O Father," etc., the emphasis is upon "Thee," to indicate the change in the address. The deepest fervor should characterize the passage, with its repetition, "O Lamb of God, who takest away the sins of the world." As in earnest entreaty, especially in the ejaculatory form of expression, the tenderest and deepest emotions are uttered, so should the voice indicate it.

In conclusion, the reader of the Litany should consider profoundly whether he is uttering this august portion of the Church Service according to its own solemn and sublime character, or whether it is rendered in the sing-song style of a school-boy, or with the apathetic utterance of a heart untouched, or a mind incapable of appreciating its beauty and its power.

CHAPTER V.

THE LESSONS, ANTE-COMMUNION SERVICE, AND BURIAL SERVICE.

THE term "Lessons" is suggestive. They should be read as if the people were to be taught something by them. Further, the Lessons are inspired. This gives a different character to the utterance from that appropriate to any other style of reading. Expression which makes the language in any sense ordinary is out of character. The attempted naturalness in the manner of the utterance of some readers is simply degrading to all ideas of inspired thought and language. And then their instructive character as Lessons can never be appropriately represented unless the thought of the end of the teaching of all Holy Scripture is kept in view. It is language to reach the very souls of men for their spiritual welfare, their salvation. And even if it appears for the time, in any passage, to be purely intellectual, yet should the voice plainly carry with its every utterance the recognition that the subject-matter is the very Word of GOD, conveying truth which commends itself to every man's conscience in His sight. It should be enough to impart gravity, sincerity, and reverential earnestness to the manner of reading, as we consider that what we are uttering is the savor of life unto life, or of death unto death, to the hearer. The truths so read will reach some hearts with the melody which is from on high, while others, on the contrary, will unconsciously respond: "Ah, doth he not speak parables?" In every utterance we are sowing the seed—some by the wayside, some on rocks, some among briers and thorns, and some in honest and good hearts, where it will produce fruit. There are some readers who seem to appreciate this ideal of a Divinely inspired Lesson, containing truths of GOD for the salvation of souls; and there are others who seem to have had no such thought in connection with the Sacred Scriptures, and certainly no such manner in delivering them as would harmonize with any high estimation of their value. Even the outward act in opening or closing, or turning the leaves of the Bible, may be found suggestive. The well-known anecdote of Garrick's inquiry of a clergyman as to what books he had with him on Sunday is applicable: "I have the Prayer-Book and Bible, of course," was the reply. "Oh! I thought from your manner of handling them that they were a ledger and a day-book." And, if outwardly the action may express a great deal, how much more the voice!

In forming a standard for study and propriety of expression, it is of primary importance that the reading be relevant in its tone. This is necessary in recognition of the inspired character of the language. It implies that the expression is deliberate; that we read with a heedful thoughtfulness which ponders the truths that are uttered; that there be no violence done to the ear, no shocking effect to the sensibilities; but a composed, grave, and earnest delivery, as though we reverenced the language we uttered, valued its precepts, heeded its counsels, rejoiced in its truth, and received it as the law of life. The reader is to show, by his expressive tones, the workings of his own mind, as fully alive to the truths proclaimed, and that he himself is a fellow-hearer with the rest of the congregation. This living, vital connection with the truth must be allowed to mark its natural impress upon every word that is uttered. It will correct the deadening effects of false habit, and give a naturalness, directness, and reality, which will help to make the expression genuine.

Some of the common faults are :

1. *Inexpressiveness.*—This may result from the error of making every passage the same in character, marking no distinction between the sublimest and the simplest passages ; none between the tender invitations of Divine mercy and the denunciations of Divine wrath ; no difference between joy and sorrow, prophecy and narrative, epistolary argument and jubilant or plaintive song.

2. *Lack of sympathy with the theme of the occasion.*— The reader may be apathetic or depressed when he should be joyful in spirit ; or jubilant in tone when he should be sorrowful. The physical conditions may be such as to interfere seriously with the power of utterance, or the reader may misinterpret the true character of the Lesson, and so violate propriety and fitness in the style. Oftentimes, indeed, we shall find that more than one interpretation is allowable. E. G., the eight woes pronounced upon the Pharisees and Sadducees would ordinarily be given with strong denunciatory effect ; but it is said that the Rev. Dr. Channing, who had an unusual degree of expressive power in reading the Scriptures, gave it with a depth of sorrow, as though it grieved the heart of the Saviour to utter such words, which is in sympathy with the exclamation : " O Jerusalem, Jerusalem, thou that killest the prophets !" etc.

3. *Impropriety.*—This may appear in various ways. In one respect, it would be found in failure to adapt the expression properly to the Fast or Festival. The difference

between the jubilant utterances of Christmas-tide, Epiphany, or Easter, and, in contrast, the solemn warnings of Advent, or the contrition of Lent, must be apparent. Who, for instance, could rightly interpret the spirit of the Church's Festival of the Epiphany by reading the glowing visions recorded in the sixtieth chapter of Isaiah's prophecy with the tenderness and pathos proper to the Evening Lesson for Good Friday, which is the fifty-third chapter of the same prophecy, where the heart-touching description of the suffering Messiah is the appointed meditation?

4. The glaring impropriety of the purely *dramatic* model, which manifests itself with the extreme of vivid and graphic effect in dialogue, adding even the demonstrative manner of gesticulation, is too palpably erroneous to require prolonged discussion. But, while this, the extreme, is to be avoided, the opposite error of giving no suggestion of character or emotion in speaking, or the force of the inspired colloquies, entirely subjecting them to an unmeaning and unnatural sameness of expression, would be open to just criticism. The proper effect, in the passages referred to, is to render them with mimetic expression, not to make them expressionless. But the whole style should be suggestive of the incidents and characters described.

5. Another error (that which is so common) is the *pathetic* or *plaintive* voice, which, in its excess, degenerates into a whine, a relic of those days when the "language of Canaan," droned through the nostrils, was the vocal indication of a peculiar type of piety. The hardy and boisterous style, appropriate to the backwoods, is, however, no proper substitution for this.

6. *An undue refinement* of expression is another defect to be sedulously avoided. The extreme delicacy of thought and feeling which such attenuation of voice implies is not adapted to manly and forcible effect. The reading of the Scriptures should, indeed, be rendered with refinement, but

not exquisitely so. Mincing tones do not suit the sublime and energetic portions of the Divine Word.

7. *Mannerism* of any kind is most unfortunate, and is sure to divert the attention of the hearer from the subject-matter to the reader himself, which offends and repels. It provokes criticism, and can scarcely be pardoned, even when prompted by the eccentricities of genius.

8. *Monotony* is another of the faults destructive to vividness and truthfulness and impressiveness, in the reading of the Lessons. It can not be that sublimity and simplicity, love and anger, denunciation and tenderness, cursing and blessing, and all the infinite and expressive variety of subjects and their treatment, found in Holy Scripture, can be properly rendered by one unmeaning and undeviating level of voice. "The dignity of the subject, the sublimity of the style, and the simplicity of the language, demand in every passage of Holy Scripture the mingling effects of grave, full, and vivid expression. To the reader of the sacred page should be brought every aid, arising from the deepest impressions of the heart, the most vivid effects of poetic imagination, the most refining influences of high intellectual culture, all the treasures of knowledge, all the riches and truer wealth of life and experience, which can be possessed; all these should be made tributary to the reading of the Scripture Lessons in Divine Service. The spiritual and intellectual nature of man is then, if ever, at its maximum of experience and power, when permitted to mingle its workings with those of the Divine Mind in Revelation."

It would be well for every reader to consider profoundly the comprehensive theory of the judicious Hooker just stated. The reader of the Scriptures is their herald or prophet. To this we may add, he is also their interpreter; for he conveys a meaning, whether right or wrong, in every utterance. In this respect the office of reading is scarcely inferior to that of preaching the Divine Word, for the truth delivered is more immediately God's Word than any human exposition of it. Every imperfection, every misreading, and misinterpretation, is just so much of misrepresentation of the truth which the reader is striving to declare. The reading of the Lessons should be made of absorbing interest, and a delight to the ear, instead of being the unmeaning, indifferent exercise of an irksome or perfunctory duty.

In reading the Lessons, the Minister should observe the simple directions to stand erect, to fill his lungs, and to be deliberate in his utterance. Distinctness of articulation, intelligent use of emphasis, a due regard to the rhythmical effect, and the observance of the other particulars above enumerated, are all well worth serious consideration. The occasional use of the eye in expressive communication, as is natural in conveying thought to the hearer, should not be deemed unworthy of observance. The downcast eye, continued throughout a long Lesson, can not be the best means of assisting the voice to convey the truth, while the incessant use of the eye, giving the effect of reciting from memory, is equally inappropriate.

I. CLASSIFICATIONS OF SCRIPTURE LESSONS FOR EXPRESSION ACCORDING TO MANNER OF COMPOSITION.

There is first the natural arrangement according to the various styles of writing, as the narrative and descriptive, didactic, prophetic, and lyric passages.

1. *Narrative and Descriptive.*

The ideal effect of this style is to read a story inspired in character. There are three marked divisions of the style: the familiar, the elevated, and the middle. The first of these is clearly indicated by the term, where all the familiar and colloquial effects, which may comport with the theories and principles previously laid down, are found. The "elevated" includes the sublime and majestic passages in narrative form, requiring greater dignity and force of expression than in the familiar. The intermediate effect is made the third division, where the reading has something of the simplicity of the first division, but is characterized by greater gravity of style from the dignity of the theme, yet is not marked by the fullest degree of sublimity.

a. Familiar.—" When therefore the Lord knew how the Pharisees had heard that Jesus made and baptized more disciples than John, (though Jesus himself baptized not, but his disciples,) he left Judea, and departed again into Galilee. And he must needs go through Samaria. Then cometh he to a city of Samaria, which is called Sychar, near to the parcel of ground that Jacob gave to his son Joseph. Now Jacob's well was there. Jesus therefore, being wearied with his journey, sat thus on the well: and it was about the sixth hour. There cometh a woman of Samaria to draw water: Jesus saith unto her, Give me to drink. (For his disciples were gone away unto the city to buy meat.) Then saith the woman of Samaria unto him, How is it that thou, being a Jew, askest drink of me, which am a woman of Samaria? for the Jews have no dealings with the Samaritans. Jesus answered and said unto her, If thou knewest the gift of God, and who it is that saith to thee, Give me to drink; thou wouldest have asked of him, and he would have given thee living water. The woman saith unto him, Sir, thou hast nothing to draw with, and the well is deep: from whence then hast thou that living water? Art thou greater than our father Jacob, which gave us the well, and drank thereof himself, and his children, and his cattle? Jesus answered and said unto her, Whosoever drinketh of this water shall thirst again: but whosoever drinketh of the water that I shall give him shall never thirst; but the water that I shall give him shall be in him a well of water springing up into everlasting life."—St. John, iv., 1–14.

Betrothing of Rebecca, Gen. xxiv.; Judah's Appeal, Gen. xliv.; Samuel before Eli, I. Sam. iii., 18, and most of the Gospel narratives.

b. Elevated.—" And God said, Let the earth bring forth the living creature after his kind, cattle, and creeping thing, and beast of the earth after his kind : and it was so. And God made the beast of the earth after his kind, and cattle after their kind, and everything that creepeth upon the earth after his kind : and God saw that it was good. And God said, Let us make man in our image, after our likeness : and let them have dominion over the fish of the sea, and over the fowl of the air, and over the cattle, and over all the earth, and over every creeping thing that creepeth upon the earth. So God created man in his own image, in the image of God created he him ; male and female created he them. And God blessed them, and God said unto them, Be fruitful, and multiply, and replenish the earth, and subdue it : and have dominion over the fish of the sea, and over the fowl of the air, and over every living thing that moveth upon the earth. And God said, Behold, I have given you every herb bearing seed, which is upon the face of all the earth, and every tree, in the which is the fruit of a tree yielding seed ; to you it shall be for meat. And to every beast of the earth, and to every fowl of the air, and to every thing that creepeth upon the earth, wherein there is life, I have given every green herb for meat : and it was so. And God saw every thing that he had made, and, behold, it was very good. And the evening and the morning were the sixth day."—Gen. i., 24–31.

The Flood, Gen. vii. and viii. ; Abraham's Vision, Gen. xv. ; the Sacrifice of Isaac (as a type), Good Friday Lesson, Gen, xxii. ; Mission of Moses, Ex. iii.; Giving of the Law, Ex. xix. ; Dedication of the Temple, I. Kings, viii. ; the Day of Pentecost, Acts, ii. ; Narratives of the Resurrection ; Triumphs of Faith, Heb. xi.; Worship in Heaven, Rev. xiv. ; the River and Tree of Life, Rev. xxii., etc.

c. Middle.—" And David rose up early in the morning, and left the sheep with a keeper, and took, and went, as Jesse had commanded him ; and he came to the trench, as the host was going forth to the fight, and shouted for the battle. For Israel and the Philistines had put the battle in array, army against army. And David left his carriage in the hand of the keeper of the carriage, and ran into the army, and came and saluted his brethren. And as he talked with them, behold, there came up the champion (the Philistine of Gath, Goliath by name) out of the armies of the Philistines, and spake according to the same words : and David heard them. And all the men of Israel, when they saw the man, fled from him, and were sore afraid. And the men of Israel said, Have ye seen this man that is come up ? surely to defy Israel is he come up : and it shall be, that the man who killeth him, the king will enrich him with great riches, and will give him his daughter, and make his father's house free in Israel. And David spake to the men that stood by him, saying, What shall be done to the man that killeth this Philistine, and taketh away the reproach from Israel ? for who is this uncircumcised Philistine, that he should defy the armies of the living God ? And the people answered him after this manner, saying, So shall it be done to the man that killeth him. . . . And David said to Saul, Let no man's heart fail because of him : thy servant will go and fight with this Philistine. And Saul said to David, Thou art not able to go against this Philistine to fight with him : for thou art but a youth, and he a man of war from his youth. And David said unto Saul, Thy servant kept his father's sheep, and there came a lion, and a bear, and took a lamb out of the flock : and I went out after him, and smote him, and delivered it out of his mouth : and when he arose against me, I caught him by his beard, and smote him, and slew him. Thy servant slew both the lion and the bear ; and this uncircumcised Philistine shall be as one of them, seeing he hath defied the armies of the living God. David said moreover, The LORD that delivered me out of the paw of the lion, and out of the paw of the bear, he will deliver me out of the hand of this Philistine.

And Saul said unto David, Go, and the LORD be with thee. And Saul armed David with his armour, and he put an helmet of brass upon his head; also he armed him with a coat of mail. And David girded his sword upon his armour, and he assayed to go; for he had not proved it. And David said unto Saul, I cannot go with these; for I have not proved them. And David put them off him. And he took his staff in his hand, and chose him five smooth stones out of the brook, and put them in a shepherd's bag which he had, even in a scrip; and his sling was in his hand: and he drew near to the Philistine. And the Philistine came on, and drew near unto David; and the man that bare the shield went before him. And when the Philistine looked about, and saw David, he disdained him: for he was but a youth, and ruddy, and of a fair countenance. And the Philistine said unto David, Am I a dog, that thou comest to me with staves? And the Philistine cursed David by his gods. And the Philistine said to David, Come to me, and I will give thy flesh unto the fowls of the air, and to the beasts of the field. Then said David to the Philistine, Thou comest to me with a sword, and with a spear, and with a shield: but I come to thee in the name of the LORD of hosts, the God of the armies of Israel, whom thou hast defied."—I. Sam. xvii., 20, etc.

Death of Abel, Gen. iv.; Jephthah's Vow, Judges, xi.; Raising of Lazarus, St. John, xi.; St. Paul before Agrippa, Acts, xxvi., etc.

2. *Didactic.*

a. Epistolary Style.—" Though I speak with the tongues of men and of angels, and have not charity, I am become as sounding brass, or a tinkling cymbal. And though I have the gift of prophecy, and understand all mysteries, and all knowledge; and though I have all faith, so that I could remove mountains, and have not charity, I am nothing. And though I bestow all my goods to feed the poor, and though I give my body to be burned, and have not charity, it profiteth me nothing. Charity suffereth long, and is kind; charity envieth not; charity vaunteth not itself, is not puffed up, doth not behave itself unseemly, seeketh not her own, is not easily provoked, thinketh no evil; rejoiceth not in iniquity, but rejoiceth in the truth; beareth all things, believeth all things, hopeth all things, endureth all things. Charity never faileth: but whether there be prophecies, they shall fail; whether there be tongues, they shall cease; whether there be knowledge, it shall vanish away. For we know in part, and we prophesy in part. But when that which is perfect is come, then that which is in part shall be done away. When I was a child, I spake as a child, I understood as a child, I thought as a child; but when I became a man, I put away childish things. For now we see through a glass, darkly; but then face to face: now I know in part; but then shall I know even as also I am known. And now abideth faith, hope, charity, these three; but the greatest of these is charity."—I. Cor. xiii.

"What shall we say then? Is there unrighteousness with God? God forbid. For he saith to Moses, I will have mercy on whom I will have mercy, and I will have compassion on whom I will have compassion. So then it is not of him that willeth, nor of him that runneth, but of God that sheweth mercy. For the Scripture saith unto Pharaoh, Even for this same purpose have I raised thee up, that I might shew my power in thee, and that my name might be declared throughout all the earth. Therefore hath he mercy on whom he will have mercy, and whom he will he hardeneth. Thou wilt say then unto me, Why doth he yet find fault? For who hath resisted his will? Nay but, O man, who art thou that repliest against God? Shall the thing formed say to him that formed it, Why hast thou made me thus? Hath not the potter power over the clay, of the same lump to make one vessel unto honour and another unto dishonour? What if God, willing to show his wrath, and to make his power known, endured with much longsuffering the vessels of wrath fitted to destruction: and that he might make known the riches of his glory on the vessels of mercy, which he had afore prepared unto glory, even us, whom he hath called, not of the Jews only, but also of the Gentiles? As he saith also in Osee, I will call them my people, which were not my people; and her beloved, which was not beloved."—Rom. ix., 14–25.

"Paul, and Silvanus, and Timotheus, unto the church of the Thessalonians in God our Father and the Lord Jesus Christ: grace unto you, and peace, from God our Father and the Lord Jesus Christ. We are bound to thank God always for you, brethren, as it is meet, because that your faith groweth exceedingly, and the charity of every one of you all toward each other aboundeth; so that we ourselves glory in you in the churches of God, for your patience and faith in all your persecutions and tribulations that ye endure; which is a manifest token of the righteous judgment of God, that ye may be counted worthy of the kingdom of God, for which ye also suffer: seeing it is a righteous thing with God to recompense tribulation to them that trouble you; and to you who are troubled, rest with us; when the Lord Jesus shall be revealed from heaven with his mighty angels, in flaming fire taking vengeance on them that know not God, and that obey not the gospel of our Lord Jesus Christ: who shall be punished with everlasting destruction from the presence of the Lord and from the glory of his power; when he shall come to be glorified in his saints, and to be admired in all them that believe (because our testimony among you was believed) in that day. Wherefore also we pray always for you, that our God would count you worthy of this calling, and fulfil all the good pleasure of his goodness, and the work of faith with power; that the name of our Lord Jesus Christ may be glorified in you, and ye in him, according to the grace of our God and the Lord Jesus Christ."—II. Thess. i., 1–12.

Rom. iii., Rom. xi., I. Cor. xv., Col. i., Heb. ix., Heb. x., etc.

b. Oral and Parabolic Style.—The style being preceptive, there is more frequent use of distinctive emphasis and pause than in flowing narration, or in the reading of letters (i. e., the Epistles). There are also the directness and naturalness of tone which imply that these were spoken words, rather than written. In the reading of the Sermon on the Mount, as it is so full, and yet so condensed in expression, the reader should aim at conveying most emphatically and distinctly a full degree of meaning, especially in the Beatitudes. If, throughout the inspired Word, every passage is of value, and to be reverently regarded, how precious are those words of Him Who spake as never man spake, and Whose deep meaning can only be partially uttered in human language!

"And seeing the multitudes, he went up into a mountain : and when he was set, his disciples came unto him : And he opened his mouth, and taught them, saying, Blessed are the poor in spirit : for theirs is the kingdom of heaven. Blessed are they that mourn : for they shall be comforted. Blessed are the meek : for they shall inherit the earth. Blessed are they which do hunger and thirst after righteousness : for they shall be filled. Blessed are the merciful : for they shall obtain mercy. Blessed are the pure in heart : for they shall see God. Blessed are the peacemakers : for they shall be called the children of God. Blessed are they which are persecuted for righteousness' sake : for theirs is the kingdom of heaven. Blessed are ye, when men shall revile you, and persecute you, and shall say all manner of evil against you falsely, for my sake. Rejoice, and be exceeding glad : for great is your reward in heaven : for so persecuted they the prophets which were before you.

. . . . . .

"No man can serve two masters : for either he will hate

the one, and love the other; or else he will hold to the one, and despise the other. Ye cannot serve God and mammon. Therefore I say unto you, Take no thought for your life, what ye shall eat, or what ye shall drink; nor yet for your body, what ye shall put on. Is not the life more than meat, and the body than raiment? Behold the fowls of the air: for they sow not, neither do they reap, nor gather into barns; yet your heavenly Father feedeth them. Are ye not much better than they? Which of you by taking thought can add one cubit unto his stature? And why take ye thought for raiment? Consider the lilies of the field, how they grow; they toil not, neither do they spin: and yet I say unto you, That even Solomon in all his glory was not arrayed like one of these. Wherefore, if God so clothe the grass of the field, which to day is, and to morrow is cast into the oven, shall he not much more clothe you, O ye of little faith? Therefore take no thought, saying, What shall we eat? or, What shall we drink, or, Wherewithal shall we be clothed? (For after all these things do the Gentiles seek:) for your heavenly Father knoweth that ye have need of all these things. But seek ye first the kingdom of God, and his righteousness; and all these things shall be added unto you. Take therefore no thought for the morrow: for the morrow shall take thought for the things of itself. Sufficient unto the day is the evil thereof."—St. Matt. v. and vi.

"Then shall the kingdom of heaven be likened unto ten virgins, which took their lamps, and went forth to meet the bridegroom. And five of them were wise, and five were foolish. They that were foolish took their lamps, and took no oil with them: but the wise took oil in their vessels with their lamps. While the bridegroom tarried, they all slumbered and slept. And at midnight there was a cry made, Behold, the bridegroom cometh; go ye out to meet him. Then all those virgins arose, and trimmed their lamps. And the foolish said unto the wise, Give us of your oil; for our lamps are gone out. But the wise answered, saying, Not so; lest there be not enough for us and you: but go ye rather to them that sell, and buy for yourselves. And while they went to buy, the bridegroom came; and they that were ready went in with him to the marriage: and the door was shut. Afterward came also the other virgins, saying, Lord, Lord, open to us. But he answered and said, Verily I say unto you, I know you not. Watch therefore; for ye know neither the day nor the hour wherein the Son of man cometh."—St. Matt. xxv., 1–13.

"And he began again to teach by the sea side: and there was gathered unto him a great multitude, so that he entered into a ship, and sat in the sea; and the whole multitude was by the sea on the land. And he taught them many things by parables, and said unto them in his doctrine, Hearken; Behold, there went out a sower to sow: and it came to pass, as he sowed, some fell by the way side, and the fowls of the air came and devoured it up. And some fell on stony ground, where it had not much earth; and immediately it sprang up, because it had no depth of earth: but when the sun was up, it was scorched; and because it had no root, it withered away. And some fell among thorns; and the thorns grew up, and choked it, and it yielded no fruit. And other fell on good ground, and did yield fruit that sprang up and increased, and brought forth, some thirty, and some sixty, and some a hundred. And he said unto them, He that hath ears to hear, let him hear. And when he was alone, they that were about him with the twelve asked of him the parable. And he said unto them, Unto you it is given to know the mystery of the kingdom of God; but unto them that are without, all these things are done in parables: That seeing they may see, and not perceive; and hearing they may hear, and not understand; lest at any time they should be converted, and their sins should be forgiven them. And he said unto them, Know ye not this parable? and how then will ye know all parables? The sower soweth the word. And these are they by the way side, where the word is sown; but when they have heard, Satan cometh immediately, and taketh away the word that was sown in their hearts. And these are they likewise which are sown on stony ground; who, when they have heard the word, immediately receive it with gladness; and have no root in themselves, and so endure but for a time: afterward, when affliction or persecution ariseth for the word's sake, immediately they are offended. And these are they which are sown among thorns; such as hear the word, and the cares of this world, and the deceitfulness of riches, and the lusts of other things entering in, choke the word, and it becometh unfruitful. And these are they which are sown on good ground; such as hear the word, and receive it, and bring forth fruit, some thirtyfold, some sixty, and some a hundred."—St. Mark, iv., 1–20.

Sermon on the Mount entire, all the Parables, the Discourses of our Lord, the Book of Proverbs, etc.

3. *Prophetic.*

The style of delivery is heraldic, as the preceding have been preceptive and descriptive. There are two natural divisions of the style—the bolder and the gentler.

a. Bold, requiring energy and fullness of voice.—" Blow ye the trumpet in Zion, and sound an alarm in my holy mountain: let all the inhabitants of the land tremble; for the day of the LORD cometh, for it is nigh at hand; a day of darkness and of gloominess, a day of clouds and of thick darkness, as the morning spread upon the mountains: a great people and a strong; there hath not been ever the like, neither shall be any more after it, even to the years of many generations. A fire devoureth before them; and behind them a flame burneth: the land is as the garden of Eden before them, and behind them a desolate wilderness; yea, and nothing shall escape them. The appearance of them is as the appearance of horses; and as horsemen, so shall they run. Like the noise of chariots on the tops of mountains shall they leap, like the noise of a flame of fire that devoureth the stubble, as a strong people set in battle array. Before their face the people shall be much pained; all faces shall gather blackness. They shall run like mighty men; they shall climb the wall like men of war; and they shall march every one on his ways, and they shall not break their ranks; neither shall one thrust another; they shall walk every one in his path: and when they fall upon the sword, they shall not be wounded. They shall run to and fro in the city; they shall run upon the wall; they shall climb up upon the houses; they shall enter in at the windows like a thief. The earth shall quake before them; the heavens shall tremble: the sun and the moon shall be dark, and the stars shall withdraw their shining: And the LORD shall utter his voice before his army; for his camp is very great: for he is strong that executeth his word: for the day of the LORD is great and very terrible; and who can abide it?"—Joel, ii., 1–11.

"Proclaim ye this among the Gentiles; Prepare war, wake up the mighty men, let all the men of war draw near; let them come up: beat your ploughshares into swords, and your pruninghooks into spears: let the weak say, I am strong. Assemble yourselves, and come, all ye heathen, and gather yourselves together round about: thither cause thy mighty ones to come down, O LORD. Let the heathen be wakened, and come up to the valley of Jehoshaphat: for there will I sit to judge all the heathen round about. Put ye in the sickle; for the harvest is ripe: come, get you down; for the press is full, the fats overflow; for their wickedness is great. Multitudes, multitudes in the valley of decision: for the day of the LORD is near in the valley of decision. The sun and the moon shall be darkened, and the stars shall withdraw their shining. The LORD also shall roar out of Zion, and utter his voice from Jerusalem; and the heavens and the earth shall shake: but the LORD will be the hope of his people, and the strength of the children of Israel."—Joel, iii., 9–16.

"Woe to the crown of pride, to the drunkards of Ephraim, whose glorious beauty is a fading flower, which are on the head of the fat valleys of them that are overcome with wine! Behold the LORD hath a mighty and strong one, which, as a tempest of hail, and a destroying storm, as a flood of mighty waters overflowing, shall cast down to the earth with the hand. The crown of pride, the drunkards of Ephraim, shall be trodden under feet."—Isaiah, xxviii., 1–3.

"Ho, every one that thirsteth, come ye to the waters, and he that hath no money; come ye, buy, and eat; yea, come, buy wine and milk without money and without price. Wherefore do ye spend money for that which is not bread? and your labour for that which satisfieth not? Hearken diligently unto me, and eat ye that which is good, and let your soul delight itself in fatness. Incline your ear, and come unto me: hear, and your soul shall live; and I will make an everlasting covenant with you, even the sure mercies of David. Behold, I have given him for a witness to the people, a leader and commander to the people. Behold, thou shalt call a nation that thou knowest not, and nations that knew not thee shall run unto thee, because of the LORD thy God, and for the Holy One of Israel; for he hath glorified thee."—Isaiah, lv., 1–5.

Denunciation and Indignation, Isaiah, i.; Reproof of Jerusalem, Zeph. iii.; Rebuke of Israel, Amos, v.; Joy and Triumph, Isaiah, lx. and lii.; etc.

a. Subdued.—The sympathetic expression should be very strongly marked in the description of the suffering Messiah. All the sorrow of the other passages is subdued. Hence the propriety of gentleness in the delivery.

"Behold, my servant shall deal prudently, he shall be exalted and extolled, and be very high. As many were astonied at thee; his visage was so marred more than any man, and his form more than the sons of men: so shall he sprinkle many nations ; the kings shall shut their mouths at him : for that which had not been told them shall they see ; and that which they had not heard shall they consider."—Isaiah, lii., 13-15.

"Who hath believed our report? and to whom is the arm of the LORD revealed? For he shall grow up before him as a tender plant, and as a root out of a dry ground : he hath no form nor comeliness ; and when we shall see him, there is no beauty that we should desire him. He is despised and rejected of men ; a man of sorrows, and acquainted with grief : and we hid as it were our faces from him ; he was despised, and we esteemed him not. Surely he hath borne our griefs, and carried our sorrows : yet we did esteem him stricken, smitten of God, and afflicted. But he was wounded for our transgressions, he was bruised for our iniquities : the chastisement of our peace was upon him ; and with his stripes we are healed. All we, like sheep, have gone astray ; we have turned every one to his own way ; and the LORD hath laid on him the iniquity of us all. He was oppressed, and he was afflicted ; yet he opened not his mouth : he is brought as a lamb to the slaughter, and as a sheep before her shearers is dumb, so he openeth not his mouth. He was taken from prison and from judgment : and who shall declare his generation ? for he was cut off out of the land of the living : for the transgression of my people was he stricken. And he made his grave with the wicked, and with the rich in his death ; because he had done no violence, neither was any deceit in his mouth. Yet it pleased the LORD to bruise him ; he hath put him to grief : when thou shalt make his soul an offering for sin, he shall see his seed, he shall prolong his days, and the pleasure of the LORD shall prosper in his hand. He shall see of the travail of his soul, and shall be satisfied : by his knowledge shall my righteous servant justify many ; for he shall bear their iniquities. Therefore will I divide him a portion with the great, and he shall divide the spoil with the strong; because he hath poured out his soul unto death : and he was numbered with the transgressors; and he bare the sin of many, and made intercession for the transgressors."—Isaiah, liii.

Comfort of the Gospel, Isaiah, xli., xlii.; Office of Christ, Isaiah, lxi., 1-4.; Lamentations of Jeremiah, Prayer of Jonah, Repentance and Promise of God's Blessing, Hosea, xiv., etc.

4. *Lyric Passages.*

These are found to be as varied as the emotions which they describe, and differ somewhat from the other classifications in being primarily emotional above all the rest. In reading we do not pour forth the full expression of a feeling as quietly as we should tell a story in the narrative style, nor would it correspond with the didactic utterance of doctrinal or preceptive truth; nor, again, would it find the same expression as the heraldic proclamations of prophecy. The following passages are musical in expression from their rhythmical structure. They are the songs, the psalms, and hymns of Holy Scripture :

"And Mary said, My soul doth magnify the Lord, and my spirit hath rejoiced in God my Saviour. For he hath regarded the low estate of his handmaiden : for, behold, from henceforth all generations shall call me blessed. For he that is mighty hath done to me great things; and holy is his name. And his mercy is on them that fear him, from generation to generation. He hath showed strength with his arm; he hath scattered the proud in the imagination of their hearts. He hath put down the mighty from their seats, and exalted them of low degree. He hath filled the hungry with good things, and the rich he hath sent empty away. He hath holpen his servant Israel, in remembrance of his mercy; as he spake to our fathers, to Abraham, and to his seed for ever."—St. Luke, i., 46–55.

The Song of Miriam, Ex. xv.; the greater part of the Book of Job; the Song of Deborah, Judges, v.; the Song of Hannah, I. Sam. ii.; the Song of Solomon; the Prayer of Daniel, Dan. ix.; the Prayer of Habbakuk, Hab. iii.; the Song of Simeon, St. Luke, ii., etc.; and the Psalter.

II. CLASSIFICATION OF LESSONS FOR EXPRESSION ACCORDING TO THE SPIRIT OF THE FAST OR FESTIVAL.

The expression in the reading of a passage is not so strongly marked when the portion occurs in the Daily Calendar as when it is used for a special Fast or Feast—e. g., at Christmas:

"And, lo, the angel of the Lord came upon them, and the glory of the Lord shone round about them; and they were sore afraid. And the angel said unto them, Fear not: for, behold, I bring you good tidings of great joy, which shall be to all people. For unto you is born this day, in the city of David, a Saviour, which is Christ the Lord. And this shall be a sign unto you: Ye shall find the babe wrapped in swaddling clothes, lying in a manger. And suddenly there was with the angel a multitude of the heavenly host, praising God, and saying: Glory to God in the highest, and on earth peace, good will toward men."—St. Luke, ii., 9–14.

So especially with the Epistle and Gospel. Every allusion to the doctrine of the Incarnation, in these passages, should be delivered with the distinctive emphasis which makes them applicable to this festival.

"God, who at sundry times and in divers manners spake in time past unto the fathers by the prophets, hath in these last days spoken unto us by his Son, whom he hath appointed heir of all things, by whom also he made the worlds; who (being the brightness of his glory, and the express image of his person, and upholding all things by the word of his power), when he had by himself purged our sins, sat down on the right hand of the Majesty on high; being made so much better than the angels, as he hath by inheritance obtained a more excellent name than they. For unto which of the angels said he at any time, Thou art my Son, this day have I begotten thee? And again, I will be to him a Father, and he shall be to me a Son? And again, when he bringeth in the First-begotten into the world, he saith, And let all the angels of God worship him. And of the angels he saith, Who maketh his angels spirits, and his ministers a flame of fire. But unto the Son he saith, Thy throne, O God, is for ever and ever; a sceptre of righteousness is the sceptre of thy kingdom. Thou hast loved righteousness, and hated iniquity; therefore God, even thy God, hath anointed thee with the oil of gladness above thy fellows. And, Thou, Lord, in the beginning hast laid the foundation of the earth; and the heavens are the works of thine hands: they shall perish, but thou remainest: and they all shall wax old as doth a garment; and as a vesture shalt thou fold them up, and they shall be changed: but thou art the same, and thy years shall not fail."—The Epistle, Heb. i., 1-12.

"In the beginning was the Word, and the Word was with God, and the Word was God. The same was in the beginning with God. All things were made by him; and without him was not anything made that was made. In him was life; and the life was the light of men. And the light shineth in darkness; and the darkness comprehended it not. There was a man sent from God, whose name was John. The same came for a witness, to bear witness of the Light, that all men through him might believe. He was not that Light, but was sent to bear witness of that Light. That was the true Light, which lighteth every man that cometh into the world. He was in the world, and the world was made by him, and the world knew him not. He came unto his own, and his own received him not. But as many as received him, to them gave he power to become the sons of God, even to them that believe on his name: which were born, not of blood, nor of the will of the flesh, nor of the will of man, but of God. And the Word was made flesh, and dwelt among us, (and we beheld his glory, the glory as of the only-begotten of the Father,) full of grace and truth."—The Gospel, St. John, i., 1–14.

Ascension Day.—The translation of Elijah, as a type of the Ascension of Christ, should be read with especial emphasis on the typical passages, in the first Lesson of the Morning Service for this day.

"And it came to pass, when the LORD would take up Elijah into heaven by a whirlwind, that Elijah went with Elisha from Gilgal. And Elijah said unto Elisha, Tarry here, I pray thee; for the Lord hath sent me to Beth-el. And Elisha said unto him, As the LORD liveth, and as thy soul liveth, I will not leave thee. So they went down to Beth-el. And the sons of the prophets that were at Beth-el came forth to Elisha, and said unto him, Knowest thou that the LORD will take away thy master from thy head to-day? And he said, Yea, I know it; hold ye your peace. And Elijah said unto him, Elisha, tarry here, I pray thee; for the LORD hath sent me to Jericho. And he said, As the LORD liveth, and as thy soul liveth, I will not leave thee. So they came to Jericho. And the sons of the prophets that were at Jericho came to Elisha, and said unto him, Knowest thou that the LORD will take away thy master from thy head to-day? And he answered, Yea, I know it; hold ye your peace. And Elijah said unto him, Tarry, I pray thee, here; for the LORD hath sent me to Jordan. And he said, As the LORD liveth, and as thy soul liveth, I will not leave thee. And they two went on. And fifty men of the sons of the prophets went, and stood to view afar off: and they two stood by Jordan. And Elijah took his mantle, and wrapped it together, and smote the waters, and they were divided hither and thither, so that they two went over on dry ground. And it came to pass, when they were gone over, that Elijah said unto Elisha, Ask what I shall do for thee, before I be taken away from thee. And Elisha said, I pray thee, let a double portion of thy spirit be upon me. And he said, Thou hast asked a hard thing: nevertheless, if thou see me when I am taken from thee, it shall be so unto thee; but if not, it shall not be so. And it came to pass, as they still went on, and talked, that, behold, there appeared a chariot of fire, and horses of fire, and parted them both asunder; and Elijah went up by a whirlwind into heaven. And Elisha saw it, and he cried, My father, my father! the chariot of Israel, and the horsemen thereof. And he saw him no more: and he took hold of his own clothes, and rent them in two pieces. He took up also the mantle of Elijah that fell from him, and went back, and stood by the bank of Jordan; and he took the mantle of Elijah that fell from him, and smote the waters, and said, Where is the LORD God of Elijah? And when he also had smitten the waters, they parted hither and thither: and Elisha went over."—II. Kings, ii., 1–14.

It is not necessary to multiply selections as illustrations of the manifest propriety of the application of the style of expression to the Fast or Festival, and Scripture Lessons, as enforcing their teaching. It is enough, to use the expression of a respected bishop of the Church, if the reading be "inflamed" with the characteristic expression.

The Epiphany.—The expressions in the Epistle relating to the Gentiles should be distinctly emphasized.

"For this cause, I Paul, the prisoner of Jesus Christ for you Gentiles; if ye have heard of the dispensation of the grace of God, which is given me to youward: How that by revelation he made known unto me the mystery (as I wrote afore in few words, whereby, when ye read, ye may understand my knowledge in the mystery of Christ) which in other ages was not made known unto the sons of men, as it is now revealed unto his holy Apostles and Prophets by the Spirit; that the Gentiles should be fellow-heirs, and of the same body, and partakers of his promise in Christ, by the Gospel: whereof I was made a minister, according to the gift of the grace of God given unto me by the effectual working of his power. Unto me, who am less than the least of all saints, is this grace given, that I should preach among the Gentiles the unsearchable riches of Christ: and to make all men see what is the fellowship of the mystery, which from the beginning of the world hath been hid in God, who created all things by Jesus Christ: to the intent that now unto the principalities and powers in heavenly places might be known, by the Church, the manifold wisdom of God, according to the eternal purpose which he purposed in Christ Jesus our Lord: in whom we have boldness and access with confidence by the faith of him.—Eph. iii., 1–12.

The Epiphany, second Lesson, A. M.

As almost every verse has some reference to the calling of the Gentiles, so should the marked emphasis show the particular teaching of the Epiphany Festival in the Lesson.

"I say then, Hath God cast away his people? God forbid. For I also am an Israelite, of the seed of Abraham, of the tribe of Benjamin. God hath not cast away his people which he foreknew. Wot ye not what the Scripture saith of Elias? how he maketh intercession to God against Israel, saying, Lord, they have killed thy prophets, and digged down thine altars; and I am left alone, and they seek my life. But what saith the answer of God unto him? I have reserved to myself seven thousand men, who have not bowed the knee to the image of Baal. Even so then at this present time also there is a remnant according to the election of grace. And if by grace, then is it no more of works: otherwise grace is no more grace. But if it be of works, then is it no more grace: otherwise work is no more work. What then? Israel hath not obtained that which he seeketh for; but the election hath obtained it, and the rest were blinded. (According as it is written, God hath given them the spirit of slumber, eyes that they should not see, and ears that they should not hear;) unto this day. And David saith, Let their table be made a snare, and a trap, and a stumblingblock, and a recompense unto them: Let their eyes be darkened, that they may not see, and bow down their back alway. I say then, Have they stumbled that they should fall? God forbid: but rather through their fall salvation is come unto the Gentiles, for to provoke them to jealousy. Now if the fall of them be the riches of the world, and the diminishing of them the riches of the Gentiles; how much more their fulness? For I speak to you Gentiles, inasmuch as I am the apostle of the Gentiles, I magnify mine office; if by any means I may provoke to emulation them which are my flesh, and might save some of them. For if the casting away of them be the reconciling of the world, what shall the receiving of them be, but life from the dead? For if the first fruit be holy, the lump is also holy: and if the root be holy, so are the branches. And if some of the branches be broken off, and thou, being a wild olive tree, wert graffed in among them, and with them partakest of the root and fatness of the olive tree; boast not against the branches. But if thou boast, thou bearest not the root, but the root thee. Thou wilt say then, The branches were broken off, that I might be graffed in. Well; because of unbelief they were broken off, and thou standest by faith. Be not highminded, but fear; for if God spared not the natural branches, take heed lest he also spare not thee. Behold therefore the goodness and severity of God: on them which fell, severity; but toward thee, goodness, if thou continue in his goodness: otherwise thou also shalt be cut off. And they also, if they abide not still in unbelief, shall be graffed in: for God is able to graff them in again. For if thou wert cut out of the olive tree which is wild by nature, and wert graffed contrary to nature into a good olive tree; how much more shall these, which be the natural branches, be graffed into their own olive tree? For I would not, brethren, that ye should be ignorant of this mystery, lest ye should be wise in your own conceits; that blindness in part is happened to

Israel, until the fulness of the Gentiles be come in. And so all Israel shall be saved : as it is written, There shall come out of Sion the Deliverer, and shall turn away ungodliness from Jacob : for this is my covenant unto them, when I shall take away their sins. As concerning the Gospel, they are enemies for your sakes : but as touching the election, they are beloved for the fathers' sakes. For the gifts and calling of God are without repentance. For as ye in times past have not believed God, yet have now obtained mercy through their unbelief : even so have these also now not believed, that through your mercy they also may obtain mercy. For God hath concluded them all in unbelief, that he might have mercy upon all. O the depth of the riches both of the wisdom and knowledge of God! how unsearchable are his judgments, and his ways past finding out ! For who hath known the mind of the Lord ? or who hath been his counsellor ? or who hath first given to him, and it shall be recompensed unto him again ! For of him, and through him, and to him, are all things : to whom be glory for ever. Amen."—Rom. xi.

The Epistle for Good Friday.—" The Law having a shadow of good things to come, and not the very image of the things, can never, with those sacrifices which they offered year by year continually, make the comers thereunto perfect. For then would they not have ceased to be offered ? because that the worshippers once purged should have had no more conscience of sins. But in those sacrifices there is a remembrance again made of sins every year. For it is not possible that the blood of bulls and of goats should take away sins. Wherefore, when He cometh into the world, he saith, Sacrifice and offering thou wouldest not, but a body hast thou prepared me : in burnt-offerings and sacrifices for sin thou hast had no pleasure. Then said I, Lo, I come (in the volume of the book it is written of me) to do thy will, O God. Above, when he said, Sacrifice and offering and burnt-offerings and offering for sin thou wouldest not, neither hadst pleasure therein; which are offered by the Law; then said he, Lo, I come to do thy will, O God. He taketh away the first, that he may establish the second. By the which will we are sanctified through the offering of the body of Jesus Christ once for all. And every priest standeth daily ministering and offering oftentimes the same sacrifices, which can never take away sins: but this Man, after he had offered one sacrifice for sins for ever, sat down on the right hand of God; from henceforth expecting till his enemies be made his footstool. For by one offering he hath perfected for ever them that are sanctified. Whereof the Holy Ghost also is a witness to us: for after that he had said before, This is the covenant that I will make with them after those days, saith the Lord, I will put my laws into their hearts, and in their minds will I write them; and their sins and iniquities will I remember no more. Now where remission of these is, there is no more offering for sin. Having therefore, brethren, boldness to enter into the holiest by the blood of Jesus, by a new and living way, which he hath consecrated for us, through the vail, that is to say, his flesh; and having an High Priest over the house of God; let us draw near with a true heart, in full assurance of faith, having our hearts sprinkled from an evil conscience, and our bodies washed with pure water. Let us hold fast the profession of our faith without wavering; (for He is faithful that promised;) and let us consider one another to provoke unto love and to good works: not forsaking the assembling of ourselves together, as the manner of some is; but exhorting one another: and so much the more, as ye see the day approaching."—Heb. x., 1-25.

III. THE EXPRESSION AS SUGGESTED BY THE EMOTION.

a. Solemnity.—"Now Jesus loved Martha, and her sister, and Lazarus. When he had heard therefore that he was sick, he abode two days still in the same place where he was. Then after that saith he to his disciples, Let us go into Judea again. His disciples say unto him, Master, the Jews of late sought to stone thee; and goest thou thither again? Jesus answered, Are there not twelve hours in the day? If any man walk in the day, he stumbleth not, because he seeth the light of this world. But if a man walk in the night, he stumbleth, because there is no light in him. These things said he: and after that he saith unto them, Our friend Lazarus sleepeth; but I go, that I may awake him out of sleep. Then said his disciples, Lord, if he sleep, he shall do well. Howbeit Jesus spake of his death: but they thought that he had spoken of taking of rest in sleep. Then said Jesus unto them plainly, Lazarus is dead; and I am glad for your sakes that I was not there, to the intent ye may believe; nevertheless let us go unto him. Then said Thomas, which is called Didymus, unto his fellow disciples, Let us also go, that we may die with him. Then when Jesus came, he found that he had lain in the grave four days already. Now Bethany was nigh unto Jerusalem, about fifteen furlongs off: and many of the Jews came to Martha and Mary, to comfort them concerning their brother. Then Martha, as soon as she heard that Jesus was coming, went and met him: but Mary sat still in the house. Then said Martha unto Jesus, Lord, if thou hadst been here, my brother had not died. But I know, that even now, whatsoever thou wilt ask of God, God will give it thee. Jesus saith unto her, Thy brother shall rise again. Martha saith unto him, I know that he shall rise again in the resurrection at the last day. Jesus said unto her, I am the resurrection, and the life: he that believeth in me, though he were dead, yet shall he live: and whosoever liveth and believeth in me shall never die. Believest thou this? She saith unto him, Yea, Lord: I believe that thou art the Christ, the Son of God, which should come into the world. And when she had so said, she went her way, and called Mary her sister secretly, saying, The Master is come, and calleth for thee. As soon as she heard that, she arose quickly, and came unto him. Now Jesus was not yet come into the town, but was in that place where Martha met him. The Jews then which were with her in the house, and comforted her, when they saw Mary, that she rose up hastily and went out, followed her, saying, She goeth unto the grave to weep there. Then when Mary was come where Jesus was, and saw him, she fell down at his feet, saying unto him, Lord, if thou hadst been here, my brother had not died. When Jesus therefore saw her weeping, and the Jews also weeping which came with her, he groaned in the spirit, and was troubled. And said, Where have ye laid him? They say unto him, Lord, come and see. Jesus wept. Then said the Jews, behold how he loved him! And some of them said, Could not this man, which opened the eyes of the blind, have caused that even this man should not have died? Jesus therefore, again groaning in himself, cometh to the grave. It was a cave, and a stone lay upon it. Jesus said, Take ye away the stone. Martha, the sister of him that was dead, saith unto him, Lord, by this time he stinketh: for he hath been dead four days. Jesus saith unto her, Said I not unto thee, that, if thou wouldest believe, thou shouldest see the glory of God? Then they took away the stone from the place where the dead was laid. And Jesus lifted up his eyes, and said, Father, I thank thee that thou hast heard me. And I knew that thou hearest me always: but because of the people which stand by I said it, that they may believe that thou hast sent me. And when he thus had spoken, he cried with a loud voice, Lazarus, come forth. And he that was dead came forth, bound hand and foot with graveclothes; and his face was bound about with a napkin. Jesus saith unto them, Loose him, and let him go."—St. John, xi., 5–44.

"Let your loins be girded about, and your lights burning; and ye yourselves like unto men that wait for their lord, when he will return from the wedding; that, when he cometh and knocketh, they may open unto him immediately. Blessed are those servants, whom the lord, when he cometh, shall find watching: verily I say unto you, that he shall gird himself, and make them to sit down to meat, and will come forth and serve them. And if he shall come in the second watch, or come in the third watch, and find them so, blessed are those servants."—St. Luke, xii., 35-38.

"And there shall be signs in the sun, and in the moon, and in the stars; and upon the earth distress of nations, with perplexity; the sea and the waves roaring; men's hearts failing them for fear, and for looking after those things which are coming on the earth: for the powers of heaven shall be shaken. And then shall they see the Son of man coming in a cloud with power and great glory. And when these things begin to come to pass, then look up, and lift up your heads; for your redemption draweth nigh. And he spake to them a parable; Behold the fig tree, and all the trees; when they now shoot forth, ye see and know of your own selves that summer is now nigh at hand. So likewise ye, when ye see these things come to pass, know ye that the kingdom of God is nigh at hand. Verily I say unto you, This generation shall not pass away, till all be fulfilled. Heaven and earth shall pass away: but my words shall not pass away."—St. Luke, xxi., 25-33.

"When the Son of man shall come in his glory, and all the holy angels with him, then shall he sit upon the throne of his glory: and before him shall be gathered all nations: and he shall separate them one from another, as a shepherd divideth his sheep from the goats: and he shall set the sheep on his right hand, but the goats on the left. Then shall the King say unto them on his right hand, Come, ye blessed of my Father, inherit the kingdom prepared for you from the foundation of the world: for I was an hungered, and ye gave me meat: I was thirsty, and ye gave me drink: I was a stranger, and ye took me in: naked, and ye clothed me: I was sick, and ye visited me: I was in prison, and ye came unto me. Then shall the righteous answer him, saying, Lord, when saw we thee an hungered, and fed thee? or thirsty, and gave thee drink? When saw we thee a stranger, and took thee in? or naked, and clothed thee? Or when saw we thee sick, or in prison, and came unto thee? And the King shall answer and say unto them, Verily I say unto you, Inasmuch as ye have done it unto one of the least of these my brethren, ye have done it unto me. Then shall he say unto them on the left hand, Depart from me, ye cursed, into everlasting fire, prepared for the devil and his angels: for I was an hungered, and ye gave me no meat: I was thirsty, and ye gave me no drink: I was a stranger, and ye took me not in: naked, and ye clothed me not: sick, and in prison, and ye visited me not. Then shall they also answer him, saying, Lord, when saw we thee an hungered, or athirst, or a stranger, or naked, or sick, or in prison, and did not minister unto thee? Then shall he answer them, saying, Verily I say unto you, Inasmuch as ye did it not to one of the least of these, ye did it not to me. And these shall go away into everlasting punishment: but the righteous into life eternal."—St. Matt. xxv., 31–46.

b. Pathos.—" And Judah said, What shall we say unto my lord? what shall we speak? or how shall we clear ourselves? God hath found out the iniquity of thy servants: behold, we are my lord's servants, both we, and he also with whom the cup is found. And he said, God forbid that I should do so: but the man in whose hand the cup is found, he shall be my servant; and as for you, get you up in peace unto your father. Then Judah came near unto him, and said, O my lord, let thy servant, I pray thee, speak a word in my lord's ears, and let not thine anger burn against thy servant: for thou art even as Pharaoh. My lord asked his servants, saying, Have ye a father, or a brother? And we said unto my lord, We have a father, an old man, and a child of his old age, a little one; and his brother is dead, and he alone is left of his mother, and his father loveth him. And thou saidst unto thy servants, Bring him down unto me, that I may set mine eyes upon him. And we said unto my lord, The lad cannot leave his father: for if he should leave his father, his father would die. And thou saidst unto thy servants, Except your youngest brother come down with you, ye shall see my face no more. And it came to pass, when we came up unto thy servant my father, we told him the words of my lord. And our father said, Go again, and buy us a little food. And we said, We cannot go down: if our youngest brother be with us, then will we go down: for we may not see the man's face, except our youngest brother be with us. And thy servant my father said unto us, Ye know that my wife bare me two sons: and the one went out from me, and I said, Surely he is torn in pieces; and I saw him not since: and if ye take this also from me, and mischief befall him, ye shall bring down my gray hairs with sorrow to the grave. Now therefore when I come to thy servant my father, and the lad be not with us; seeing that his life is bound up in the lad's life; it shall come to pass, when he seeth that the lad is not with us, that he will die: and thy servants shall bring down the gray hairs of thy servant our father with sorrow to the grave. For thy servant became surety for the lad unto my father, saying, If I bring him not unto thee, then I shall bear the blame to my father for ever. Now therefore, I pray thee, let thy servant abide instead of the lad a bondman to my lord; and let the lad go up with his brethren. For how shall I go up to my father, and the lad be not with me? lest peradventure I see the evil that shall come on my father."—Gen. xliv., 16–34.

 c. Consolation.—"The Spirit of the Lord God is upon me; because the LORD hath anointed me to preach good tidings unto the meek; he hath sent me to bind up the brokenhearted, to proclaim liberty to the captives, and the opening of the prison to them that are bound; to proclaim the acceptable year of the Lord, and the day of vengeance of our God; to comfort all that mourn; to appoint unto them that mourn in Zion, to give unto them beauty for ashes, the oil of joy for mourning, the garment of praise for the spirit of heaviness; that they might be called Trees of righteousness, The planting of the Lord, that he might be glorified."—Isaiah, lxi., 1–3.

d. Sublimity.—" I was in the Spirit on the Lord's day, and heard behind me a great voice, as of a trumpet, Saying, I am Alpha and Omega, the first and the last: and, What thou seest, write in a book, and send it unto the seven churches which are in Asia; unto Ephesus, and unto Smyrna, and unto Pergamos, and unto Thyatira, and unto Sardis, and unto Philadelphia, and unto Laodicea. And I turned to see the voice that spake with me. And being turned, I saw seven golden candlesticks; and in the midst of the seven candlesticks one like unto the Son of man, clothed with a garment down to the foot, and girt about the paps with a golden girdle. His head and his hairs were white like wool, as white as snow; and his eyes were as a flame of fire; and his feet like unto fine brass, as if they burned in a furnace; and his voice as the sound of many waters. And he had in his right hand seven stars: and out of his mouth went a sharp twoedged sword: and his countenance was as the sun shineth in his strength. And when I saw him, I fell at his feet as dead. And he laid his right hand upon me, saying unto me, Fear not; I am the first and the last: I am he that liveth, and was dead; and behold, I am alive for evermore, Amen; and have the keys of hell and of death. Write the things which thou hast seen, and the things which are, and the things which shall be hereafter: the mystery of the seven stars which thou sawest in my right hand, and the seven golden candlesticks. The seven stars are the angels of the seven churches: and the seven candlesticks which thou sawest are the seven churches."—Rev. i., 10–20.

"The earth trembled and quaked, the very foundations also of the hills shook, and were removed, because he was wroth. There went a smoke out in his presence, and a consuming fire out of his mouth, so that coals were kindled at it. He bowed the heavens also, and came down, and it was dark under his feet. He rode upon the cherubim, and did fly; he came flying upon the wings of the wind. He made darkness his secret place, his pavilion round about him with dark water, and thick clouds to cover him. At the brightness of his presence his clouds removed; hailstones and coals of fire. The LORD also thundered out of heaven, and the Highest gave his thunder; hailstones and coals of fire. He sent out his arrows and scattered them; he cast forth lightnings, and destroyed them. The springs of waters were seen, and the foundations of the round world were discovered at thy chiding, O LORD, at the blasting of the breath of thy displeasure."—Ps. xviii., 7-15.

e. Denunciation.—"Then began he to upbraid the cities wherein most of his mighty works were done, because they repented not: Woe unto thee, Chorazin! woe unto thee, Bethsaida! for if the mighty works, which were done in you, had been done in Tyre and Sidon, they would have repented long ago in sackcloth and ashes. But I say unto you, It shall be more tolerable for Tyre and Sidon at the day of judgment, than for you. And thou, Capernaum, which art exalted unto heaven, shalt be brought down to hell: for if the mighty works, which have been done in thee, had been done in Sodom, it would have remained until this day. But I say unto you, That it shall be more tolerable for the land of Sodom in the day of judgment, than for thee."—St. Matt. xi., 20-24.

The illustrations might be extended indefinitely, according to the varied conditions of feeling, but it is designed to give only a sufficient number, to suggest further analysis and practice on the part of the student himself.

IV. Expression as Suggested by the Thought.

Pointed emphasis is required to enforce the meaning of the succeeding passages:

"Take heed that ye do not your alms before men, to be seen of them: otherwise ye have no reward of your Father which is in heaven. Therefore when thou doest thine alms, do not sound a trumpet before thee, as the hypocrites do in the synagogues and in the streets, that they may have glory of men. Verily I say unto you, They have their reward. But when thou doest alms, let not thy left hand know what thy right hand doeth : that thine alms may be in secret : and thy Father which seeth in secret himself shall reward thee openly.

"And when thou prayest, thou shalt not be as the hypocrites are: for they love to pray standing in the synagogues and in the corners of the streets, that they may be seen of men. Verily I say unto you, They have their reward. But thou, when thou prayest, enter into thy closet, and when thou hast shut thy door, pray to thy Father which is in secret; and thy Father which seeth in secret shall reward thee openly. But when ye pray, use not vain repetitions, as the heathen do ; for they think that they shall be heard for their much speaking. Be not ye therefore like unto them ; for your Father knoweth what things ye have need of, before ye ask him."—St. Matt. vi., 1–8.

"Judge not, that ye be not judged. For with what judgment ye judge, ye shall be judged : and with what measure ye mete, it shall be measured to you again. And why beholdest thou the mote that is in thy brother's eye, but considerest not the beam that is in thine own eye ? Or how wilt thou say to thy brother, Let me pull out the mote out of thine eye ; and, behold, a beam is in thine own eye ? Thou hypocrite, first cast out the beam out of thine own eye ; and then shalt thou see clearly to cast out the mote out of thy brother's eye.

"Give not that which is holy unto the dogs, neither cast ye your pearls before swine, lest they trample them under their feet, and turn again and rend you.

"Ask, and it shall be given you; seek, and ye shall find; knock, and it shall be opened unto you: for every one that asketh receiveth; and he that seeketh findeth; and to him that knocketh it shall be opened. Or what man is there of you, whom if his son ask bread, will he give him a stone? Or if he ask a fish, will he give him a serpent?

"If ye then, being evil, know how to give good gifts unto your children, how much more shall your Father which is in heaven give good things to them that ask him? Therefore all things whatsoever ye would that men should do to you, do ye even so to them: for this is the law and the prophets.

"Enter ye in at the straight gate: for wide is the gate, and broad is the way, that leadeth to destruction, and many there be which go in thereat: because straight is the gate, and narrow is the way, which leadeth unto life, and few there be that find it."—St. Matt. vii., 1-14.

"Verily, verily, I say unto you, He that entereth not by the door into the sheepfold, but climbeth up some other way, the same is a thief and a robber. But he that entereth in by the door is the shepherd of the sheep. To him the porter openeth; and the sheep hear his voice: and he calleth his own sheep by name, and leadeth them out. And when he putteth forth his own sheep, he goeth before them, and the sheep follow him: for they know his voice. And a stranger will they not follow, but will flee from him; for they know not the voice of strangers. This parable spake Jesus unto them; but they understood not what things they were which he spake unto them. Then said Jesus unto them again, Verily, verily, I say unto you, I am the door of the sheep. All that ever came before me are thieves and robbers: but the sheep did not hear them. I am the door: by me if any man enter in, he shall be saved, and shall go in and out, and find pasture. The thief cometh not, but for to steal, and to kill, and to destroy: I am come that they might have life, and that they might have it more abundantly. I am the good shepherd: the good shepherd giveth his life for the sheep. But he that is an hireling, and not the shepherd, whose own the sheep are not, seeth the wolf coming, and leaveth the sheep, and fleeth; and the wolf catcheth them, and scattereth the sheep. The hireling fleeth, because he is an hireling, and careth not for the sheep. I am the good shepherd, and know my sheep, and am known of mine. As the Father knoweth me, even so know I the Father: and I lay down my life for the sheep. And other sheep I have, which are not of this fold: them also I must bring, and they shall hear my voice; and there shall be one fold, and one shepherd."—St. John, x., 1–16.

"I am the true vine, and my Father is the husbandman. Every branch in me that beareth not fruit he taketh away: and every branch that beareth fruit, he purgeth it, that it may bring forth more fruit. Now ye are clean through the word which I have spoken unto you. Abide in me, and I in you. As the branch cannot bear fruit of itself, except it abide in the vine; no more can ye, except ye abide in me. I am the vine, ye are the branches. He that abideth in me, and I in him, the same bringeth forth much fruit; for without me ye can do nothing. If a man abide not in me, he is cast forth as a branch, and is withered; and men gather them, and cast them into the fire, and they are burned. If ye abide in me, and my words abide in you, ye shall ask what ye will, and it shall be done unto you. Herein is my Father glorified, that ye bear much fruit; so shall ye be my disciples. As the Father hath loved me, so have I loved you: continue ye in my love. If ye keep my commandments ye shall abide in my love; even as I have kept my Father's commandments, and abide in his love. These things have I spoken unto you, that my joy might remain in you, and that your joy might be full."—St. John, xv., 1–11.

"For Christ is the end of the law for righteousness to every one that believeth. For Moses describeth the righteousness which is of the law, That the man which doeth those things shall live by them. But the righteousness which is of faith speaketh on this wise, Say not in thine heart, Who shall ascend into heaven? (that is, to bring Christ down from above:) or, Who shall descend into the deep? (that is, to bring up Christ again from the dead.) But what saith it? The word is nigh thee, even in thy mouth, and in thy heart: that is, the word of faith, which we preach. That if thou shalt confess with thy mouth the Lord Jesus, and shalt believe in thine heart that God hath raised him from the dead, thou shalt be saved. For with the heart man believeth unto righteousness; and with the mouth confession is made unto salvation. For the Scripture saith, Whosoever believeth on him shall not be ashamed. For there is no difference between the Jew and the Greek: for the same Lord over all is rich unto all that call upon him. For whosoever shall call upon the name of the Lord shall be saved. How then shall they call on him in whom they have not believed? and how shall they believe in him of whom they have not heard? and how shall they hear without a preacher? And how shall they preach, except they be sent? as it is written, How beautiful are the feet of them that preach the gospel of peace, and bring glad tidings of good things! But they have not all obeyed the gospel: for Esaias saith, Lord, who hath believed our report? So then faith cometh by hearing, and hearing by the word of God."—Rom. x., 4–17.

V. EXPRESSION BY INFLECTION CHIEFLY.

a. The falling inflection for irony.—"He heweth him down cedars, and taketh the cypress and the oak, which he strengtheneth for himself among the trees of the forest: he planteth an ash, and the rain doth nourish it. Then shall it be for a man to burn : for he will take thereof, and warm himself; yea, he kindleth it, and baketh bread; yea, he maketh a god, and worshippeth it; he maketh it a graven image, and falleth down thereto. He burneth part thereof in the fire; with part thereof he catch flesh; he roasteth roast, and is satisfied : yea, he warmeth himself, and saith, Aha, I am warm, I have seen the fire : and the residue thereof he maketh a god, even his graven image : he falleth down unto it, and worshippeth it, and prayeth unto it, and saith, Deliver me; for thou art my god."—Isaiah, xliv., 14–17.

b. The circumflex, for irony.—" And it came to pass at noon, that Elijah mocked them, and said, Cry aloud : for he is a god; either he is talking, or he is pursuing, or he is in a journey, or peradventure he sleepeth, and must be awaked."

c. The monotone, for awe and sublimity.—" And I saw another angel ascending from the east, having the seal of the living God : and he cried with a loud voice to the four angels, to whom it was given to hurt the earth and the sea, saying, Hurt not the earth, neither the sea, nor the trees, till we have sealed the servants of our God in their foreheads. And I heard the number of them which were sealed; and there were sealed an hundred and forty and four thousand, of all the tribes of the children of Israel.

"Of the tribe of Judah were sealed twelve thousand.
"Of the tribe of Reuben were sealed twelve thousand.
"Of the tribe of Gad were sealed twelve thousand.
"Of the tribe of Aser were sealed twelve thousand.
"Of the tribe of Nephthali were sealed twelve thousand.
"Of the tribe of Manasses were sealed twelve thousand.
"Of the tribe of Simeon were sealed twelve thousand.
"Of the tribe of Levi were sealed twelve thousand.
"Of the tribe of Issachar were sealed twelve thousand.
"Of the tribe of Zabulon were sealed twelve thousand.

"Of the tribe of Joseph were sealed twelve thousand.

"Of the tribe of Benjamin were sealed twelve thousand.

"After this I beheld, and lo, a great multitude, which no man could number, of all nations, and kindreds, and people, and tongues, stood before the throne, and before the Lamb, clothed with white robes, and palms in their hands; and cried with a loud voice, saying, Salvation to our God which sitteth upon the throne, and unto the Lamb! And all the angels stood round about the throne, and about the elders, and the four beasts, and fell before the throne on their faces, and worshipped God, saying, Amen; Blessing, and glory, and wisdom, and thanksgiving, and honour, and power, and might, be unto our God for ever and ever! Amen."—Rev. vii., 2–12.

"In thoughts from the visions of the night, when deep sleep falleth on men, fear came upon me, and trembling, which made all my bones to shake. Then a spirit passed before my face; the hair of my flesh stood up: it stood still, but I could not discern the form thereof: an image was before mine eyes, there was silence, and I heard a voice, saying, Shall mortal man be more just than God? shall a man be more pure than his Maker?"—Job, iv., 13–17.

d. Denunciation, falling inflection.—"But woe unto you, scribes and Pharisees, hypocrites! for ye shut up the kingdom of heaven against men: for ye neither go in yourselves, neither suffer ye them that are entering to go in. Woe unto you, scribes and Pharisees, hypocrites! for ye devour widows' houses, and for a pretence make long prayer: therefore ye shall receive the greater damnation. Woe unto you, scribes and Pharisees, hypocrites! for ye compass sea and land to make one proselyte; and when he is made, ye make him twofold more the child of hell than yourselves. Woe unto you, ye blind guides, which say, Whosoever shall swear by the temple, it is nothing; but whosoever shall swear by the gold of the temple, he is a debtor! Ye fools and blind: for whether is greater, the gold, or the temple that sanctifieth the gold? And, Whosoever shall swear by the altar, it is nothing; but whosoever sweareth by the gift that is upon it, he is guilty. Ye fools and blind: for whether is greater, the gift, or the altar that sanctifieth the gift? Whoso therefore shall swear by the altar, sweareth by it, and by all things thereon. And whoso shall swear by the temple, sweareth by it, and by him that dwelleth therein. And he that shall swear by heaven, sweareth by the throne of God, and by him that sitteth thereon. Woe unto you, scribes and Pharisees, hypocrites! for ye pay tithe of mint and anise and cummin, and have omitted the weightier matters of the law, judgment, mercy, and faith: these ought ye to have done, and not to leave the other undone. Ye blind guides, which strain at a gnat, and swallow a camel. Woe unto you scribes and Pharisees, hypocrites! for ye make clean the outside of the cup and of the platter, but within they are full of extortion and excess. Thou blind Pharisee, cleanse first that which is within the cup and platter, that the outside of them may be clean also. Woe unto you, scribes and Pharisees, hypocrites! for ye are like unto whited sepulchres, which indeed appear beautiful outward, but are within full of dead men's bones, and of all uncleanness. Even so ye also outwardly appear righteous unto men, but within ye are full of hypocrisy and iniquity. Woe unto you, scribes and Pharisees, hypocrites! because ye build the tombs of the prophets, and garnish the sepulchres of the righteous, And say, If we had been in the days of our fathers, we would not have been partakers with them in the blood of the prophets. Wherefore ye be witnesses unto yourselves, that ye are the children of them which killed the prophets. Fill ye up then the measure of your fathers. Ye serpents, ye generation of vipers, how can ye escape the damnation of hell?"—St. Matt. xxiii., 13-33.

Further divisions under each of the above heads for expression could readily be made, and several more of the elocutionary topics further illustrated. If, however, the student will exercise himself sufficiently upon these, with the leading effect in view in the use of each topic, he will have matter enough for study, and still wider fields will open themselves before him. The reader may rest assured that there are few compensations more immediate in the return, as a reward for close study, than those which relate to the expressive reading of the Lessons. And, while consciously imperfect utterance is a source of the greatest annoyance, the approval of the ear in heartfelt and appropriate expression is one of the richest sources of comfort which attends honest, earnest, intelligent effort to read impressively and appropriately the Word of God.

The Decalogue.

A full analysis of this portion of the Service would properly fill many pages. Its treatment here must be brief, and simply suggestive. The first thing to be insisted upon is that the Commandments should be read as Commandments of God. This thought gives dignity and authority to the expression. The two extremes of the faulty reading are : 1. The feeble effect of a petition, or a pathetic request that these laws should be observed, setting the words to a minor tune, and imparting the sound of complaint, in place of command. 2. The pompous authority which gives a personal effect, as though the reader himself had enacted these laws, and was personally requiring obedience to them. Besides these there are many other errors, such as undue rapidity, suppression of the force, too high a key, pauses too long or too short, etc. The utterance should be deliberately and expressively emphatic, so as to leave no room in the mind of the hearer for misinterpretation or doubt as to the meaning and application of the law. The voice of authority must be sustained throughout. The reading should be expression of the Law, from which there is no appeal, mandatory and absolute, not a narrative, not the feeble expression of a desire, but the firm utterance of unyielding and inexorable law—"Thou shalt," and "Thou shalt not."

It is well to observe the change in the character of the utterance as the reader passes from the voice of instruction or prayer to the voice of command. The use of it in this part of the Service calls for a different expression from that found in its narrative form, when read as a Lesson, and it would be well for every reader of the Commandments to recall, before he reads them, the awful scene on Sinai, and the majesty and the mystery attendant upon the giving of the Law.

"And it came to pass on the third day in the morning, that there were thunders and lightnings, and a thick cloud upon the mount, and the voice of the trumpet exceeding loud; so that all the people that was in the camp trembled. And Moses brought forth the people out of the camp to meet with God; and they stood at the nether part of the mount. And mount Sinai was altogether on a smoke, because the LORD descended upon it in fire: and the smoke thereof ascended as the smoke of a furnace, and the whole mount quaked greatly. And when the voice of the trumpet sounded long, and waxed louder and louder, Moses spake, and God answered him by a voice."—Deut. xix., 16-19.

With such a scene in mind, and the preceding prayer for purity of heart, before Him Who is of purer eyes than to behold iniquity, and unto Whom all hearts are open, let the reader consider the dignity, character, and authority of the introduction, "God spake these words and said." Anything less than a deliberate, firm, and emphatic utterance of the preface is not a fitting preparation for the reading of the entire Law.

First Commandment.—The deliberation is to be fully marked, the authority more emphatically expressed than in the preface.

"I am the Lord thy God: Thou shalt have none other gods but me."

Second Commandment.—"Thou *shalt* not—" the negative in the Commandments throughout takes a secondary emphasis. No one would read, "Ye can*not* serve God and Mammon," except in contradiction. Goddard, in his "Reading of the Liturgy," changes the authorized punctuation of the period, and gives a comma after the phrase "under the earth," to avoid the prohibition of all forms of graven images. But surely there is little danger of imperiling the noble art of sculpture by the stolid, literal rendering, when the application is so obvious. Following Sheridan, Bishop Henshaw, Goddard, and others, it is correct to make it apparent that the sins of the fathers are visited unto the third or fourth generation of their children, which places the pause after "generation." With deliberate emphasis upon "children" and "hate," we are the better prepared to give the rhythmical emphasis of antithesis upon "thousands," and "love me and keep my commandments." The expressive emphasis of the lamented Dr. Francis Hawks on the word "thousands" was peculiarly suggestive of the infinitude of the Divine mercy.

"Thou shalt not make to thyself any graven image, nor the likeness of any thing that is in heaven above, or in the earth beneath, or in the water under the earth. Thou shalt not bow down to them, nor worship them : For I the Lord thy God am a jealous God ; and visit the sins of the fathers upon the children, unto the third and fourth generation of them that hate me ; and show mercy unto thousands in them that love me, and keep my commandments."

Third Commandment.—The prohibition should be purposely emphatic, and the warning so solemnly and threateningly given, that the profane swearer may indeed feel that he is not held guiltless before his GOD. Strong emphasis and full pause at "guiltless" enforce the expression.

"Thou shalt not take the name of the Lord thy God in vain : For the Lord will not hold him guiltless that taketh his name in vain."

Fourth Commandment.—Emphasize "remember," and pause after it, making it monitory. The emphatic word in the first sentence is not "day," but "*Sabbath*-day." The falling inflection upon every clause gives the best expression of prohibition and command. The pause after "sea" connects it properly with "heaven and earth." A common error is to unite "sea" directly with "and all that in them is." Full emphasis should be given upon "rested"; also upon "blessed and hallowed." The sounding of the syllable "-ed" in "blessed and hallowed" destroys the grammatical character, making the verbs take the construction of adjectives.

"Remember that thou keep holy the Sabbath-day. Six days shalt thou labour, and do all that thou hast to do; but the seventh day is the Sabbath of the Lord thy God. In it thou shalt do no manner of work; thou, and thy son, and thy daughter, thy man-servant, and thy maid-servant, thy cattle, and the stranger that is within thy gates. For in six days the Lord made heaven and earth, the sea, and all that in them is, and rested the seventh day; wherefore the Lord blessed the seventh day and hallowed it."

Fifth Commandment.—"Honour," "father," and "mother" are especially emphatic. The pause and emphasis are upon "long" rather than "land."

"Honour thy father and thy mother; that thy days may be long in the land which the Lord thy God giveth thee."

Sixth, Seventh, and Eighth Commandments.—A very effective reader of the Commandments is said to make murder horrible, adultery vile, and theft mean, by the interpretation of his reading. This would be suggestive as a study, but no mere imitation should be attempted, unless the reader is sure that his utterance imparts the same effect. These three words are primarily emphatic, and the emphasis upon the negative should be secondary. In the Seventh Commandment the pause is after "not" rather than "commit."

"Thou shalt do no *murder.*"

"Thou shalt not commit *adultery.*"
"Thou shalt not *steal.*"

Ninth Commandment.—"False witness" receives the emphasis on both words, with a pause following.

"Thou shalt not bear *false witness* | against thy neighbour."

Tenth Commandment.—The falling slide, with emphasis upon each clause, makes the expression prohibitory. Emphasis should be placed upon "anything" and "his."

"Thou shalt not covet thy neighbour's house, thou shalt not covet thy neighbour's wife, nor his servant, nor his maid, nor his ox, nor his ass, nor *anything* that is *his.*"

Now, if the reading has given interpretation to the unyielding rigor and the inexorable authority of the law of works, we are prepared for the comforting and sympathetic instructions of the law of love. The fullness of the voice of authority is chastened and subdued by the gentler attribute which is described. Especial meaning and emphasis should be given upon the clause, "as thyself."

"Thou shalt love the Lord thy God with all thy heart, and with all thy soul, and with all thy mind : This is the first and great commandment. And the second is like unto it ; Thou shalt love thy neighbour as thyself. On these two commandments hang all the law and the prophets."

The Sentences of the Offertory.

These passages are very useful as studies of expression in the effort to awaken good impulses and generosity in almsgiving. If they are read as so many instructive exhortations, and with the actual purpose of moving Christian people to their duty, it will give a clearness, an emphasis, and an effect, not to be secured equally well by any other process.

A general summary of the varying character of the passages would classify them as : 1, injunctions ; 2, explanatory declarations ; 3, oratorical interrogations implying exhortation ; 4, comforting promises, encouraging the duty of almsgiving ; and 5, example inciting to liberality.

All of these divisions would vary somewhat in expression, one from another.

1. *The Injunctions.*—These passages have more of the preceptive and pronounced utterance of authoritative direction or command, softened by the moral purpose in view of persuading men to be merciful after their power.

"Let your light so shine before men, that they may see your good works, and glorify your Father, which is in heaven."—St. Matt. v., 16.

"Lay not up for yourselves treasures upon earth ; where moth and rust doth corrupt, and where thieves break through and steal : but lay up for yourselves treasures in heaven ; where neither moth nor rust doth corrupt, and where thieves do not break through nor steal."—St. Matt. vi., 19, 20.

"Whatsoever ye would that men should do to you, even so do to them : for this is the Law and the Prophets."—St. Matt. vii., 12.

"Let him that is taught in the Word minister unto him that teacheth, in all good things. Be not deceived, God is not mocked : for whatsoever a man soweth that shall he reap."—Gal. vi., 6, 7.

"While we have time, let us do good unto all men ; and especially unto them that are of the household of faith."—Gal. vi., 10.

"Charge them who are rich in this world, that they be ready to give, and glad to distribute ; laying up in store for themselves a good foundation against the time to come, that they may attain eternal life."—I. Tim. vi., 17-19.

"To do good, and to distribute, forget not ; for with such sacrifices God is well pleased."—Heb. xiii., 16.

"Give alms of thy goods, and never turn thy face from any poor man ; and then the face of the Lord shall not be turned away from thee."—Tobit, iv., 7.

"Be merciful after thy power. If thou hast much, give plenteously ; if thou hast little, do thy diligence gladly to give of that little : for so gatherest thou thyself a good reward in the day of necessity."—Tobit, iv., 8, 9.

2. *Explanatory Declarations.*—These portions have the effect of both explanations and statements. They are less emphatic than the direct injunctions.

"Not every one that saith unto me, Lord, Lord, shall enter into the Kingdom of heaven; but he that doeth the will of my Father which is in heaven."—St. Matt. vii., 21.

"He that soweth little, shall reap little ; and he that soweth plenteously, shall reap plenteously. Let every man do according as he is disposed in his heart, not grudgingly, or of necessity ; for God loveth a cheerful giver.—II. Cor. ix., 6, 7.

"Godliness is great riches, if a man be content with that he hath : for we brought nothing into this world, neither may we carry anything out."—I. Tim. vi., 6, 7.

"God is not unrighteous, that he will forget your works, and labor that proceedeth of love ; which love ye have showed for his Name's sake, who have ministered unto the saints, and yet do minister."—Heb. vi., 10.

3. *Oratorical Interrogation.*—The interrogative appeal is equivalent to emphatic assertion. In the first of the sentences below the inquiry is given in the form of reasoning by parallel instances ; in the second, it is reasoning based on a principle of justice ; in the third, it is reasoning from example, in the interrogative form, with the statement, "even so hath the Lord ordained," etc. ; and in the fourth, affectionate expostulation.

"Who goeth a warfare at any time at his own cost ? Who planteth a vineyard, and eateth not of the fruit thereof ? or who feedeth a flock, and eateth not of the milk of the flock ?"—I. Cor. ix., 7.

"If we have sown unto you spiritual things, is it a great

matter if we shall reap your worldly things?"—I. Cor. ix., 11.

"Do ye not know, that they who minister about holy things, live of the sacrifice ; and they who wait at the altar, are partakers with the altar ? Even so hath the Lord also ordained, that they who preach the Gospel, should live of the Gospel."—I. Cor. ix., 13, 14.

"Whoso hath this world's good, and seeth his brother have need, and shutteth up his compassion from him, how dwelleth the love of God in him ?"—St. John, iii., 17.

4. *Comforting Promises encouraging to Duty.*—More of gentleness, and consequently more of sympathy, in expression, characterize the two sentences following :

"He that hath pity upon the poor, lendeth unto the Lord : and look, what he layeth out, it shall be paid him again."—Prov. xix., 17.

"Blessed be the man that provideth for the sick and needy : the Lord shall deliver him in the time of trouble."—Psalm xli., 1.

5. *Example inciting to Liberality.*—The particulars of the act described below, to be impressive, should be delivered with marked emphasis :

"Zaccheus stood forth, and said unto the Lord, Behold, Lord, the half of my goods I give to the poor ; and if I have done any wrong to any man, I restore fourfold."—St. Luke, xix., 8.

If the sentences are to be used instructively, and as incitements to Christian duty, especially when that duty relates to our offerings to the Lord, as a part of the most solemn act of our religious offices, every expression should bear some proportionate character to the solemnity of the duty. In other words, the correct reading of these sentences should actually so instruct and exhort the people to almsgiving that they would be thus provoked to love and good works.

As it is not the intention to attempt an analysis, nor

suggest the character, of the reading of all portions of the Liturgy, it may be sufficient to state that, after the prayer for the Church Militant, the Service following, in all its varied divisions, is marked by greater solemnity and reverence than any of the other Services; and, therefore, to be read with expressive propriety, should receive the emphasis of these characteristics.

The Burial Service.

This is the one Service, above all others, which, out of the Church and within it, is acknowledged to be as nearly perfect as any humanly ordered Service can be. The reading of it, therefore, should be with the laudable purpose of making it not merely appropriate, in an expression free from marked defects, but also to interpret it according to the most impressive effect.

The sub-bass, so to speak, of the characteristic reading of the Service is the depth of solemnity pervading every portion of it. Even in the triumphant part of the Apostle's argument, in the Lesson, the majesty of the solemnity is still heard. And with this feeling we find accompanying the tenderest sympathy for the bereaved, and the kindly prompting of the heart which yearns to give the oil of joy for mourning, and the garment of praise for the spirit of heaviness. A single sound of the voice, out of keeping with these characteristics in the Service, is like the utterance of a thoughtless word, or the doing of some incongruous act, which shows the heart out of sympathy with the occasion. There is no Service where the voice of the pastor may be made to convince his people that he, with St. Paul, has them in his heart, and there is no occasion when unsympathetic, unfeeling, and inappropriate reading can estrange so completely the interest and affection of parishioners.

The Sentences.—The first is designed to inspire faith in the One mighty to save. Any utterance which does not imply the profoundest solemnity and tenderness of feeling, or fails to suggest that we may rest securely in our faith in Him who is the Resurrection and the Life, does not rightly interpret this opening passage in the Burial Service. We should endeavor to utter them as the very words of the great Conqueror of Death, employed by the Church for the instruction and comfort of bereaved hearts in the trying hour of the burial of their dead. All hurried, unfeeling, and careless utterance shocks the ear, and does not suggest the sustaining comforts of the Christian faith in the thought of the Saviour's triumph.

"I am the resurrection and the life, saith the Lord : he that believeth in me, though he were dead, yet shall he live : and whosoever liveth and believeth in me, shall never die."—St. John, xi., 25, 26.

The Second Sentence.—As in the first Sentence it is the words of Christ we hear, encouraging faith, so in the second is heard the response. The language seems to apply to the assured belief of the departed. Deliberate emphasis, with confident, yet tranquil, trust, will give the key-note to the reading.

"I know that my Redeemer liveth, and that he shall stand at the latter day upon the earth. And though after my skin worms destroy this body, yet in my flesh shall I see God : whom I shall see for myself, and mine eyes shall behold, and not another."—Job, xix., 25-27.

The Third Sentence.—With more subdued voice now follows the utterance of the reverential submission and resignation of the bereaved. Hurried utterance and negligent expression do not comport with the thoughtfulness of the quiet trust which acknowledges the Divine mercy and wisdom in ways past finding out.

"We brought nothing into this world, and it is certain we can carry nothing out. The Lord gave, and the Lord hath taken away ; blessed be the Name of the Lord."—I. Tim. vi., 7 ; Job, i., 21.

The First Anthem.—If this is *read*, the deepest solemnity of feeling and sustained rhythmical utterance, with deliberately slow movement, low pitch of voice, and strongly marked emphasis, should characterize the reading.

"Lord, let me know my end, and the number of my days; that I may be certified how long I have to live.

"Behold, thou hast made my days as it were a span long; and mine age is even as nothing in respect of thee; and verily every man living is altogether vanity.

"For man walketh in a vain shadow, and disquieteth himself in vain; he heapeth up riches, and cannot tell who shall gather them.

"And now, Lord, what is my hope? Truly my hope is even in thee.

"Deliver me from all mine offences; and make me not a rebuke unto the foolish.

"When thou with rebukes dost chasten man for sin, thou makest his beauty to consume away, like as it were a moth fretting a garment: every man therefore is but vanity.

"Hear my prayer, O Lord, and with thine ears consider my calling: Hold not thy peace at my tears.

"For I am a stranger with thee, and a sojourner; as all my fathers were.

"O spare me a little, that I may recover my strength; before I go hence, and be no more seen.

"Lord, thou hast been our refuge, from one generation to another.

"Before the mountains were brought forth or ever the earth and the world were made, thou art God from everlasting, and world without end.

"Thou turnest man to destruction; again thou sayest, Come again, ye children of men.

"For a thousand years in thy sight are but as yesterday; seeing that is past as a watch in the night.

"As soon as thou scatterest them, they are even as a sleep; and fade away suddenly like the grass.

"In the morning it is green, and groweth up; but in the evening it is cut down, dried up, and withered.

"For we consume away in thy displeasure; and are afraid at thy wrathful indignation.

"Thou hast set our misdeeds before thee; and our secret sins in the light of thy countenance.

"For when thou art angry, all our days are gone: We bring our years to an end, as it were a tale that is told.

"The days of our age are threescore years and ten; and though men be so strong that they come to fourscore years, yet is their strength then but labour and sorrow; so soon passeth it away, and we are gone.

"So teach us to number our days, that we may apply our hearts unto wisdom.

"Glory be to the Father, and to the Son, and to the Holy Ghost;

"As it was in the beginning, is now, and ever shall be, world without end. Amen."

The Lesson should be read with the intelligent purpose of really instructing and comforting bereaved hearts with the consolations of the Christian faith. It should be read in fullest and tenderest sympathy with the mourners, and yet in full sympathy also with the majesty, glory, and triumph of the Resurrection. It is to be remembered that it is a *Lesson*, and therefore the voice of instruction is heard; but the intellectual rendering should not, in the least, interfere with the solemnity, the reverence, the sympathy, the majesty, and the triumph, which render the whole passage so remarkably adapted to its use in this Service. If the voice be flippant here, in its effect, it utterly destroys the character of the inspired passage in its instructive use for this place. And again, if the utterance be too heavily weighted in depth and volume of voice, while the mystery and the awe may find expression, the tenderness and the triumph are lost. The italicized and capitalized portions below are used simply to suggest where the expressive, interpretative emphasis falls.

"Now is Christ *risen* from the dead, and become the *first-fruits* of them that slept. For since by *man* came *death*, by *man* came also the *resurrection* of the dead. For as in *Adam* all *die*, even so in *Christ* shall all be made *alive*. But every man in his own order : Christ the first-fruits ; afterward they that are Christ's, at his coming. Then cometh the *end*, when he shall have delivered up the kingdom to God, even the Father ; when he shall have put down all rule, and all authority, and power. For he must reign, till he hath put all enemies under his feet. The *last enemy* that shall be destroyed is *death*. For he hath put *all* things *under his feet*. But when he saith, all things are put under him, it is manifest that he is excepted, which did put all things under him. And when all things shall be subdued unto him, then shall the *Son also himself* be subject unto Him that put all things under him, that God may be *all in all*. Else what shall they do which are baptized for the dead, if the dead rise not at all ? Why are they then baptized for the dead ? and why stand we in jeopardy every hour ? I protest by your rejoicing, which I have in Christ Jesus our Lord, I die daily. If after the manner of men I have fought with beasts at Ephesus, what advantageth it me, if the dead rise not ? let us eat and drink, for to-morrow we die. *Be not deceived:* evil communications corrupt good manners. Awake to righteousness, and sin not ; for some have not the knowledge of God. I speak this to your shame. But some man will say, *How* are the dead raised up ? and with what *body* do they come ? Thou fool ! that which thou sowest is *not quickened,* except it *die*. And that which thou *sowest,* thou sowest not *that body* that shall be, but *bare* grain, it may chance of wheat, or of some other grain. But God giveth it a *body* as it hath pleased him, and to every seed his own body. All flesh is not the same flesh ; but there is one kind of flesh of men, another flesh of beasts, another of fishes, and another of birds. There are also celestial bodies, and bodies terrestrial; but the glory of the celestial is one, and the glory of the terrestrial is another. There is one glory of the sun, and another glory of the moon, and another glory of the stars; for one star differeth from another star in glory. *So also is the resurrection of the dead. It is sown in corruption;* IT IS RAISED IN INCORRUPTION: *it is sown in dishonour;* IT IS RAISED IN GLORY: *it is sown in weakness;* IT IS RAISED IN POWER: *it is sown a natural body;* IT IS RAISED A SPIRITUAL BODY. There is a *natural* body, and there is a *spiritual* body. And so it is written, The first man Adam was made a living soul; the last Adam was made a quickening spirit. Howbeit, that was not first which is spiritual, but that which is natural; and afterward that which is spiritual. The first man is of the earth, earthy: the second man is the Lord from heaven. As is the earthy, such are they that are earthy: and as is the heavenly, such are they also that are heavenly. And as we have borne the image of the earthy, we shall also bear the image of the heavenly. Now this I say, brethren, that flesh and blood cannot inherit the kingdom of God; neither doth corruption inherit incorruption. Behold, I show you a *mystery:* we shall not *all sleep,* but we shall *all be changed, in a moment, in the twinkling of an eye,* at the last trump: for the trumpet shall sound, and the dead shall be raised incorruptible, and *we shall be changed.* For this *corruptible* must put on *incorruption,* and this *mortal* must put on *immortality.* So when this *corruptible* shall have put on *incorruption,* and this *mortal* shall have put on *immortality;* then shall be brought to pass the saying that is written, *Death is swallowed up in victory.* O DEATH, WHERE IS THY STING? O GRAVE, WHERE IS THY VICTORY? The *sting* of death is *sin;* and the *strength* of sin is the *Law.* But thanks be to God, which giveth us the *victory through our Lord Jesus Christ.* Therefore, my beloved brethren, be ye steadfast, unmovable, always abounding in the work of the Lord, forasmuch as ye know that your labour is not in vain in the Lord."

The Second Anthem.—The same feelings characterizing the first Anthem mark this also, with the increased reverential fervor of the importunate supplication in repetitious forms of prayer.

" Man, that is born of a woman, hath but a short time to live, and is full of misery. He cometh up, and is cut down, like a flower; he fleeth as it were a shadow, and never continueth in one stay.

" In the midst of life we are in death : of whom may we seek for succor, but of thee, O Lord, who for our sins art justly displeased ?

" Yet, O Lord God most holy, O Lord most mighty, O holy and most merciful Saviour, deliver us not into the bitter pains of eternal death.

" Thou knowest, Lord, the secrets of our hearts ; shut not thy merciful ears to our prayers ; but spare us, Lord most holy, O God most mighty, O holy and merciful Saviour, thou most worthy Judge eternal, suffer us not, at our last hour, for any pains of death, to fall from thee."

The Committal.—This passage should be delivered with the utmost solemnity and dignity, with the voice of subdued sorrow, deliberate movement, long pauses, and low pitch, to the portion describing the might and the triumph of the Resurrection, when the voice changes to greater volume and force.

" Forasmuch as it hath pleased Almighty God, in his wise providence, to take out of this world the soul of our deceased brother, we therefore commit his body to the ground ; earth to earth, ashes to ashes, dust to dust ; looking for the general Resurrection in the last day, and the life of the world to come, through our Lord Jesus Christ ; at whose second coming in glorious majesty to judge the world, the earth and the sea shall give up their dead ; and the corruptible bodies of those who sleep in him shall be changed, and made like unto his own glorious body; according to the mighty working whereby he is able to subdue all things unto himself."

The Third Anthem, to be given with its lofty and inspiring character, is rendered most expressively with the sustained and equable flow of the monotone, and slow and reverential movement.

"I heard a voice from heaven, saying unto me, Write, From henceforth blessed are the dead who die in the Lord: even so saith the Spirit; for they rest from their labours." —Rev. xiv., 13.

The Closing Prayers.—The utterance of the first which follows the Lord's Prayer should be given with a voice tenderly alive to thoughts of the blessed rest upon which the faithful departed have entered. "After life's fitful fever they sleep well." And at the grave-side, where we have committed dust to dust, the tranquillity of the repose with chastened sorrow finds expression in the subdued voice and deliberate utterance.

The second prayer has more of earnest supplication, and is, therefore, quicker in movement; the voice is higher in its key, with the emphasis more fully marked.

The Benediction, with more than unusual depth and solemnity of reverent feeling, closes this Service.

"Almighty God, with whom do live the spirits of those who depart hence in the Lord, and with whom the souls of the faithful, after they are delivered from the burden of the flesh, are in joy and felicity; We give thee hearty thanks for the good examples of all those thy servants, who, having finished their course in faith, do now rest from their labours. And we beseech thee, that we, with all those who are departed in the true faith of thy holy Name, may have our perfect consummation and bliss, both in body and soul, in thy eternal and everlasting glory; through Jesus Christ our Lord. *Amen.*

THE BURIAL SERVICE. 235

"O merciful God, the Father of our Lord Jesus Christ, who is the resurrection and the life ; in whom whosoever believeth, shall live, though he die ; and whosoever liveth, and believeth in him, shall not die eternally ; who also hath taught us, by his holy Apostle Saint Paul, not to be sorry, as men without hope, for those who sleep in him ; We humbly beseech thee, O Father, to raise us from the death of sin unto the life of righteousness ; that, when we shall depart this life, we may rest in him ; and that, at the general Resurrection in the last day, we may be found acceptable in thy sight ; and receive that blessing which thy well-beloved Son shall then pronounce to all who love and fear thee, saying, Come, ye blessed children of my Father, receive the kingdom prepared for you from the beginning of the world. Grant this, we beseech thee, O merciful Father, through Jesus Christ, our Mediator and Redeemer. *Amen.*

" The grace of our Lord Jesus Christ, and the love of God, and the fellowship of the Holy Ghost, be with us all evermore. *Amen.*"

The Order for Morning and for Evening Prayer, for the Holy Communion, and for Baptism, will be found at the end of the volume, for convenience of reference.

PART III.

MANNER IN THE PULPIT.

INTRODUCTION.

It has been already suggested that the style of expression in clerical elocution has a standard distinct from the mimetic effect of the stage, the colloquially unrestrained standard of the bar, and the haranguing effect of the public platform, or the formality of the parliamentary style. Its standard is raised for the direct purpose of reaching the very souls of men, and to inspire within them a sense of their accountability to God, and their obedience to His commandments; and it deals directly with Divine truth in accomplishing these ends. There must be, therefore, a gravity and dignity of demeanor, a simplicity and godly sincerity, and an earnestness of purpose, which do not characterize the other standards of public speaking. No one can consciously hold the God-given authority, or aim at the Divinely appointed end of such work, of breaking the true Bread of Life to needy, hungering souls, without being inspired with a moral earnestness of purpose, which must render him superior to all trivial and unworthy associations in such sacred work.

We are now to consider some of the leading physical, moral, and intellectual qualifications for proclaiming the truth of God from the Christian pulpit. In writing of these, the standard must be high—higher than can ordinarily be attained. For it is extremely rare that there is such a happy and perfect combination of faculties and powers united as would make a faultless speaker. In fact, if a preacher has the perfection of power in almost any one direction, or according to any one standard, he will probably be found deficient in some other.

Let no one, therefore, be discouraged because he must necessarily fall short of a high ideal of a standard for manner. For the presence of any single excellence in expressive power is sufficient to secure success, although, of course, all the additional elements which may, by nature or by culture, accompany a single faculty, are just so much increase of power. Moreover, the consciousness of a fault or deficiency is the very best predisposition to secure its remedy. Moreover, the exertion to attain what is aimed at generates a reserve-power of great force.

We begin our discussion of the qualifications of the clerical speaker by considering those that are *physical*. The best effects in public speaking come primarily from health. An enfeebled condition of the body is not the ideal state for one who is to communicate wholesome and life-giving truth. And while men suffering under physical infirmities have accomplished little less than miraculous effects in public speaking, yet it was extraordinary will-power, or unusual intensity of nervous action, which produced the result. Public speaking has so much of sympathetic and contagious power that, to strengthen strong-minded men, or to command and lead their thoughts, the well-being of the body is made an essential condition. "A sound mind in a healthy body" is nowhere more important than here. To speak with spent force, or the appearance of exhausting effort, or to show in any way that the speaker has given forth his best effort, and has nothing in reserve, produces a dispiriting effect in his hearers which no labor of his can counteract.

All means, therefore, of preserving the health should be

observed with rigorous fidelity, under a most solemn sense of the binding obligations of duty. For further treatment of the subject the student is referred to the introductory discussion of this topic in the earlier pages of the present work.

Secondly, the *moral* qualifications. The first and most important of these—the power that comes from conscious rectitude of purpose and deep-seated desire to fulfill the Divine will—is a moral effect for the loss of which nothing can compensate. Quintilian's theory, that the good speaker must be a good man, could nowhere better apply than in the consideration of what the herald of the Church should be. Nobility of purpose, purity of heart, communion with God by prayer and by devout use of all the means of grace, are all essential to moral power, even in speaking in the pulpit. In addition to these, there must be the desire and the determination to declare the truth of God. "The love of Christ constraineth us." "Yea, woe is me if I preach not the Gospel." It is the *desire* to proclaim the truth which makes the expression unlabored and spontaneous.

An immense amount of *will-power* is required in all successful public speaking, for it awakens into effort every energy of an impelling force, steadied by a self-controlling effort, which adds weight and dignity to the style. If in anything the will makes the way, it is in the effect in public speaking. The determination to be heard, to convey and enforce the truth, opens the way for effectiveness in speaking.

Kindliness and *sympathy* may not compel a hearing, or impress the congregation as a strong amount of will-power may do, but they win by their attractiveness, and the heart of the hearer is led a more willing subject under the domination of greater force. "Speaking the truth in love" will be the ideal of the gentler influence of the preacher's moral power.

The Intellectual Qualifications.—These are manifestly more varied gifts in number and in power than those which relate to the physical and moral faculties of the public speaker. It is enough to say, in consideration of the theme with which we have to do, that there is no intellectual gift, however brilliant, or however great, and no amount of culture, however vast or profound, which does not find its fullest scope in expressive communication to others of Gospel truth. But the majority of us must be content with very moderate gifts, and with the imperfections of insufficient culture. Still, even with this impaired power, it must be apparent that every clergyman declaring truth from the pulpits of the Church must be possessed with the consciousness that the thought which he would convey to others is fairly awakened in his own mind, and that he purposes to express it, in all its clearness, to the minds of others. This implies, at the least, mental life and activity.

CHAPTER I.

ESSENTIAL REQUISITES FOR EFFECTIVENESS.

THE essential requisites for effectiveness in style are life, *force, warmth,* and *grace*—life to inspirit, force to impress, warmth to inflame, and grace to attract. Under these comprehensive terms may be considered all the elements that relate to an effective manner in public speaking.

1. *Life.*—There can be no excuse for the lack of this element of style on the part of any speaker moderately well gifted intellectually, and blessed with good bodily health. The just degree of animation imparts a quickening effect to the thoughts and spirits of the hearer. The absence of this effect throws the hearer into an apathetic and somnolent state, which no effort of the will can over-

come. The satirist good-naturedly says that "it is the parson's privilege to prose." But, if there is this danger, the preacher should set himself resolutely against it, and show himself both alive and awake. There is constantly a danger on the part of a speaker endeavoring to overcome this defect, that he will become unduly vivacious. The Christian philosopher in the pulpit, proclaiming the truth of God to human souls, can not be merely sprightly in his manner, with any undue degree of vivacity, but he can manifest activity and health in the play of his thought, and the impulse of spirited feeling in communicating it. Freshness and vitality of thought and expression, however acquired, should characterize every effort of communicating the truth from the pulpit. The truth with which we have to deal is wholesome. The principles which it instills are quickening. The hopes which it awakens are inspiriting. All the ways of religion are pleasantness, and the speaker who communicates such truth can not achieve his purpose without having a manner which corresponds with these vitalizing influences. It becomes, therefore, the bounden duty of every public speaker to ascertain, by subjective effect of his own manner upon himself, whether it is quickening and inspiriting, or the reverse. By practice in the faculty of self-criticism he will become able to decide whether his manner is sufficiently animated. This he can properly test by a consideration of the elocutionary elements treated of in the succeeding paragraph.

Animated expression inclines to the lighter uses of the voice, inasmuch as it deals more with thought than with feeling. Weight, volume, and depth of voice are not the primary elements of life in expression, although they may accompany it. The elasticity or play of the voice is hampered in its effect by anything that retards its movement, or imparts solemnity as the primary emotion. The pauses are short, and the emphasis strongly marked. The percussive radical stress is heard more frequently than any other element in the expression, although the others are used with frequent changes in effect, thus producing animation. The action is frequent and spirited. And in this property of style the *expressive use of the eye* has greater effect than elsewhere. The "lack-lustre" look, the casting of the eye upward or askance at a fixed object, or any other avoidance of its direct expressive and communicative use, is at variance with the desired impression. The speaker who keeps his eye riveted upon his manuscript may give the effect of the school-boy reading his composition, or of the aged man troubled with imperfection of sight, but he can no more be expressively communicative than in conversation should he so misuse the electric power of the eye. This defect is sometimes the result of a nervous timidity which does not comport with the idea of a *man* speaking earnestly to *men* on the most important of all truths.

To secure the lively utterance of which the most inspiriting lyric passages furnish good examples, it is well to practice upon such compositions as Browning's "How we brought the Good News from Ghent to Aix" with intense activity and vividness in the expression. The following prose extracts will also be found of service, with drill upon the selection from Sewell, printed elsewhere.

Julius Cæsar.—J. S. Knowles.

"To form an idea of Cæsar's energy and activity, observe him when he is surprised by the Nervii. His soldiers are employed in pitching their camp. The ferocious enemy sallies from his concealment, puts the Roman cavalry to rout, and falls upon the foot. Everything is alarm, confusion, and disorder. Every one is doubtful what course to take—every one but Cæsar. He causes the banner to be erected, the charge to be sounded, the soldiers at a distance to be recalled—all in a moment. He runs from place to place; his whole frame is in action; his words, his looks, his motions, his gestures, exhort his men to remember their former valor. He draws them up, and causes the signal to be given—all in a moment. The contest is doubtful and dreadful; two of his legions are entirely surrounded. He seizes a buckler from one of the private men, puts himself at the head of his broken troops, darts into the thick of the battle, rescues his legions, and overthrows the enemy!"

Self-denial.—Newman.

"There are other modes of self-denial to try your faith and sincerity which it may be right just to mention. It may so happen that the sin you are most liable to is not called forth every day. For instance: anger and passion are irresistible, perhaps, when they come upon you, but it is only at times that you are provoked, and then you are off your guard; so that the occasion is over, and you have failed, before you were well aware of its coming. It is right, then, for you almost to *find out* for yourself daily self-denials, and this because our Lord bids you take up your cross daily, and because it proves your earnestness, and because by doing so you strengthen your general power of self-mastery, and come to have such an habitual command of yourself as will be a defence ready prepared when the season of temptation comes. Rise up, then, in the morning with the purpose that (please God) the day shall not pass without its self-denial, with a self-denial in innocent pleasures and tastes, if none occurs to mortify sin. Let your very rising from your bed be a self-denial; let your meals be self-denials. Determine to yield to others in things indifferent, to go out of your way in small matters, to inconvenience yourself (so that no direct duty suffers by it), rather than you should not meet with your daily self-discipline. This was the Psalmist's method, who was, as it were, 'punished all day long, and chastened every morning.' It was St. Paul's method, who 'kept under' or bruised 'his body, and brought it into subjection.' . . . Let not your words run on; force every one of them into action as it goes, and thus, cleansing yourself from all pollution of the flesh and spirit, perfect holiness in the fear of God. In dreams we sometimes move our arms to see if we are awake or not, and so we are awakened. This is the way to keep your heart awake also. Try yourself daily in little deeds, to prove that your faith is more than a deceit."

Variety is one of the constituent elements of *life* in style. The monotonous speaker is by necessity dull. A due degree of variety is necessary to the best effect in speaking. Dullness and apathy can not exist where there is just variety. But, like all other expressive elements, it must be used with propriety, as its misapplication is more injurious than the defect it seeks to remedy. Startling and abrupt changes, simply for the sake of change, are mechanical and artificial, and so nullify their own design. For instance, if a speaker proceeds with great force and rapidity for several sentences, and then suddenly startles the attention by the sudden break of a pause of unusual length, and a mechanical transition to a very low key and a very slow movement, the impression will be at variance with all that nature prompts in continuous and animated communication of thought.

As the theme which we have to present is infinite in its variety, having all nature and grace for its province, and spiritual mysteries into which angels desire to look ; treating of that which "daily before us lies," and of thoughts where the mind loses itself, from the vast extent of its subject ; appealing to the entire sweep of the endless changes of human feeling, and addressing men in every possible rhetorical form of approach—there must be a correspondingly varied play of the voice to express correctly in its proper place each emotion and thought of this boundless range of the intellect.

In enumerating the expressive elocutionary elements for variety, we are led through nearly all technical topics previously considered. In "*quality*" we have all the changes from the "head-voice" to the "orotund" and "pectoral"; the entire scope of "*force*," from the gentlest to the loudest degrees; the full compass of "*pitch*," "high" and "low"; the degrees of "*movement*," from "slow" to "quick." The "*stress*," "*slide*," "*pause*," the "*emphasis*," are all called into play in some one of their manifold changes. If, now, we take the extremes in all these elements, and consider that the intermediate stages are equally employed, we see how infinitely varied the style of expression may become, in opposition to the undeviating sameness of an intolerable monotony. Yet every speaker, it should be remembered, is inclined to some one element more than another, and is in constant danger of becoming monotonous in some one thing. In addition to the vocal elements, we have also the aid of variety in action, to break in upon apathetic habit. To be always emphatically assertive, or picturesquely descriptive, or to fall into some unmeaning habit of action, whether awkward or graceful, is at variance with the demands of variety of style. "Suit the action to the word, and the word to the action."

In conclusion, the power there is in variety, both as regards the relief to the ear of the listener, and to the vocal organs of the speaker, not less than its natural and expressive propriety, should cause every public speaker to satisfy himself that, whatever other defects may mark his style, it is, at least, *varied*.

In order to train the voice and ear to flexibility, ready appreciation, and a good degree of sensitive power, the practice of reading highly wrought lyric passages would be serviceable, as Southey's "Fall of Lodore." The examples given here will also serve the same purpose:

The Call of Christ.—Dr. James De Koven.

"Perhaps there is no period of life when the advent of Christ to the soul of man, if I may call it so, seems to come so evidently as to the child just entering into manhood. Whether he be baptized or unbaptized, whether it be the speaking of the grace already within him, or the voice of God's ineffable election, Christ stands by his side. His voice is very gentle, His accents most loving. He lays His hand upon his brow, and almost leads him with His love. His words are like the sound of many waters, and harpers harping with their harps. It would be only a little self-government, the restraint of the passions, the life by rule, the steady habit of duty, reverence, obedience, and devotion; and he almost tries it. But life is sunny, and hopes are bright, and the world seems strewed with flowers; and, half sorrowful, he falls at the feet of his Lord, and beseeches Him to depart. And He leaves him for a little while to himself and the busy world.

"He grows older and stronger, and is more full of manhood and power. The world, indeed, is not so bright as it was, but it more fills his soul. He works and is strong, and he eats and is satisfied. Busy action delights him. He is tempted and he sins; there are spots on his soul; the prayers of his childhood, the simplicity of his boyhood—these are gone. But all the while Christ beholds him; He loves him still; He watches him every day, and once more He stands by his side. It is in the height of his happiness, it may be in the tenderness of his love, in the first joy of a father's heart, in the brightness of his promise, that He calls him. But can he leave the world and its pleasures? Can he leave the pursuit of gain? Can he become humble as a little child? Nay, it is too deep a loss, and once more he bids Him depart.

"He is middle-aged now, and his locks are somewhat silvered. His passions are tamed, and his blood runs coldly. Nothing excites him greatly, but he lives in the routine of his business. He is a man of habits. He does every day what he did yesterday. His dreams are over, and realities beset him. Things have disappointed him, and he thinks much of his comfort. There is a charm about his home and his children. It is a quiet place for him, where he can rest. There, at least, he is sure of truth and sincerity and unselfish love, and there his heart centers. It is there, once more, with chastising love, that the Master meets him. He can only be made perfect through suffering. The grave yawns for his loved ones. It is the fair child, or the wife beloved, that he must bury out of his sight. By the side of the open grave, in the midst of his sorrow and his heart-broken anguish, once more he sees that form Divine. He hears the only words that can comfort him. A vision of that love, better than of sons and daughters, flashes upon him. But it is but for a moment; earth is too strong for him, and he beseeches Him to depart.

"Age, weary age, is upon him. His staff will hardly support him as he totters along. Sadly, sadly pass the days, cold and desolate. There is a voice in his ear saying evermore, 'Earth to earth, dust to dust.' Father and mother and early friends, where are they? Hopes and expectations and aims of youth, what have they come to? Life, life, what has it been? In the wakeful nights memory torments him. Ghosts of sins long since committed haunt him. Melancholy shapes beset him. As one that stands upon the sea-shore, with impassable rocks behind, and sees the advancing tide that shall overwhelm, and hears no sound of answer but the ceaseless beating of the waves, and the wild cry of the sea-birds, so he stands on the brink of eternity. The years of his life stretch out before him, they mock him with their emptiness. Like a spectral host they march along, and as they pass by, one by one, cry aloud, with accents of terror, 'Lost, lost, for ever!'

"He knows it not, perchance, but, veiled in wrath, still Christ is standing by him. His very remorse is the voice of the Lord. It is the last opportunity, the last hour of his probation, the last effort of mercy. Will he let Him go away, with heaven and hell before him, and the grave open at his feet? Alas! He is passing by. There is no sound that bids Him stay, no voice that says 'Abide with me,' no hand that touches the hem of His garment, no supplicating cry, 'Jesus, Master, have mercy on me!' Will no one warn him? can friend or brother help him? shall the Lord pass out of his coasts for ever? close his eyes gently, and part his silver hair upon his forehead, and cross his hands upon his bosom, and say your prayers, and write his epitaph, for all is over, over, until you and I, and the people of Gadara, with kindreds and nations and languages, shall see him once again, in the clouds of heaven."

The Endearing Attribute.—*Monod.*

"God is love."—I. John, iv., 8.

"In a small town in Italy, which, eighteen hundred years since, an eruption of Mount Vesuvius buried beneath a flood of lava, some ancient manuscripts, so scorched as to resemble cinders more nearly than books, have been discovered, and, by an ingenious process, slowly and with difficulty unrolled. Let us imagine that one of these scrolls of Herculaneum contained a copy, and the only one in the world, of the epistle from which the text is taken, and that, having come to the fourth chapter, and eighth verse, they had just deciphered these two words, 'God *is*,' and were as yet ignorant of what should follow.

"What suspense! That which philosophers have so ardently and vainly sought—that of which the wisest among them have abandoned the pursuit—a definition of God! Here it is, and given by the hand of God himself—'God *is!*' What is he about to tell us? What is God, 'who dwelleth in the light whereunto no man can approach, whom no man hath seen, nor can see'; whom we 'feel after, if haply we may find Him, though He is not far from every one of us'; who constrains us to cry out with Job, 'O that I knew where I might find Him! if I go forward, He is not there; backward, but I can not perceive Him; on the left hand, where He doth work, but I can not behold Him; He hideth himself on the right hand that I can not see Him?' What is He, that all-powerful God, whose word hath created, and whose word could annihilate, everything which exists—'in whom we live, and move, and have our being'—who holds us each moment under His hand, and who can dispose as He will of our existence, our situation, our abode, our circle of friends, our body, and our soul even? What, in short, is this holy God, 'who is of purer eyes than to behold iniquity,' and whom our conscience accuses us of having offended; of whose displeasure nature has conveyed to us some vague impression, but of whose pardon neither conscience nor nature has given us any intimation—this just Judge, into whose hands we are about to fall, it may be to-morrow, it may be to-day, ignorant of the sentence which awaits us, and knowing only that we deserve the worst—*What is He?* Our *repose,* our *salvation,* our eternal *destiny—all* is at stake; and methinks I see all the creatures of God bending over the sacred record in silent and solemn expectation of what is about to be revealed concerning this question of questions.

"At length the momentous word *love* appears! Who could desire a better? What could be conceived comparable to it by the boldest and loftiest imagination? This hidden God, this powerful God, this holy God—He is LOVE! What need we more? God loves us. Do I say He loves us? *All* in God is love. Love is His very essence. He who speaks of God speaks of love. God is love! O answer, surpassing all our hopes! O blessed revelation, putting an end to all our apprehensions! O glorious pledge of our happiness, present, future, eternal!"

Naturalness of manner, that rarely attained perfection, should be considered in connection with life or animation. The hindrances to natural expression are many. The restraints of the place in which we speak, the solemnity of the duties of the office, the unusual method of precomposing thought, and returning to its written form, days—it may be weeks—after its composition, and then, hardest of all, the delivery from manuscript of the message which should be spontaneous in its prompting, instead of restraining in its effect upon the voice, and restrictive in action, the oft-repeated theme, the natural inertness and impassibility of the hearers—all these are influences which repress and chill rather than develop the power of expression. Every speaker who extemporizes easily must have noticed the change in favor of naturalness of manner when the manuscript is laid aside. But it would not serve to introduce into the style of the delivery of a manuscript sermon all the variety instinctively prompted while speaking extemporaneously. Yet there is something of the freshness of the extemporaneous style which should be incorporated into the manner of delivering the written discourse. The written sermon has more or less of formality to characterize it, which would suit the extemporaneous style no better than the freedom and familiarity of the extemporized discourse would properly characterize the other. Even naturalness, then, may have its degrees, not only in the varying styles of preparation, but also in the delivery of each. A style perfectly natural should be free from all mannerisms, and as simple and direct in vocal expression as possible. Even individuality, which enters so largely into naturalness, if the personality be made too prominent, can not safely be followed as a standard. The proprieties of the place, the occasion, the theme, have the superior informing power, and necessarily suppress all that is too plainly characteristic of the individual. In deciding upon a true standard of naturalness in manner, it would be well for the student to practice upon the delivery of passages in his own or selected matter precisely as though he were uttering the same to an individual parishioner, and then increase by degrees, in his repetitions, an imaginary number of hearers, until he attains to the fullness of expression required for his own congregation. He will find by this that, beyond the increase of volume of voice, a slower movement, together with longer pauses and stronger emphasis, there is scarcely any other change required. But every preacher, in inquiring into his own defects, should learn to distinguish the wide difference between what is merely *habitual* and what is strictly *natural* in his utterance. It is habitual, for instance, for one man to talk through his nose, but this is far from being strictly natural. So on through many particulars of expression which are unnatural, although habitual, the discussion might be carried.

From a sermon by the Bishop of Bedford to the Salvation Army:

"But turn and look. See these crowds of poor souls all about us. Walk through Bethnal Green, or Ratcliffe, or Spitalfields, or Whitechapel, on a fine summer evening, when all the people are out in the streets; or go into the lodging-houses and talk with the men there; or go with some district visitor from room to room in the miserable places they call home, and see the poor families huddled together so that it is hard to see how there can be any self-respect, or even cleanliness or decency; and then just think a moment of that picture I drew. Why, what do these poor souls know of all this? You might as well talk Greek to them as tell them much of what I have told you. Talk of heavenly affections and love of holiness to men wallowing in the filth of the foulest lusts! Talk of the blessedness of a life of prayer to men who use God's name only for curses! Talk of the power and grace of Sacraments to men who have no conception of anything beyond what their senses tell them of! Talk of the grand old Creeds to men who have never realized the very first words, 'I believe in God!' Talk of unselfishness to men who have never acted on any other motive than self! Talk of happiness in religion to men whose only idea of happiness is the indulgence of the passing passions!

"O, my friends, there is something to do before all this. We want to tell these poor souls just the very first and simplest things we have got to tell. We want to tell them, as we would our own little children, of a God Who loves them that they might live, of a Spirit Who will help them to break their fetters and be free. I know it is just this you are trying to tell them. God guide, and help, and bless all who are striving to carry to the lost the message of salvation, and to bring them to the Saviour.

"I should be strangely constituted if, being called to preside, as Bishop, over the Church of England in East London, I should be indifferent to any efforts to win the masses of our people, who, alas! lie for the most part outside all present religious influences, to a knowledge of Christ and a hope beyond the grave. You do not work in our ways, and I should be untruthful to let you suppose I can approve of all your ways, but there are the masses of the godless and indifferent. We will have no jealousies. Go, in God's name, and drag them out of the mire, if you can! Perhaps they need a trumpet-call louder and more startling than we have learned to blow. At any rate, we are not ashamed to confess that you are teaching us by your zeal and courage to ask ourselves some questions, which I asked publicly at the Mansion House last Monday—Is it possible that we have been too straightlaced? Is it possible that we have been lacking in the intensity of our longing to seek and to save the lost? If you teach us Church people to ask ourselves such questions as these, we shall owe you a debt of gratitude. . . .

"But mark. The Spirit is a Spirit of obedience and of order. Don't let us despise ordinances. Jesus did not. Why, think of baptism. How expressly commanded! How highly honored! St. Peter uses stronger language about it than I should have dared to use; and yet Christians think lightly of it! Look at Holy Communion, except the Lord's Prayer, the only act of Worship enjoined by the Lord. How high and heavenly are the words that are written about it! How blessed are its promises! How manifold its privileges! And yet men think they can serve the Lord without it! Then, again, there is Confirmation, so sanctioned by Apostolic practice, so stamped with approval as one of the 'principles' or foundation truths of the doctrine of Christ, so honored by God in its power in the lives of His children! And yet men hold it as naught. Now, Sacraments and Ordinances cannot save. Only Christ can save. But they are blessed helps to the soul, blessed channels of God's good gifts. And we, who know their blessedness, are always ready and thankful to instruct and prepare any who are longing to seek grace in these means of grace."

Force.—As "life" has to do with inspiriting effect, so "force" relates to all that is commanding and impressive. It is primarily the manly element in public speaking, and, therefore, commands a hearing. Feeble utterance and pathetic expression may touch the sympathies of those whom the "dear man" addresses, but such a speaker does not compel or direct thought and feeling. And, whatever other excellence in style he may possess, he still can not be fully or deeply impressive. The excess of this attribute of style, when magnified to a fault, renders the speaker simply pompous or boisterous, both qualities being poor substitutes for "force." The moral source of this power is found in the will, by which a speaker learns that *authoritative* utterance which enforces a hearing. It rests likewise upon the quiet influence of that power of self-possession and self-respect which constitute the essence of *dignity.* The speaker who can not first control himself can not expect to control his hearers. Any mere imitation of this effective quality degenerates into arrogance and extreme formality. And still further, all manly force is absolutely *free* in its expression, anything like constraint, reserve, and inexpressiveness, being at variance with this genuine quality. Akin to this is *boldness* of style, where the force, impelled by interest in the theme, by conscious sincerity of purpose, and by the determination boldly to speak the truth, gives the speaker a power not otherwise to be acquired. All these properties combined, quickened by the element of *animation*, and enkindled by *warmth*, produce *energy*, the very maximum of force and of commanding effect in public speaking. The bolder and fuller uses of the voice are then heard, the emphasis is strongly and deliberately marked, the action is muscularly emphatic, and the whole bearing of the body and the expression of the eye will display the conscious authority of the office, the dignity which befits the theme, the freedom which recognizes no restraints but those imposed by propriety, and the boldness which, knowing the commission to be from GOD, fears not the face of man. While writing with the intention solely of encouraging force, the author is liable to be misunderstood, in censuring the feebler effects, of unduly magnifying the subject under discussion. Without *reverence*, the "savor of life unto life," the consciousness of the presence of God, there can be no true presentation of the divine herald's character. In writing against violence of manner, however, it should be understood that this does not exclude, in some instances, a sufficient degree of force to be characterized as vehemence.

The succeeding extract may be practiced with reference to the notion of calm authority:

Authority.—Dr. James De Koven.

"What then? I shall be asked, Is there some charm in this Episcopacy that it is to work all these wonders? Yes, I reply, the sovereign charm of right reason, due authority, and the Divine blessing. For who, that ever looked intelligently into the Scriptures, failed to find that the plan of salvation is everywhere set forth as a covenant, in which God by His representatives—first, 'the one Mediator between God and man, the man Christ Jesus,' then by His ambassadors clothed by Him, as St. John relates, with plenary power, 'as my Father hath sent me, even so send I you'—offers, through faith in His Son, pardon, adoption, and salvation, and to the true believer seals and pledges them for ever. Now, who that has not this authority can exercise it? Who can have it that has not received it from Christ? To whom did Christ ever give it but to the Apostles and their successors? 'Go *ye* and make disciples of all nations.' 'Lo I am with you alway, even unto the end of the world.' 'Whosoever sins ye remit, they are remitted unto them, and whosoever sins ye retain, they are retained.' 'Is God a man that he should lie, or the son of man that he should repent? He said, and shall he not do it? Hath He spoken, and shall He not make it good?' Will He not bless His own institutions? or can they who depart from His institutions expect His blessing. Abana and Pharpar, though rivers, are not the river of Jordan. The opinion of the most learned member of the bar is not the decision of the judge. The holiest of men can have no authority to represent God, unless 'called of God,' as was Aaron, and, of course, can not convey the blessing which Aaron was appointed to convey. Yes, could I swell my voice till it should reach from Canada to Mexico, and from the Atlantic to the Pacific shore, it should be lifted up to entreat of all who heard it to seek with their whole hearts the Gospel of Christ *in* the Church of Christ—not to be content with the Word of God, without that ministry and those sacraments which are equally His ordinance, and equally essential to salvation, but, for Christ's sake, for their own soul's sake, to cling to that Divine institution of Episcopacy of which the Holy Ghost was the author. I would offer to them the office of a Bishop as the angel flying in the midst of heaven, having the everlasting Gospel to preach unto them that dwell in the earth, and 'to every nation and kindred and tongue and people,' the agency on earth to which the care of souls has been intrusted, divinely authorized to propose the covenant of salvation, and to affix the seals. I would urge it upon them, not as of Divine appointment merely, but as fitted, beyond anything that human wisdom can conceive of, to promote, in every possible way, the present interests and the speedy consummation of the Redeemer's kingdom."

The passage given here illustrates well the proper dignity of the pulpit:

The Study of the Scriptures.—Dr. E. A. Washburn.

"I have so endeavored to show you the true spirit in which we shall study together this Statute Book of Israel. May He who is 'Truth and Life' guide us in the study. Each sentence, illuminated by the light of Christ's wisdom, shall be full of deeper, broader meanings than are found on its surface; and it may seem to some as if it had been hitherto only a Hebrew tongue, sacred, yet dead to us. We shall see no longer the sins that walked in Jerusalem, but the sins that to-day wear as large phylacteries, and sound the trumpet in our streets. This is the moral history that concerns us. This is the lesson we need to learn of the vices of our own hearts and of our own Christian time; the knowledge that befits the disciples of our Divine Master. What is it to be under such a law? Again, as I turn to that stately monument of a Hebrew past, there rises before me the mount of Sinai, and I behold the law-giver, veiled in the light of GOD's presence, descending with the tables of stone in his hand, and speaking to the awe-struck crowd the words of blessing and cursing. But when I stand before that mount of Beatitudes, not burning with fire, but a lower slope, gently reaching down like the love of GOD to man, I see another face, diviner than that of

Moses. I know there 'how awful goodness is'; I hear in that voice which says 'Blessed are the pure in heart' a word mightier than the thunders of the Jewish law-giver; a law that speaks from heaven, yet quickens, cheers, uplifts us; a law sharper than a two-edged sword to pierce the motives, to unveil the secret sins; yet it aids us in every true aim, it warns us in every temptation, it smiles on us in every struggle, it leads us, weak and sinful as we are, toward that life of holiness which is the gate of the life eternal."

The selection following is an excellent example of freedom of style:

Life's Probation.—Archer Butler.

"We are pilgrims to a dwelling-place of blessedness, and the light which streams through its open portals ought to suffuse us as we approach them. An anticipated beatitude, a sanctity that even now breathes of Paradise, a grace which is already tinged with the richer hues of glory—these should mark the Christian disciple: and these, as he advances in years, should brighten and deepen upon and around him, until the distinction of earth and heaven is almost lost, and the spirit, in its unearthly and placid repose, is gone before the body, and at rest already with its GOD. This may seem but an ideal, and too sad it is that it should commonly be only such; for once adequately conceive the Christian's gift and privilege, and what have I described which ought not naturally to characterize him? A being already invested with a deathless life, already adopted into the immediate family of GOD, already enrolled in the brotherhood of angels—yea, of the Lord of angels; a being who, amid all the revolutions of earth and skies, feels and knows himself indestructible, capacitated to outlast the universe, a sharer in the immortality of GOD—what is there that can be said of such an one which falls not below the awful glory of his position? O misery, that with such a calling man should be the groveling thing that he is! that, summoned but to pause awhile in the vestibule of the eternal temple, ere he be introduced into its sanctuaries, he should forget, in the dreams of his lethargy, or learn, poor scoffer! to despise, the eternity that awaits him! O wretchedness beyond words, that, surrounded by love and invited by glory, he should have no heart for happiness; but should still love to cower in the dark, while light ineffable solicits him to behold and to enjoy it! O horror yet more terrific, that him whom love and joy can not attract, even vengeance and torment can not alarm; that, unwilling to receive GOD as merciful, he can not be taught to remember him as just, or to reflect that he who refuses to prepare for the inheritance of the saints in light is by that very refusal hardening his own heart to the temper of the inheritors of darkness!"

The impassioned appeal for the abolition of the slave-trade is a fine example of boldness:

The Slave-Trade.—Dewey.

"'The world is full of wrongs and evils, and full of wronged and suffering men. But still I do say that, of all wrongs, slavery is the greatest. It denies to man his humanity, and all its highest and holiest rights. And of all slavery, the African is the most monstrous. Other men have fallen under this doom by the fate of war. They have bought life at the price of bondage. With Africa there has been no war but that of the prowling man-stealer! He has gone up among the river glades of that ill-fated land; he has torn men, women, and children from their country and their homes, who never did him any wrong; he has hurried them to his prison-ship; he has plunged them into the dungeon of 'the middle passage'—'*middle passage!*' phrase that passes in universal speech for all the atrocities that human nature can inflict or endure; he has thrust them down into that dark, unbreathing confine, in mingling and writhing agony, and despair and disease and corruption and death ; he has borne them away, regardless of their tears and entreaties, and sold them into hopeless bondage in a strange land ; forty millions, it is calculated— forty millions of human beings have suffered this awful fate ! Oh ! it is the great felon act in humanity ! Oh ! it is the monster crime of the world !"

Warmth.—A style that is cold and unfeeling will never form a true standard for the pulpit, for its office is to speak the truth in *love.* The glow of kindly, cordial feeling must suffuse the speaker's manner, or his words will be unfelt. Apathetic statements and unimpassioned appeals never yet moved the human heart. The mind, indeed, may be reached and impressed by quickening and impressive utterances from the pulpit, but to touch and melt the soul, to set it aglow with love to GOD and man, is the result of heart speaking to heart, of cordial and enthusiastic interest in the theme, and the great mission it is to accomplish for men. A pulpit manner, to be truly efficient in accomplishing its high purposes, must be touched with living coals from off the altar of the heart. No dead embers, and no frenzied fires, can supplant the need of a continued, cordial, and unfailing interest in the declaration of the truth. The very foundation, therefore, of warmth of manner is earnest interest on the part of the speaker. Earnestness is the first stage of that enkindling interest which increases in ardor and in fervor until it attains to a consuming zeal. The voice in earnestness becomes more or less *aspirated*, and in intensity of feeling, as in colloquial intercourse, where the heart is deeply moved, this occasionally becomes very marked. The *force* is *suppressed*, although intensified by the weight of feeling which struggles for expression. The *pitch* varies from *low* to *high*, according to the nature of the emotion to be expressed, intensity and ardor representing the former, and deep solicitude and solemnity of feeling the latter. The *pauses* are *brief* and the *emphasis* very *marked* and emphatic, the action is energetic, and the very body, as well as the heart, is warmed with the glow of feeling. The following may be read with these properties of voice, aiming at the moral effect and feeling just described :

Death-bed Repentance.—Bishop Hobart.

"Alas! that any should rest their immortal interests on a death-bed repentance. We do not declare such repentance impossible ; on the contrary, we declare it to be possible, through the extraordinary mercy and grace of God ; and therefore we encourage and soothe the contrition and sorrow of the dying penitent. But still a death-bed repentance is inexpressibly difficult, eminently hazardous, and recompensed at best with only imperfect rewards. Will any, then, rest their eternal happiness on a death-bed repentance ? That repentance may never come ; some sudden accident may in a moment cut asunder the tie that unites you to life ; disease may instantly terminate your mortal existence ; delirium, seizing your departing spirit, may render you incapable of reflection, of resolution, even of one prayer for mercy. Oh, fatal delusion ! that has placed the interests of eternity on a death-bed repentance—which never comes.

"Beloved brethren ! defer not to this uncertain hour—this hour of solicitude, of weakness, of pain, of agony—the work of repentance. Employ the season of health, of strength, and of vigor, in this difficult, this arduous, but indispensable work. Let your death-bed be the scene, not of your tears, your anguish, your conflicts, but of your praises, your joys, your triumphs. Then have recourse to your God, not as your Judge, to be appeased, but as your Father already reconciled. Then have recourse to your Saviour, not solely to shelter you from the tempest of the Divine displeasure, but to support and conduct you through

the darkness and trials of this dread hour to the light and
glories of eternity. Oh, brethren ! delay not until the last
moment ; sue for mercy, lest the door be shut."

Another of the obvious elements of *warmth* in expression proceeds from *sincerity* of conviction on the part of
the speaker. It is the conviction of the truth of what he
utters which leads to earnestness of feeling and telling expression. The speaker half-convinced can speak with but
a partial degree of power; but, if thoroughly persuaded,
he is inflamed with an expressive *earnestness* which nothing
else can awaken. This accounts for his warmth of manner.
This quality may be well illustrated by the following selection from one of Robertson's sermons :

Conscience.—F. W. Robertson.

"You will observe in all this the terrible supremacy of
conscience. There was struck a chord deep in the nature
of these men [i. e., the possessors of curious books at Ephesus], and it vibrated in torture. They could not bear their
own secret, and they had no remedy but immediate confession. It is this arraigning accuser within the bosom that
compels the peculator, after years of concealed theft, to
send back the stolen money to his employer, with the
acknowledgment that he has suffered years of misery. It
was this that made Judas dash down his gold in the Temple,
and go and hang himself. It is this that again and again
has forced the murderer from his unsuspected security in
social life to deliver himself up to justice, and to choose a
true death rather than the dreadful secret of a false life.
Observe how mightily our moral nature works, for health
and peace, if there be no obstruction ; but for disease and
torture if it be perverted."

The warnings of Dr. Chalmers, given below, also serve
as an example of earnestness :

Christian Warning.—Chalmers.

"Perhaps it may have been little thought of, in the days of careless and thoughtless and thankless unconcern which you have spent hitherto, but I call upon you to think of it now, to lay it seriously to heart, and no longer to delay when the high waters of death and judgment and eternity are thus set so evidently before you, and the tidings wherewith I am charged; the blood lieth upon your own head, and not upon mine, if you will not listen to them. The object of my coming among you is to let you know what more things are to come; it is to carry you beyond the regions of sight and sense, to the regions of faith, and to assure you, in the name of Him who can not lie, that as sure as the hour for the laying the body in the grave comes, so surely will also come the hour of the spirit returning to Him who gave it. Yes, the day of the final reckoning will come, and the appearance of the Son of God in heaven, and His mighty angels around Him, will come, and the opening of the books will come, and the standing of men of all generations before the judgment-seat will come, and the solemn passing of that sentence which is to fix your destiny for eternity will come."

Cordiality of expression is an exhibition of the warmth of the interest felt in the subject. We know the difficulty of directing our thoughts at all times in obedience to the will. It is still more difficult to control and order our feelings. But if any will-power can be made to move the heart to a positive degree of cordial interest, that should be exercised to the uttermost to exhibit such a degree of "warmth." And one of the best methods of making the heart readily responsive for the purposes of expression is practice upon such passages as the following. We still find warnings interspersed, but they are stated in a cordial, friendly manner.

Forgiveness of Injuries.—*Massillon.*

"But I go still further, and entreat you to listen to me. I admit your brother to have more faults than even you accuse him of having. Alas! you are so gentle and so friendly toward those from whom you expect your fortune and your establishment, and whose temper, haughtiness, and manner shock you. You bear with all their pride, their repulses, their scorns; you swallow all their inequalities and caprices; you are never disheartened; your patience is always greater than your antipathy and repugnance, and you neglect nothing to please. Ah! if you regarded your brother as he upon whom depends your eternal salvation, as he to whom you are to be indebted, not for a fortune of dross, and an uncertain establishment, but for the fortune even of your eternity, would you follow, with regard to him, the caprice of your fancy? Would you not conquer the unjust antipathy which estranges you from him? Would you suffer so much in putting your inclinations in unison with your eternal interests, and in doing upon yourself so useful and so necessary a violence? You bear with everything for the world, and for vanity; and you cry out, How hard! from the moment that a single painful proceeding is exacted of you for eternity."

A full degree of warmth implies *enthusiasm* on the part of the speaker, a degree of feeling most important to possess, if we would have the power to pour into other hearts the feelings which inspire our own. The enthusiastic speaker carries his audience with him, for his whole expression is contagious, and the hearers are swept along by the full tide of feeling which the speaker's interest creates.

Christian Courage.—*Moodie.*

"The heathen, unsupported by those prospects which the Gospel opens, might be supposed to have sunk under every trial, yet, even among them, was sometimes displayed an exalted virtue—a virtue which no interest, no danger, could shake; a virtue which could triumph amidst tortures and death; a virtue which, rather than forfeit its conscious integrity, could be content to resign its consciousness for ever. And shall not the Christian blush to repine? the Christian from before whom the veil is removed? to whose eyes are revealed the glories of heaven?

"Your indulgent Ruler doth not call you to run in vain, or to labor in vain. Every difficulty, and every trial, that occurs in your path, is a fresh opportunity presented by His kindness of improving the happiness after which he hath taught you to aspire. By every hardship which you sustain in the wilderness, you secure an additional portion of the promised land. What though the combat be severe? A kingdom, an everlasting kingdom, is the prize of victory. Look forward to the triumph which awaits you, and your courage will revive. Fight the good fight, finish your course, keep the faith; there is laid up for you a crown of righteousness, which the Lord, the righteous Judge, shall give unto you at that day. What though in the navigation of life you have sometimes to encounter the war of elements? What though the winds rage, though the waters roar, and dangers threaten around? Behold, at a distance, the mountains appear; your friends are impatient for your arrival; already the feast is prepared; and the rage of the storm shall serve only to waft you sooner to the haven of rest. No tempests assail those blissful regions which approach to view; all is peaceful and serene; there you shall enjoy eternal comfort; and the recollection of the hardships which you now encounter shall heighten the felicity of better days."

From "The Offers and Obligations of the Cross."—Bp. William Croswell Doane.

"In the manger of the stable of an inn at Bethlehem a new-born child is laid. There are with it but the meek mother and a mild and meditative man. And yet a company of shepherds throng the door. The midnight sky is radiant with a more than earthly light. The music of celestial songs dies out upon the ear. There is a fluttering above it as of angels' wings, and all the air is fragrant with an angel's breath. 'Who is this?'

. . . .

"There is a stranger in Jerusalem. He has no house. He has no home. As He passes, people stop, and turn around to gaze upon the loveliness which lights His countenance. He does not lift His voice up in the street, but His words are wisdom, truth, and love. He looks upon the sick, and they are cured. He speaks to the deaf, and they hear. He touches the blind, and they see. He meets a bier, and the widow's son revives. He takes a dead girl by the hand, and she arises. He speaks to Lazarus in his grave, and he comes forth. 'Who is this?'

"There is a garden over the brook Kedron. It is a sweet and solitary place. The paschal moon is broad and bright in heaven. In a secluded clump of olive-trees there is one prostrate, in an agony of prayer. He is alone. The three who were with Him are sleeping by themselves. Three times He falls upon the earth, and every time His prayer is one: 'If it be possible, let this cup pass from me; nevertheless, not as I will, but as Thou wilt!' As He rises to rejoin the slumbering three, we see that it is He who healed the broken heart at Nain, and sent the lepers back to their deserted homes. 'Who is this?'

"There are three crosses on Mount Calvary. Upon the outer two there are two thieves, in writhing anguish. The central sufferer meekly bows His head. What sacred words break from His pallid lips? 'Father, forgive them, for they know not what they do!' And again: 'Into Thy hands I commend my spirit.' And again: 'It is finished.' He has breathed out His life. The sun is dark. The earth is shaken. The rocks are rent. The graves are opened. The dead come forth. 'Who is this?'

"In a garden there is a sepulchre. It is hewn from the solid rock. It is covered with a massive stone. It is sealed with Pilate's seal. It is a new tomb. But one was ever laid in it, and He but yesterday. And, that His sleep may be unbroken, a guard of Roman soldiers has been set upon it. Before the day there is the sound of feet approaching it. It is love's pilgrimage, and women are, of course, the pilgrims. They would weep once more upon their darling. They would anoint his body with sweet spices. His memory is embalmed in their hearts. But He is gone. The seal is broke. The guard are as dead men. The stone is rolled away. The sleeper has arisen. 'Who is this?'

"At evening, the small company that had been with Him in His life, and were bereaved in His death, are gathered in an upper room. The doors are shut. Fear mingles with their sorrow. But, while they talk and weep, He stands among them. The doors have not been opened, and yet He is there. It is He, for they have seen His wounds. It is He, for they have heard His voice. It is He, for they have felt His peace. 'Who is this?'

"There is a little company upon Mount Olivet. There is one upon whose lips they hang, upon whose face their eyes are fixed, whom they cling to as about to leave them. Again the heavens are opened. Again the clouds are radiant with the light from the immediate throne. Again there is the fluttering of angelic wings. Again there is the fragrance of angelic breath, and He ascends to heaven. They gaze up after Him. But He is gone. 'Who is this?'

"Upon the dullness of a slumbering world a trumpet rings abroad that shakes the solid earth. The heavens are opened, and let down the throne. From every spot which death has consecrated, from the mountains, from the valleys, from the sea, the dead come forth. They make, with all that live, one solemn, endless caravan. They gather to one place. They gaze upon one object. They are riveted with one thought. Slowly the throne descends. Angelic hosts accompany it. One sits on it, in form like unto the Son of Man. His hands are pierced. His feet are pierced. His side is pierced. He looks on that innumerable multitude, and they divide in silence, such as human heart has never felt, and are for ever parted, to the right hand and to the left, sharers with Him of His eternal, glorious kingdom, or for ever exiled from His presence and His peace. 'Who is this?'"

"Beloved, in these poor sketches, with their flickering lights and feeble shadows, you behold the dim prospective of the panorama of redemption. What a revelation of the sinfulness of sin! What a demonstration of the love of God! What other words so sure to break from every heart that is not hardened into stone as those of holy Paul? 'How shall we escape, if we neglect so great salvation?' Think what a ruin that must have been which needed such salvation. Think what a ruin that must be for which such salvation shall be unavailing."

If the speaker is to express in full degree warmth of feeling, he must also have the faculty of giving the impress of *reality* to all he says. It is like the conviction of sincerity, but even more clear and pointed in its vivid power of making truths *real*. He literally *realizes* the truth, as the English people use that word.

The Church of God.—Dr. James De Koven.

"I see a vision stately fair of the one Church of God. Built on the foundation of the apostles and prophets, with Jesus Christ for its chief corner-stone, I see it rise before me. Built in its walls as living stones are the martyrs of God, the bishops and doctors, the poor and unknown, little children and virgin souls. With many a blow and biting sculpture each stone is laid. Now one and now another is called to take his place—the bishop who has gone to his rest, you and I. Unfinished yet, with neither sound of hammer nor instrument of steel, in silence wonderful, it rises still. As I gaze, the mists of earth, or else the tears that blind my eyes, or murky clouds that gather I know not whence, shut out the view. But as I strain my weary sight, lo! the clouds are rifted, and from heaven descending comes the New Jerusalem, like a bride adorned for her husband. The two are blended into one. The gates are pearl; the streets are gold; the crystal waters shine; the tree of life is full of healing leaves. There is no weary controversy, or bitter words, or cruel misunderstandings, or mistaken divisions. There are hymns that know no discord, worship that never ceases, praise that never ends, and the Lamb of God to be our joy and peace, for ever and ever."

There are other and further degrees of warmth of manner, but, as they relate chiefly to sudden impulses, or inspirations of feeling, and do not wait upon ordinary methods, much less for the directions of rule, are not recorded here. They are like the scintillations of genius, which do not sparkle at our bidding, but which flash forth in fires of their own lighting. They are enkindling, exhilarating, or thrilling, and sometimes produce lasting effects, but with results more commonly evanescent, and belong to the category of things extraordinary, which, should they be frequently repeated, would speedily sink to the level of effects which, because they are common, become simply ordinary. This would apply to many of those startling effects which are produced by popular revival preaching. Many of them are undoubtedly genuine, aside from all questions of the propriety of their use: and when the speaker, like the Italian, Gavazzi, makes use of them, few can withstand their power, although the suppressed, or rather condensed, enthusiasm of the style of Père Hyacinthe is undoubtedly a safer model.

4. *Grace.*—It is the preacher's duty to persuade and attract men, as well as to convince, to arouse, and to impress them. There must be something in his manner which pleases, or he can not win a hearing. As a necessary condition to pleasing effect, there must be nothing in the voice which repels. All harsh, forbidding, and unsympathetic sounds should be avoided as destructive to the true effect. We are such victims of habit that even the most shocking and disagreeable uses of the voice may become customs, and the speaker himself be in utter ignorance of the defect. The student is here referred to what has been said on this topic under the head of "Quality" of voice. So, too, with action. The speaker may not be naturally graceful, but, with slight attention to the matter, he can avoid being ungainly, awkward, grotesque, and inexpressive. The hints under the head of "Gesture" may be found helpful in this respect. It is far from the purpose of the author to suggest any assumed "honey-tongued eloquence" as the ideal standard, or that the speaker should make it apparent that he has devoted himself very assiduously to the study of Hogarth's line of beauty in action, or that he has acquired the "start theatric practiced at the glass." But as the message which he has to deliver is winning and attractive, so should he study to acquire such a presentation of it as shall not seem utterly at variance with the character of his theme.

Ease of expression is one of the leading constituents of a graceful delivery. It arises from perfect self-possession, and renders the utterance mellifluous and the action flowing. All appearance of effort impairs this element of power. Even in the strongest uses of the voice it must still appear that they have not been produced with great exertion. All anxiety, nervousness, and timidity are just so much loss of power, because the speaker is ill at ease. To be fussy and fidgety is simply unpardonable. To be clutching and grasping and scratching in action, to be wriggling and twisting and jerking and jumping in the movements of the body in the pulpit, is utterly at variance with the calm, deep thinking and the chastened and reverential feeling of the Christian philosopher proclaiming Divine truth. But wretched as all these substitutes are for ease of manner, they had better all be tolerated than that the idea of dignified ease should so restrain the style as to deprive it of all inspiriting effect.

If the succeeding extract is delivered in the same manner in which it is written, it will partake of the graceful ease of its literary style:

Evening.—Allison.

"There is an even-tide in the day—an hour when the sun retires and the shadows fall, and when Nature assumes the appearance of soberness and silence. It is an hour from which everywhere the thoughtless fly, as peopled only in their imagination with images of gloom; it is the hour, on the other hand, which, in every age, the wise have loved, as bringing with it sentiments and affections more valuable than all the splendors of the day.

"Its first impression is to still all the turbulence of thought or passion which the day may have brought forth. We follow with our eye the descending sun, we listen to the decaying sounds of labor and of toil, and, when all the fields are silent around us, we feel a kindred stillness to breathe upon our souls, and to calm them from the agitations of society.

"From this first impression there is a second which naturally follows it: in the day we are living with men, in the even-tide we begin to live with nature; we see the world withdrawn from us; the shades of night darken over the habitations of men, and we feel ourselves alone. It is an hour fitted, as it would seem, by Him who made us, to still, but with gentle hand, the throb of every unruly passion and the ardor of every impure desire; and, while it veils for a time the world that misleads us, to awaken in our hearts those legitimate affections which the heat of the day may have dissolved."

Serenity, akin to *ease*, and yet with a very perceptible shade of difference, forms another element of graceful manner. The excess of it degenerates into mere blandness, which is peculiarly offensive. The absence of it allows no composure or sense of rest to the speaker or the hearer. It is the result of profound and elevated thought, upon which the mind rests with satisfaction and pleasure. Fitful action and impulsive utterance would be at variance with this characteristic, and, like the glowing hues of the setting sun to the eye, it suffuses the whole manner with a tranquillity and a beauty grateful to the ear. The hurried, business-like air, as the habitual manner of some speakers, would seem to show that they never possessed their souls in peace. We can not take the eternal verities of the Christian faith and auction them off in our speech as though we were cheapening merchandise. We can not soar to the serene heights of Christian truth, we can not lift our hearts and minds to Christ, and with him continually dwell and draw others heavenward, without the tranquillity of spirit which manifests itself in placidity of expression.

Age.—Godman.

"Now comes the autumn of life, the season of the 'sere and yellow leaf.' The suppleness and mobility of the limbs diminish, the senses are less acute, and the impressions of external objects are less remarked. The fibers of the body grow more rigid, the emotions of the mind are more calm and uniform, the eye loses its lustrous keenness of expression. The mind no longer roams abroad with its original excursiveness; the power of imagination is, in great degree, lost. Experience has robbed external objects of their illusiveness; the thoughts come home; it is the age of reflection. It is the period in which we receive the just tribute of veneration and confidence from our fellow-men, if we have so lived as to deserve it, and are entitled to the respect and confidence of the younger portion of mankind, in exact proportion to the manner in which our own youth has been spent, and our maturity improved."

Sympathy is pleasing, and, therefore, belongs to gracefulness of manner. All the more tender, gentler, and personal feelings will find expression thus. Of all the winning powers of speech, sympathy is the greatest. It is apparent through this, that the speaker literally feels *with* and *for* his hearer. It at once establishes community of interest, and awakens that sense of kinship in feeling and in life's experience which induces the hearer to yield himself captive to the speaker's power, knowing that he will lead him to interpretations of his own thoughts and feelings, or to those by which he would enlarge the scope of his own sympathies. The speaker using such power has but to touch the chords of the human heart, and they respond in sympathetic vibration. The sense of strangeness is, by this union, immediately removed, and the listener feels, as it were, a friendly interest in the speaker. The practice of reading and writing upon themes which develop the tender emotions is serviceable in creating a standard of style for study. Where this element of manner is cultivated at the expense of an equal balance of the other elements of expression, the result is unfortunate. The extreme sensibility which renders the speaker susceptible, and nothing more, loses its due degree of power. Manliness in the style, under this excessive defect, gives place to effeminacy, and extreme tenderness of feeling is liable to sink into the habit of the *weeping utterance*. As one has justly said, "infirmity of the lachrymal glands is not reckoned as one of the Christian graces."

From " Enigmas of Life."—Greg.

"When the portals of this world have been passed, when time and sense have been left behind, and this " body of death " has dropped away from the liberated soul, everything which clouded the perceptions, which dulled the vision, which drugged the conscience, while on earth, will be cleared off like a morning mist. *We shall see all things as they really are*—ourselves and our sins among the number. No other punishment, whether retributive or purgatorial, will be needed. Naked truth, unfilmed eyes, will do all that the most righteous vengeance could desire. Every now and then we have a glimpse of such perceptions while on earth. Times come to all of us when the passions, by some casual influence or some sobering shock, have been wholly lulled to rest, when all disordered emotions have drunk repose

'From the cool cisterns of the midnight air,'
and when, for a few brief and ineffectual instants, the temptations which have led us astray, the pleasures for which we have bartered away the future, the desires to which we have sacrificed our peace, appear to us in all their wretched folly and miserable meanness. From our feelings *then* we may form a faint imagination of what our feelings will be hereafter, when this occasional and imperfect glimpse shall have become a perpetual flood of light, irradiating all the darkest places of our earthly pathway, piercing through all veils, scattering all delusions, burning up all sophistries; when the sensual man, *all desires and appetites now utterly extinct,* shall stand amazed and horror-struck at the low promptings to which he once yielded himself up in such ignominious slavery, and shall sink in loathing and shame from the reflected image of his own animal brutality; when the hard, grasping, sordid man, *come now into a world where wealth can purchase nothing, where gold has no splendors and luxury no meaning,* shall be almost unable to com-

prehend how he could ever have valued such unreal goods; when the malignant, the passionate, the cruel man, *everything which called forth his vices now swept away with the former existence,* shall appear to himself as he appeared to others upon earth, shall hate himself as others hated him upon earth. We shall see, judge, feel about all things there perfectly and constantly, as we saw, judged, and felt about them partially in our rare better and saner moments here. We shall think that we must have been mad if we did not too well know that we had been willful. Every urgent appetite, every boiling passion, every wild ambition. which obscured and confused our reason here below, will have been burnt away in the valley of the shadow of death; every subtle sophistry with which we blinded or excused ourselves on earth will have vanished before the clear glance of a disembodied spirit; nothing will intervene between us and the truth. Stripped of all the disguising drapery of honeyed words and false refractions, we shall see ourselves as we are; we shall judge ourselves as God has always judged us. Our lost or misused opportunities; our forfeited birthright; our glorious possibility, ineffable in its glory; our awful actuality, ineffable in its awfulness; the nature which God gave us, the nature we have made ourselves; the destiny for which He designed us, the destiny to which we have doomed ourselves—all these things will grow and fasten on our thoughts till the contemplation must terminate in madness, were not madness a mercy belonging to the world of flesh alone."

In closing this discussion upon *manner,* the student will realize, as in other parts of this treatise, the extreme difficulty of describing *sound,* and defects of manner, by the use of words alone. But it is hoped that some thought has been awakened, in connection with this topic, which may be found serviceable. If it shall assist in self-criticism, it will serve as a test by which the speaker can recognize the elements of his own effectiveness, or show reason for the want of it, should it be lacking. If, for instance, after reviewing the topic of "*life*," and reading experimentally the illustrative extracts under that head, he can satisfy himself that he possesses what will be reasonably required of this animating effect; and if he will pursue a similar course under all the divisions of the present topic, he will find that he has at hand elements which will guide him in the formation of an expressive manner. The object is, of course, "to hold the mirror up to nature," and, in the light of such reflection, the speaker may, in his study, properly thus catechise himself: "Have I sufficient *animation?* Am I impressively *forcible?* Is my style *cordial* enough? And am I so far *pleasing* as a speaker that I can say that there is nothing repellant in my manner?"

CHAPTER II.

GESTURE.

The public speaker should remember that everything pertaining to his voice, action, posture, or dress, relates immediately to expression. The embattlements of the pulpit do not protect him from this. Even if the body be almost hidden from view, the effect of the right bearing is still apparent in the carriage of the shoulders, the chest, and the head; and there is the language of facial expression, and the graphic gesture of the hand. Speech is to be made not only audible, but also visible in action. To disregard any of these effects, or to convert that which was meant to be expressively communicative into positive subversion of its appointed use (whether it follows from the perversions of bad habit or of false taste), this is to be at variance with Nature, and needlessly to impair the speaker's power. Let him then remember that, as a communicative creature, he is to make his voice and his action naturally, effectively, and appropriately expressive.

The precise degree of power in expression will, of course, be greatly varied, according to the temperament of the individual. To some, reticence is as natural as utterance to others, and stillness of body to one as incessant action to another. But just as the inexpressive man is to learn the art of expression, so is the inactive speaker to learn the habit of action. In any case, the action should be expressive, even reserved action may be made so, and every posture, every look, every gesture, should mean something, and should be made to enforce or convey the precise meaning which the speaker intends, and no other.

The Position of the Body.—It should be easily balanced on one foot or the other, seldom on both alike, except for sturdy resistance or some similar action. The body expresses repose of thought or feeling when the position is retired; when thrown forward, activity and energy is the language of the attitude. No one position should be assumed as a habit, as the tranquillity of the retired position would, if long sustained, betray a want of earnestness, and the forward position, if habitually taken, would show an earnestness which does not comport with more quiet expression. Again, the retired position, for repose, if carried too far back, produces the effect of *hauteur* in the bearing. The erect posture is preferable to any other, for the reason that it recognizes propriety and self-respect rather than the negligence and indifference of lounging and slouching attitudes. The chest should be carried square to the audience, and no " cold shoulder " should be turned to them. The lungs should be well filled, not merely as an aid to expression, but also as characteristic of manly and dignified bearing.

Carriage of the head has much to do with the impression produced in public speaking. To be expressive and communicative, it should be held erect for all dignified and impressive effect; and for all earnest expression it inclines forward. A stiff carriage of the head and neck gives a post-like appearance to this part of the body, while too much vibration detracts from the dignity and force of the erect bearing. Some speakers have the unfortunate habit of beating time with the head, by which they mark emphatic passages. This, in frequent repetition, gives a *bobbing* effect, which is only ridiculous. An occasional vibration of the head in earnestness is natural, but the *wabbling* or *bowing* of the head is no more expressive than the china image of the mandarin.

The Expression of the Face.—Every speaker in the pulpit is supposed to be superior to the mere vanity of "looking pretty." He should be equally careful, if he can possibly avoid the imputation, not to look ugly. The author has known speakers who were not themselves conscious of these defects, displaying them very offensively to their congregations by the nervous habit of facial distortion. One clergyman, who is inclined to anything but simpering in character or in rhetorical expression, wears a nervous smirk upon his countenance whether speaking of the joys of his faith or the torments of the doomed; another, by distortion of his features, would give a strange hearer the mistaken impression that he was either very unhappy whenever he proclaimed his message, or was in a state of bodily pain, which ought to excuse him from the work. If the eye and the face and the body all agree in the expression of the feeling at the moment conveyed, harmony of effect and unity of impression are the result. But, where the expressive powers do not work in unison or in harmony, the power of expression is necessarily impaired.

The Arm.—In the action of the arm, the speaker, in his practice, should remember that the simple habit of moving the arm freely, forcibly, and with wide sweeps, will, in a short time, make it easy for him, if he is inclined to in-

GESTURE. 277

ertness of action, to respond readily to the promptings of feeling. This gymnastic exercise, if it is nothing more, to begin with, will open the way for spontaneity and expressiveness, when the impulse of action comes upon the speaker. It is because the muscles have not been exercised that action is restrained. The arms seem, under some circumstances, ponderous, the joints stiff, and action unnatural. Much of this may be avoided by the simple exercises suggested.

In all action designed to make speech expressive, the primary laws of *force*, *freedom*, and *grace* should be observed. And to these may be added expressiveness and propriety. We should remember that gesture is not a thing assumed independently of the thought expressed. It is simply its natural accompaniment and picturesque enforcement of it. There must be harmony, therefore, between the nature of the thought and the character of its descriptive action. If they do not harmonize in the general effect, one element vitiates the power of the other. For instance, if the thought be emphatic, and the gesture feeble, or the reverse, the action injures and does not help the expression. But this is no reason why the speaker should abstain from action, because he has not learned to employ it appropriately. It would be equally fitting for the speaker to remain silent, because his voice was inexpressively or inappropriately used, as that his arms should hang lifeless at his side, because he does not know how to use them. Observation and practice will, in due time, instinctively create expressive power in action. To read a sermon as an essay, is to imply that the thoughts have not the electric power to move men, and that it is not the design of the preacher to affect their characters and lives to impel them toward good, to restrain them from evil, and to move their very souls; but that the very sermon is only a refined intellectual essay addressed solely to the reason, and not in the least to the moral and motive powers of men. The arm in repose, and the arm in appropriate action, suggest these thoughts. While, however, maintaining the necessity and propriety of some gesture, we should be equally anxious to avoid unmeaning redundancy in the mere swaying and sweeping, like the arms of the windmill. Attention to the primary laws already suggested will preserve the speaker from the marked defects. *Force, freedom, grace, expressiveness*, and *propriety*—if the gestures are tested by these principles, they can not be far astray. One caution is in place here: The habit of falling into the use of a single action should be avoided, whether that be the clinched fist of a Chalmers, the index-finger of a Randolph, the prone hand of a Choate, or the vibratory, vertical action of an Everett. Clerical speakers, being confined to a manuscript, within the circumscribed limits of an ordinary pulpit, are much more liable to fall into habits and tricks of action than other orators.

The Hand.—There are many different natural positions, and no one of them should become of habitual use, but should be varied one with another. Each position has, in different lines of elevation, depression, and extension, its own significance. Would that every clerical speaker could learn by his own practice to realize that the hand is naturally as expressive as the eye or the tongue. The only language of the hapless deaf-mutes shows this.

Positions of the Hand.—a. Supine [palm up].—This is the most common position of all, because, ordinarily, it *imparts, asserts, describes, appeals, welcomes.* Attention should be given to the fitting position of the hand supine. It is the palm of the hand which is primarily expressive. That should be held so that it may be plainly seen by the audience. To screen it, by partially closing the fingers, is not only to give feebleness to the effect, but actually to rob the gesture of its designed expression. No gesture can be eloquent with the hand partially closed. The force of feeling which impels the action extends to the minor joints, as well as the larger ones, and even the tip of the little finger has eloquence in its position, its flexibility, and its extension. It has been said that the hand is eloquent in proportion to the length of line from the tip of the little finger to the tip of the thumb. This will not imply a strained position, but one easily held.

In the supine position the two middle fingers incline together, as they are moved by a single tendon. The forefinger is straight, not stiff, the little finger slightly curved inward, and the thumb outward. That this is the natural position may be verified by reference to almost any of the standard works of art in sculpture and painting. We can not insist too strongly upon this free, flexible opening of the hand for impartation of thought. The feeble position, on the contrary, of the fingers inclined inward suggests the receiving, not giving. The flexible spring of the fingers is of itself expressive, in the free and forcible opening of the hand.

b. Hand prone [palm down].—This is simply the same position of the hand as above, except that it is reversed. It is used for *repression, restraint, superposition,* and some forms of *description.*

c. Hand vertical [palm perpendicular and outward].— This is chiefly used for *repulsion, resistance,* and *defense.* The same relative position of thumb and fingers is maintained as before.

d. Hand clinched.—This is used in *energy, determination, boldest assertion, defiance,* and *belligerent expression.* The awkward habit which some speakers have formed of belaboring the sermon or the pulpit with clinched fist, as if to arouse these insensate things, expresses feeling indeed, but not of a right kind, or is simply misdirected action.

Both hands may be used appropriately in the same positions and through the same lines with increased effect, if the emphasizing of the thought requires it.

The index-finger is used expressively in reference, and may occasionally be used in designation, and in close analysis in argument.

To return to the fuller definition of the characteristic principles:

Strict attention should be given to the just degree of *force*. As all action should not be uniformly forcible, neither should it be uniformly gentle. And, if the gentleness becomes feebleness, it will be better to have no action. A speaker inspired with an energetic and forcible thought should feel its thrill and its strong impulses throughout the frame. The muscles are on tension, and their action is energetic, and thus he emphasizes his thought. It may be that the entire frame is moved with the force of the action. How different from the cold, inert, impassive speaker, who stands with post-like rigidity, and the incommunicativeness of a sphinx, save his voice. *Freedom*, if it be not excessive, is one of the pleasing effects in action. It leads to a fullness of scope and extension, and flowing movement. It is as though nothing but a sense of propriety in any way restrained the speaker. All gesture, to be really effective, must be free, spirited, and unconstrained. The only danger under the impelling of this principle is redundancy in action, which, like all other defects, impairs more than it strengthens it. *Grace* is simply the result of following out, in the movement of every joint, the *curved* rather than the *straight* line. But an excessive use of the curved line, while it would encourage freedom, would be very liable to weaken the lines of force, for they are direct. The speaker must learn in the school of his own experience when to please and when to emphasize by his action. An excess of graceful movement would be like the excess of agreeable effects in the use of the voice—too much sweetening for manly taste. But the avoidance of this error does not excuse anything ungainly, boorish, or awkward in the gesture of the pulpit. We have further to consider that some gestures may be peculiarly expressive which are inappropriate and not permissible. Of this kind would be found all mimetic action, and especially the low comedy of the drama. Some of the popular speakers do not hesitate to resort to devices for expression which would be unseemly in any place, except for public entertainment of an inferior order.

The action should harmonize with the entire standard of manner in the pulpit, which, in its most earnest desire to reach men effectively, does not exceed the proprieties of time and place, and the character of the sacred office. It is, indeed, a possible thing to carry these solemnizing and restraining thoughts and principles too far, so that we fail to reach men in a manner corresponding to their every-day interests. But every public speaker, as a herald of Divine truth, must see that he does not lose with one hand what he is striving to grasp with the other; that he does not lower the standard of his high office, and does not degrade the character of the truth he proclaims, by any unwisdom in the manner of its presentation.

MISCELLANEOUS EXTRACTS.

Trust.—Dean Alford.

"I know not, if dark or bright
   Shall be my lot;
If that wherein my hopes delight
   Be best or not.

"It may be mine to drag for years
   Toil's heavy chain,
Or day or night my meat be tears,
   On bed of pain.

"Dear faces may surround my hearth
   With smiles and glee,
Or I may dwell alone, and mirth
   Be strange to me.

"My bark is wafted from the strand
   By breath Divine,
And on the helm there rests a hand
   Other than mine.

"One who has known in storms to sail
   I have on board;
Above the raging of the gale
   I have my Lord.

"He holds me when the billows smite—
   I shall not fall ;
If sharp, 'tis short—if long, 'tis light—
   He tempers all.

"Safe to the land ! Safe to the land !
   The end is this—
And then with Him go hand in hand
   Far into bliss."

Night.—James Montgomery.

" Night is the time for rest :
   How sweet, when labors close,
To gather round an aching breast
   The curtain of repose,
Stretch the tired limbs, and lay the head
Down on our own delightful bed !

" Night is the time for dreams :
   The gay romance of life,
When truth that is and truth that seems,
   Mix in fantastic strife ;
Ah ! visions less beguiling far
Than waking dreams by daylight are !

" Night is the time for toil :
   To plow the classic field,
Intent to find the buried spoil
   Its wealthy furrows yield ;
Till all is ours that sages taught,
That poets sang, and heroes wrought.

" Night is the time to weep :
   To wet with unseen tears
Those graves of Memory, where sleep
   The joy of other years ;

Hopes that were angels at their birth
But died when young, like things of earth.

"Night is the time to watch :
 O'er ocean's dark expanse
To hail the Pleiades, or catch
 The full moon's earliest glance,
That brings into the homesick mind
All we have loved and left behind.

"Night is the time for care :
 Brooding on hours misspent,
To see the spectre of Despair
 Come to our lonely tent ;
Like Brutus, midst his slumbering host,
Summoned to die by Cæsar's ghost.

"Night is the time to think :
 When from the eye the soul
Takes flight ; and on the utmost brink
 Of yonder starry pole
Discerns beyond the abyss of night
The dawning of uncreated light.

"Night is the time to pray :
 Our Saviour oft withdrew
To desert mountains far away ;
 So will his followers do—
Steal from the throng.to haunts untrod,
And commune there alone with God.

"Night is the time for Death :
 When all around is peace,
Calmly to yield the weary breath,
 From sin and suffering cease,
Think of heaven's bliss, and give the sign
To parting friends—such death be mine."

To a Waterfowl.—Bryant.

"Whither, midst falling dew,
While glow the heavens with the last steps of day,
Far, through their rosy depths, dost thou pursue
  Thy solitary way?

"There is a Power whose care
Teaches thy way along that pathless coast—
The desert and illimitable air—
  Lone wandering, but not lost.

"Thou'rt gone, the abyss of heaven
Hath swallowed up thy form; yet, on my heart
Deeply hath sunk the lesson thou hast given,
  And shall not soon depart.

"He who, from zone to zone,
Guides through the boundless sky thy certain flight,
In the long way that I must tread alone,
  Will lead my steps aright."

Milton.—Prof. Reed.

"To return to Milton. He whose delight it had once been to roam through woods, and over the green fields, was now chained by blindness to the sunny porch of a suburban dwelling. He whose heart's pulse was a love of independence was now a helpless dependent for every motion, for all communion with books; every step of him who had walked through all the ways of life so firmly was at the mercy of another. His spirit was darkened, too, with disappointment in his countrymen, and with bitter memories of domestic discords. As the 'Comus' was a beautiful reflection of happy youth, the 'Samson Agonistes' shadows forth the gloomy grandeur of the poet's old age. In some passages there is the breaking out of a bitter agony; but a stern magnanimity pervades the poem—a high-souled pathos befitting the sorrows of a vanquished, captive giant. With our thoughts of the hero of the tragedy mingle thoughts of the poet himself, for what was John Milton in the degenerate days of Charles the Second but a blind Samson in the citadel of the Philistines? In the words the hero speaks, we seem to hear the voice of Milton's own spirit, subdued to a gentle melancholy:

 " 'I feel my genial spirits droop,
 . . . . . .
  My race of glory run, and race of shame;
  And I shall shortly be with them that rest.'"

  Despised and Rejected.—C. G. Rosetti.

" My sun has set, I dwell
 In darkness as a dead man out of sight;
And none remain, not one, that I should tell
To him mine evil plight
This bitter night.
I will make fast my door,
That hollow friends may trouble me no more.

" 'Friend, open to Me.'—Who is this that calls?
Nay, I am deaf as are my walls:
Cease crying, for I will not hear
Thy cry of hope or fear.
Others were dear,
Others forsook me: what art thou indeed
That I should heed
Thy lamentable need?
Hungry should feed,
Or stranger-lodge thee here?

" 'Friend, My Feet bleed;
Open thy door to Me and comfort Me.'

I will not open ; trouble me no more.
Go on thy way footsore,
I will not rise and open unto thee.

" ' Then is it nothing to thee ?   Open, see
Who stands to plead with thee.
Open, lest I should pass thee by, and thou
One day entreat my face
And howl for grace,
And I be deaf as thou art now.
Open to Me.'

" Then I cried out upon him : ' Cease,
Leave me in peace ;
Fear not that I should crave
Aught thou mayst have.
Leave me in peace, yea, trouble me no more,
Lest I arise and chase thee from my door.
What, shall I not be let
Alone, that thou dost vex me yet ?'

" But all night long that voice spake urgently :
'Open to Me.'
Still harping in mine ears :
' Rise, let Me in.'
Pleading with tears :
' Open to Me that I may come to thee.'
While the dew dropped, while the dark hours were
    cold :
" ' My Feet bleed, see My Face.
See My Hands bleed that bring thee grace,
My Heart doth bleed for thee.
Open to Me.'

" So till the break of day :
Then died away

That voice, in silence as of sorrow;
Then footsteps echoing like a sigh
Passed me by,
Lingering footsteps slow to pass.
On the morrow
I saw upon the grass
Each footprint marked in blood, and on my door
The mark of blood forevermore."

From " Enigmas of Life."—Greg.

"*Here* we never see into each other's souls; characters the most opposite and incompatible dwell together upon earth, and may love each other much, unsuspicious of the utter want of fundamental harmony between them. The aspiring and the worldly may have so much in common, and may both instinctively conceal so much, that their inherent and elemental differences may go undiscovered to the grave. The soul that will be saved and the soul that will be lost may cling round each other here with wild affection, all unconscious of the infinite divergence of their future destiny. The mother will love her son with all the devotion of her nature, in spite or in ignorance of his unworthiness. That son may reciprocate his mother's love, and in this only he is not unworthy; the blindness which is kindly given us hides so much, and affection covers such a multitude of sins. The pure and holy wife and the frail and sinful husband can live together harmoniously and can love fondly here below, because the vast moral gulf between them is mercifully veiled from either eye. But when the great curtain of ignorance and deception shall be withdrawn, 'when the secrets of all hearts shall be made known,' when the piercing light of the Spiritual World shall at once and for ever disperse those clouds which have hidden what we really are from those who have loved us, and almost from ourselves; when the trusting confidence of friendship shall discover what a serpent has been nourished in its bosom; when the yearning mother shall perceive on what a guilty wretch all her boundless and priceless tenderness has been lavished; when the wife shall at length see the husband whom she cherished, through long years of self-denying and believing love, revealed in his true colors, a wholly alien creature—what a sudden, convulsive, inevitable, because natural, separation between the clean and the unclean will then take place!"

Good-By.—Ralph Waldo Emerson.

"Good-by, proud world, I'm going home:
Thou art not my friend, and I'm not thine.
Long through thy weary crowds I roam;
A river-ark on the ocean brine,
Long I've been tossed like the driven foam,
But now, proud world, I'm going home.

"I'm going to my own hearth-stone,
Bosomed in yon green hills alone,
A secret nook in a pleasant land,
Whose groves the frolic fairies planned;
Where arches green, the livelong day,
Echo the blackbird's roundelay,
And vulgar feet have never trod
A spot that is sacred to thought and God.

"O, when I am safe in my sylvan home,
I tread on the pride of Greece and Rome;
And when I am stretched beneath the pines,
Where the evening star so holy shines,
I laugh at the lore and the pride of man,
At the sophist schools, and the learned clan;
For what are they all, in their high conceit,
When man in the bush with God may meet."

Tacking Ship off Shore.—W. F. *Mitchell.*

"The weather leach of the topsail shivers,
    The bowlines strain and the lee shrouds slacken,
The braces are taut and the lithe boom quivers,
    And the waves with the coming squall-cloud blacken.

"Open one point on the weather bow
    Is the light-house tall on Fire Island head;
There's a shade of doubt on the captain's brow,
    And the pilot watches the heaving lead.

"I stand at the wheel, and with eager eye
    To sea and to sky and to shore I gaze,
Till the muttered order of 'Full and by!'
    Is suddenly changed to 'Full for stays!'

"The ship bends lower before the breeze
    As her broadside fair to the blast she lays;
And she swifter springs to the rising seas
    As the pilot calls, 'Stand by for stays!'

"It is silence all, as each in his place,
    With the gathered cord in his hardened hands,
By tack and bowline, by sheet and brace,
    Waiting the watchword impatient stands.

"And the light on Fire Island head draws near
    As, trumpet-winged, the pilot's shout
From his post on the bowsprit's heel I hear,
    With the welcome cry of 'Ready! About!'

"No time to spare! it is touch and go,
    And the captain growls, 'Down helm! Haul down!'
As my weight on the whirling spokes I throw,
    While heaven grows black with the storm-cloud's frown.

"High o'er the knight-heads flies the spray,
    As we meet the shock of the plunging sea ;
And my shoulder stiff to the wheel I lay,
    As I answer, 'Ay, ay, sir ! Hard a lee !'

"With the swerving leap of a startled steed
    The ship flies fast in the eye of the wind,
The dangerous shoals on the lee recede,
    And the headland white we have left behind.

"The topsails flutter, the jibs collapse,
    And belly and tug at the groaning cleats ;
The spanker slaps and the mainsail flaps,
    And thunders the order, 'Tacks and sheets !'

"Mid the rattle of blocks and the tramp of the crew
    Hisses the rain of the rushing squall ;
The sails are aback from clew to clew,
    And now is the moment for 'Mainsail, Haul !'

"And the heavy yards like a baby's toy
    By fifty strong arms are swiftly swung ;
She holds her way, and I look with joy
    For the first white spray o'er the bulwarks flung.

"'Let go, and haul !' 'tis the last command,
    And the head-sails fill to the blast once more ;
Astern and to leeward lies the land,
    With its breakers white on the shingly shore.

"What matters the reef, or the rain, or the squall,
    I steady the helm for the open sea ;
The first mate clamors, 'Belay there, all !'
    And the captain's breath once more comes free.

"And so off shore let the good ship fly ;
    Little care I how the gusts may blow,
In my fo'castle-bunk in a jacket dry,
    Eight bells have struck, and my watch is below."

Naturalness in Appeal.—*Prof. Phelps.*

"Appeals, above all other utterances from the pulpit, demand a natural elocution. The close contact implied in direct hortation needs to avoid all possibly repellant adjuncts of speech. Nowhere else, therefore, is an unnatural delivery so hurtful. We need but to name the chief defects of pulpit elocution to be made sensible of the truth of this. Inanimate appeals, singsong in appeals, theatrical appeals, declamatory appeals, excessive passion in appeals, unmeaning or unfit or inordinate gesture in appeals, whining appeals, hysteric appeals, appeals through the nose, guttural appeals, the peculiarity of an untrained voice which resembles the quacking of a duck in appeals, screaming and bellowing, with alternate whisperings, in appeals, rolling of the eye-balls in appeals, the scowl, the grin, the froth of saliva in appeals—is there any other feature or process of oral speech in which these faults of delivery are so repulsive as in this, in which we aim to speak to the inmost being of a hearer, and to get possession of his heart? That which we tolerate elsewhere is unendurable here. That which is only unpleasant elsewhere is disgusting here. That which we smile at elsewhere nauseates us here."

The Bridge of Sighs.—*Thomas Hood.*

" One more unfortunate,
 Weary of breath,
 Rashly importunate,
 Gone to her death!

"Take her up tenderly,
 Lift her with care;
 Fashioned so slenderly,
 Young, and so fair!

"Look at her garments,
 Clinging like cerements;

Whilst the wave constantly
Drips from her clothing.
Take her up instantly,
Loving, not loathing.

"Touch her not scornfully;
Think of her mournfully,
Gently, and humanly;
Not of the stains of her,
All that remains of her
Now is pure womanly.

. . .

"Loop up her tresses
Escaped from the comb,
Her fair auburn tresses;
Whilst wonderment guesses
Where was her home!

"Who was her father?
Who was her mother?
Had she a sister?
Had she a brother?
Or was there a dearer one
Still, and a nearer one
Yet, than all other?

"Alas! for the rarity
Of Christian charity
Under the sun!
Oh! it was pitiful!
Near a whole city full,
Home she had none.

. . .

"Perishing gloomily,
Spurred by contumely,

>   Cold inhumanity,
>   Burning insanity,
>   Into her rest.
>   Cross her hands humbly,
>   As if praying dumbly,
>   Over her breast!
>   Owning her weakness,
>   Her evil behavior,
>   And leaving with meekness
>   Her sins to her Saviour!"

From Eulogy of William Hungerford.—Governor Hubbard.

"When I consider this long life closed—these many years ended of eminent labor in the highest ranks of the forum, and nothing left of it but a tolling bell, a handful of earth, and a passing tradition—a tradition already half past—I am reminded of the infelicity which attends the reputation of a great lawyer. To my thinking, the most vigorous brain-work of the world is done in the ranks of our profession. And then our work concerns the highest of all temporal interests—property, reputation, the peace of families, liberty, life, even the foundations of society, the jurisprudence of the world, and, as a recent event has shown, the arbitrations and peace of nations. The world accepts the work, but forgets the workers. The waste hours of Lord Bacon and Sergeant Talfourd were devoted to letters, and each is infinitely better remembered for his mere literary diversions than for his whole long and laborious professional work. The cheap caricatures of Dickens on the profession will outlive, I fear, in the popular memory, the judgments of Chief Justice Marshall, for the latter were not clownish burlesques, but only masterpieces of reason and jurisprudence. The victory gained by the counsel of the seven bishops was infinitely more to the people of England than all the triumphs of the Crimean War. But one Lord Cardigan led a foolishly brilliant charge against a Russian battery at Balaklava, and became immortal. Who led the great charge of the seven great confessors of the English Church against the English Crown at Westminster Hall? You must go to your books to answer. They were not on horseback. They wore gowns instead of epaulets. The truth is, we are like little insects that in the unseen depths of the ocean lay the coral foundations of uprising islands. In the end come the solid land, the olive and the vine, the habitations of man, the acts and industries of life, the havens of the sea, and ships riding at anchor. But the busy toilers which laid the beams of a continent in a dreary waste are entombed in their work, and forgotten in their tombs."

From Eulogy on Judge Seymour.—Governor Hubbard.

"I think we can all say, in very truth and soberness, and with nothing of extravagance in eulogy, that we have lost the foremost—undeniably the foremost—lawyer, and, take him for all in all, the noblest citizen of our State.

"He possessed, to begin with, an intellect which, if not brilliant or original, was receptive and absorbent in a very high degree, and which not only held and assimilated its stores, but weighed them, as it were, in balances. Besides this judicial temper of mind, he brought to the bench very ample attainments in the science of the law, a large and varied experience in practice at the bar, and a certain sinewy common sense which added to his other attainments a practical working value that nothing else could have given. I hardly need add—what would naturally result from the premises—that he had a large measure of what is known among lawyers as judicial wisdom, that supreme endowment of a judge. . . .

"You would have said in advance that he was the last lawyer in the State to rebel against an old hereditary bondage of the law. Like the man in the iron mask, he had got used to it, and lived and grown old in it. But he saw and felt—what some of our best lawyers have found it so difficult to see and feel—that the law has remained for centuries a dead and cowardly conservatism, rusted and crusted all over with what Burke, in the glamour of his eloquence, calls 'the awful hour of innumerable ages.' How bold and courageous he was for reform, and yet how careful, discreet, and wise, let our new system of civil procedure testify. By this work, more than by all else he has done, he has left his mark on the jurisprudence of the State. The fame of the best lawyer ordinarily goes with him into his coffin; but I can not doubt that this service of his rendered to law reform will make his name and fame abide in honor when the lives of the rest of us shall be as a watch in the night that is past.

"And now, in conclusion, this half-century of just and useful life-work done, this race of honor run and won, not without sweat and toil, we commend, with one accord and a common love, grief and homage, this Christian sleeper to the hospitable bosom of our common mother till the day break and the shadows flee away; and so, in the saintly language of the saintly Fuller, 'We leave our good judge to receive a just reward of his integrity from the Judge of judges at the great assize of the world.'"

From Eulogy of Judge Waldo.—Governor Hubbard.

"Frugal and temperate in his habits, afflicted with neither poverty nor wealth, his manhood was passed in the practice of all those virtues which conduce so largely to the health both of body and mind; and he ripened at last into an old age that was almost youthful. If gray hairs be, as is so often said, a crown of glory, the crown is not seldom set with thorns; for with old age there come in the order of nature I know not what infirmities of temper, what physical dishonors, like, as it were, a moth fretting a garment, what darkenings of the sun and of the moon and of the stars, what vain struggles by spent swimmers against the swift current, what enforced marches, with reverted eyes and sealed orders, into the land of shadows.

"Nothing of all this in the declining years of our friend. The day was far spent and the night at hand; yet he was as trustful and even-tempered as a child. Nothing barren or wintry in this old age of his—I speak that which I have myself seen—but everything ripe and genial, as when the mellow autumn sets in upon the toil and scorch and sweat of summer; and though verdure and flower and the voice of the bird are gone, yet the song of labor is on the hill-sides, and the harvests gather themselves into garners, and the wasting foliage flushes into purple, and the sloping sun yellows into gold. All this, perhaps, I have little need to relate, for you have seen it all under your own eyes; only I may add that with this disappearing old man disappears a life which would be thought as gentle as good old George Herbert's, if as gentle a pen as good old Izaak Walton's could be found to sketch it. You may easily find greater men, but where a better, a more white-souled one?

"I have thus given you my idea, founded on much observation, of the character of our deceased brother. 'Tis a friendly portrait, I will not deny. I would not have it otherwise, but true, I hope, to the modesty of nature.

"I can not close without calling to mind in a common memory those other patriarchs of our profession—the fellows of the deceased in age and rank—the roll of them I will not call—who have passed away since yesterday, as it were, leaving behind them—am I not right, or does affection mislead my judgment?—no successors of equal rank and stature. The last of that great patriarchate is gone. The roll closes.

"'Abiit ad plures.'

"And now, as I look over our broken ranks, and my eyes miss this white-haired and venerable leader, this loved and fatherly presence gone hence where go the judges and counselors of the earth till the heavens be no more, may I not here and now, before our ranks close again and we move on and leave our dead comrade behind, may I not here and now, in the presence of this brotherhood who knew him best and loved him most, borrow for my last words that golden benediction of our Supreme Counselor and Judge—'Blessed are the peacemakers, for they shall be called the children of God.'"

Emphasis of Distinction and Contrast.
Extract from Quarles.

"If *evil* men speak *good*, or *good* men *evil*, of thy conversation, examine all thy actions and *suspect thyself*. But if *evil* men speak *evil* of thee, hold it as thy honor, and by way of thankfulness *love* them; but upon condition that they continue to *hate* thee.

"To *tremble* at the sight of thy sin makes thy *faith* the *less apt* to tremble. The *devils believe* and *tremble*, because they *tremble* at what they *believe*. *Their belief* brings *trembling*; *thy trembling* brings *belief*."

THE ORDER FOR DAILY MORNING PRAYER.

¶ *The Minister shall begin the* MORNING PRAYER, *by reading one or more of the following Sentences of Scripture.*

THE LORD is in his holy temple ; let all the earth keep silence before him.—Hab. ii., 20.

From the rising of the sun even unto the going down of the same, my Name shall be great among the Gentiles ; and in every place incense shall be offered unto my Name, and a pure offering : for my Name shall be great among the heathen, saith the LORD of hosts.—Mal. i., 11.

Let the words of my mouth, and the meditation of my heart, be alway acceptable in thy sight, O LORD, my strength and my redeemer.—Psalm xix., 14, 15.

When the wicked man turneth away from his wickedness that he hath committed, and doeth that which is lawful and right, he shall save his soul alive.—Ezek. xviii., 27.

I acknowledge my transgressions ; and my sin is ever before me.—Psalm li., 3.

Hide thy face from my sins ; and blot out all mine iniquities.—Psalm li., 9.

The sacrifices of God are a broken spirit : a broken and a contrite heart, O God, thou wilt not despise.—Psalm li., 17.

Rend your heart, and not your garments, and turn unto the LORD your God ; for he is gracious and merciful, slow to anger, and of great kindness, and repenteth him of the evil.—Joel, ii., 13.

To the Lord our God belong mercies and forgivenesses, though we have rebelled against him; neither have we obeyed the voice of the LORD our God, to walk in his laws which he set before us.—Dan. ix., 9, 10.

O LORD, correct me, but with judgment; not in thine anger, lest thou bring me to nothing.—Jer. x., 24. Psalm vi., 1.

Repent ye; for the Kingdom of Heaven is at hand.—St. Matt. iii., 2.

I will arise, and go to my father, and will say unto him, Father, I have sinned against heaven, and before thee, and am no more worthy to be called thy son.—St. Luke, xv., 18, 19.

Enter not into judgment with thy servant, O LORD; for in thy sight shall no man living be justified.—Psalm cxliii., 2.

If we say that we have no sin, we deceive ourselves, and the truth is not in us; but if we confess our sins, God is faithful and just to forgive us our sins, and to cleanse us from all unrighteousness.—I. John, i., 8, 9.

¶ *Then the Minister shall say,*

DEARLY beloved brethren, the Scripture moveth us, in sundry places, to acknowledge and confess our manifold sins and wickedness; and that we should not dissemble nor cloak them before the face of Almighty God our heavenly Father; but confess them with an humble, lowly, penitent, and obedient heart; to the end that we may obtain forgiveness of the same, by his infinite goodness and mercy. And although we ought, at all times, humbly to acknowledge our sins before God; yet ought we chiefly so to do, when we assemble and meet together to render thanks for the great benefits that we have received at his hands, to set forth his most worthy praise, to hear his most holy Word, and to ask those things which are requisite and necessary, as well for the body as the soul. Wherefore I pray and beseech you, as many as are here present, to accompany me with a pure heart and humble voice, unto the throne of the heavenly grace, saying—

A General Confession.

¶ *To be said by the whole Congregation, after the Minister, all kneeling.*

ALMIGHTY and most merciful Father; We have erred, and strayed from thy ways like lost sheep. We have followed too much the devices and desires of our own hearts. We have offended against thy holy laws. We have left undone those things which we ought to have done; And we have done those things which we ought not to have done; And there is no health in us. But thou, O Lord, have mercy upon us, miserable offenders. Spare thou those, O God, who confess their faults. Restore thou those who are penitent; According to thy promises declared unto mankind in Christ Jesus our Lord. And grant, O most merciful Father, for his sake; That we may hereafter live a godly, righteous, and sober life, To the glory of thy holy Name. Amen.

The Declaration of Absolution, or Remission of Sins.

¶ *To be made by the Priest alone, standing; the People still kneeling.*

ALMIGHTY God, the Father of our Lord Jesus Christ, who desireth not the death of a sinner, but rather that he may turn from his wickedness and live, hath given power, and commandment, to his Ministers, to declare and pronounce to his people, being penitent, the Absolution and Remission of their sins. He pardoneth and absolveth all those who truly repent, and unfeignedly believe his holy Gospel. Wherefore let us beseech him to grant us true repentance, and his Holy Spirit, that those things may please him which we do at this present; and that the rest of our life hereafter may be pure and holy ; so that at the last we may come to his eternal joy ; through Jesus Christ our Lord.

¶ *The People shall answer here, and at the end of every Prayer,* Amen.

¶ *Or this.*

ALMIGHTY God, our heavenly Father, who of his great mercy hath promised forgiveness of sins to all those who, with hearty repentance and true faith, turn unto him ; Have mercy upon you ; pardon and deliver you from all your sins ; confirm and strengthen you in all goodness ; and bring you to everlasting life ; through Jesus Christ our Lord. *Amen.*

¶ *Then the Minister shall kneel, and say the Lord's Prayer ; the People still kneeling, and repeating it with him, both here, and wheresoever else it is used in Divine Service.*

OUR Father, who art in heaven, Hallowed be thy Name. Thy kingdom come. Thy will be done on earth, As it is in heaven. Give us this day our daily bread. And forgive us our trespasses, As we forgive those who trespass against us. And lead us not into temptation ; But deliver us from evil : For thine is the kingdom, and the power, and the glory, for ever and ever. Amen.

¶ *Then likewise he shall say,*

O Lord, open thou our lips.

Answer. And our mouth shall show forth thy praise.

¶ *Here, all standing up, the Minister shall say,*

Glory be to the Father, and to the Son, and to the Holy Ghost ;

Answer. As it was in the beginning, is now, and ever shall be, world without end. Amen.

Minister. Praise ye the Lord.

Answer. The Lord's Name be praised.

¶ *Then shall be said or sung the following Anthem ; except on those days for which other Anthems are appointed ; and except also, when it is used in the course of the Psalms, on the nineteenth day of the month.*

Venite, exultemus Domino.

O COME, let us sing unto the LORD ; let us heartily rejoice in the strength of our salvation.

Let us come before his presence with thanksgiving ; and show ourselves glad in him with psalms.

For the LORD is a great God ; and a great King above all gods.

In his hand are all the corners of the earth ; and the strength of the hills is his also.

The sea is his, and he made it ; and his hands prepared the dry land.

O come, let us worship, and fall down, and kneel before the LORD our Maker.

For he is the Lord our God ; and we are the people of his pasture, and the sheep of his hand.

O worship the LORD in the beauty of holiness ; let the whole earth stand in awe of him.

For he cometh, for he cometh to judge the earth ; and with righteousness to judge the world, and the people with his truth.

¶ *Then shall follow a* Portion *of the Psalms, as they are appointed, or one of the* Selections *of Psalms set forth by this Church. And at the end of every Psalm, and likewise at the end of the* Venite, Benedicite, Jubilate, Benedictus, Cantate Domino, Bonum est confiteri, Deus misereatur, Benedic, anima mea—*MAY be said or sung the* Gloria Patri ; *and at the end of the whole* Portion, *or* Selection *of Psalms for the day, SHALL be said or sung the* Gloria Patri, *or else the* Gloria in excelsis, *as followeth.*

Gloria in excelsis.

GLORY be to God on high, and on earth peace, good will towards men. We praise thee, we bless thee, we worship thee, we glorify thee, we give thanks to thee for thy great glory, O Lord God, heavenly King, God the Father Almighty.

O Lord, the only-begotten Son, Jesus Christ ; O Lord God, Lamb of God, Son of the Father, that takest away the sins of the world, have mercy upon us. Thou that takest away the sins of the world, have mercy upon us. Thou that takest away the sins of the world, receive our prayer. Thou that sittest at the right hand of God the Father, have mercy upon us.

For thou only art holy; thou only art the Lord; thou only, O Christ, with the Holy Ghost, art most high in the glory of God the Father. Amen.

¶ *Then shall be read the first Lesson, according to the Table or Calendar.*
¶ *After which shall be said or sung the following Hymn.*

¶ *Note, That before every Lesson, the Minister shall say,* Here beginneth such a Chapter, or Verse of such a Chapter, of such a Book: *and after every Lesson,* Here endeth the first, or the second Lesson.

Te Deum laudamus.

WE praise thee, O God; we acknowledge thee to be the Lord.

All the earth doth worship thee, the Father everlasting.

To thee all Angels cry aloud; the Heavens, and all the Powers therein.

To thee Cherubim and Seraphim continually do cry,

Holy, Holy, Holy, Lord God of Sabaoth;

Heaven and earth are full of the Majesty of thy Glory.

The glorious company of the Apostles praise thee.

The goodly fellowship of the Prophets praise thee.

The noble army of Martyrs praise thee.

The holy Church throughout all the world doth acknowledge thee;

The Father, of an infinite Majesty;

Thine adorable, true, and only Son;

Also the Holy Ghost, the Comforter.

Thou art the King of Glory, O Christ.

Thou art the everlasting Son of the Father.

When thou tookest upon thee to deliver man, thou didst humble thyself to be born of a Virgin.

When thou hadst overcome the sharpness of death, thou didst open the Kingdom of Heaven to all believers.

Thou sittest at the right hand of God, in the Glory of the Father.

We believe that thou shalt come to be our Judge.

We therefore pray thee, help thy servants, whom thou hast redeemed with thy precious blood.

Make them to be numbered with thy Saints, in glory everlasting.

O Lord, save thy people, and bless thine heritage.

Govern them, and lift them up forever.

Day by day we magnify thee;

And we worship thy Name ever, world without end.

Vouchsafe, O Lord, to keep us this day without sin.

O Lord, have mercy upon us, have mercy upon us.

O Lord, let thy mercy be upon us, as our trust is in thee.

O Lord, in thee have I trusted; let me never be confounded.

¶ *Or this Canticle.*

Benedicite, omnia opera Domini.

O ALL ye Works of the Lord, bless ye the Lord; praise him, and magnify him for ever.

O ye Angels of the Lord, bless ye the Lord; praise him, and magnify him for ever.

O ye Heavens, bless ye the Lord; praise him, and magnify him for ever.

O ye Waters that be above the firmament, bless ye the Lord; praise him, and magnify him for ever.

O all ye Powers of the Lord, bless ye the Lord; praise him, and magnify him for ever.

O ye Sun and Moon, bless ye the Lord; praise him, and magnify him for ever.

O ye Stars of Heaven, bless ye the Lord; praise him, and magnify him for ever.

O ye Showers and Dew, bless ye the Lord; praise him, and magnify him for ever.

O ye Winds of God, bless ye the Lord; praise him, and magnify him for ever.

O ye Fire and Heat, bless ye the Lord; praise him, and magnify him for ever.

O ye Winter and Summer, bless ye the Lord; praise him, and magnify him for ever.

O ye Dews and Frosts, bless ye the Lord; praise him, and magnify him for ever.

O ye Frost and Cold, bless ye the Lord; praise him, and magnify him for ever.

O ye Ice and Snow, bless ye the Lord; praise him, and magnify him for ever.

O ye Nights and Days, bless ye the Lord; praise him, and magnify him for ever.

O ye Light and Darkness, bless ye the Lord; praise him, and magnify him for ever.

O ye Lightnings and Clouds, bless ye the Lord; praise him, and magnify him for ever.

O let the Earth bless the Lord; yea, let it praise him, and magnify him for ever.

O ye Mountains and Hills, bless ye the Lord; praise him, and magnify him for ever.

O all ye Green Things upon the earth, bless ye the Lord; praise him, and magnify him for ever.

O ye Wells, bless ye the Lord; praise him, and magnify him for ever.

O ye Seas and Floods, bless ye the Lord; praise him, and magnify him for ever.

O ye Whales, and all that move in the waters, bless ye the Lord; praise him, and magnify him for ever.

O all ye Fowls of the Air, bless ye the Lord; praise him, and magnify him for ever.

O all ye Beasts and Cattle, bless ye the Lord; praise him, and magnify him for ever.

O ye Children of Men, bless ye the Lord; praise him, and magnify him for ever.

O let Israel bless the Lord; praise him, and magnify him for ever.

O ye Priests of the Lord, bless ye the Lord; praise him, and magnify him for ever.

O ye Servants of the Lord, bless ye the Lord; praise him, and magnify him for ever.

O ye Spirits and Souls of the Righteous, bless ye the Lord; praise him, and magnify him for ever.

O ye holy and humble Men of heart, bless ye the Lord; praise him, and magnify him for ever.

¶ *Then shall be read, in like manner, the second Lesson, taken out of the New Testament, according to the Table or Calendar.*

¶ *And after that, the following Psalm.*

Jubilate Deo. Psalm c.

O BE joyful in the LORD, all ye lands: serve the LORD with gladness, and come before his presence with a song.

Be ye sure that the LORD he is God; it is he that hath made us, and not we ourselves; we are his people, and the sheep of his pasture.

O go your way into his gates with thanksgiving, and into his courts with praise; be thankful unto him, and speak good of his Name.

For the LORD is gracious, his mercy is everlasting; and his truth endureth from generation to generation.

¶ *Or this Hymn.*

Benedictus. St. Luke, i., 68.

BLESSED be the Lord God of Israel; for he hath visited and redeemed his people;

And hath raised up a mighty salvation for us, in the house of his servant David;

As he spake by the mouth of his holy Prophets, which have been since the world began;

That we should be saved from our enemies, and from the hand of all that hate us.

¶ *Then shall be said the Apostles' Creed by the Minister and the People, standing. And any Churches may omit the words,* He descended into hell, *or may, instead of them, use the words,* He went into the place of departed spirits, *which are considered as words of the same meaning in the Creed.*

I BELIEVE in God the Father Almighty, Maker of heaven and earth :

And in Jesus Christ his only Son our Lord ; Who was conceived by the Holy Ghost, Born of the Virgin Mary ; Suffered under Pontius Pilate, Was crucified, dead, and buried ; He descended into hell, The third day he rose from the dead ; He ascended into heaven, And sitteth on the right hand of God the Father Almighty ; From thence he shall come to judge the quick and the dead.

I believe in the Holy Ghost ; The holy Catholic Church, The Communion of Saints ; The Forgiveness of sins ; The Resurrection of the body ; And the Life everlasting. Amen.

¶ *Or this.*

I BELIEVE in one God the Father Almighty, Maker of heaven and earth, And of all things visible and invisible :

And in one Lord Jesus Christ, the only-begotten Son of God, Begotten of his Father before all worlds, God of God, Light of Light, very God of very God, Begotten, not made, Being of one substance with the Father ; By whom all things were made ; Who, for us men, and for our salvation, came down from heaven, And was incarnate by the Holy Ghost of the Virgin Mary, And was made man ; And was crucified also for us under Pontius Pilate. He suffered, and was buried ; And the third day he rose again, according to the Scriptures ; And ascended into heaven, And sitteth on the right hand of the Father ; And he shall come again with glory to judge both the quick and the dead, Whose kingdom shall have no end.

And I believe in the Holy Ghost, the Lord and Giver of Life, Who proceedeth from the Father and the Son, Who with the Father and the Son together is worshipped and glorified, Who spake by the Prophets; and I believe one Catholic and Apostolic Church; I acknowledge one Baptism for the remission of sins; And I look for the Resurrection of the dead, And the Life of the world to come. Amen.

¶ *And after that, these Prayers following, all devoutly kneeling; the Minister first pronouncing,*

The Lord be with you.

Answer. And with thy spirit.

Minister. Let us pray.

O Lord, show thy mercy upon us.

Answer. And grant us thy salvation.

Minister. O God, make clean our hearts within us.

Answer. And take not thy Holy Spirit from us.

¶ *Then shall follow the Collect for the day, except when the Communion Service is read; and then the Collect for the day shall be omitted here.*

A Collect for Peace.

O GOD, who art the author of peace and lover of concord, in knowledge of whom standeth our eternal life, whose service is perfect freedom; Defend us thy humble servants in all assaults of our enemies; that we, surely trusting in thy defence, may not fear the power of any adversaries, through the might of Jesus Christ our Lord. *Amen.*

A Collect for Grace.

O LORD, our heavenly Father, Almighty and everlasting God, who hast safely brought us to the beginning of this day; Defend us in the same with thy mighty power; and grant that this day we fall into no sin, neither run into any kind of danger; but that all our doings, being ordered by thy governance, may be righteous in thy sight; through Jesus Christ our Lord. *Amen.*

A Prayer for the President of the United States, *and all in Civil Authority.*

O LORD, our heavenly Father, the high and mighty Ruler of the universe, who dost from thy throne behold all the dwellers upon earth; Most heartily we beseech thee with thy favour to behold and bless thy servant THE PRESIDENT OF THE UNITED STATES, and all others in authority; and so replenish them with the grace of thy Holy Spirit, that they may always incline to thy will, and walk in thy way. Endue them plenteously with heavenly gifts; grant them in health and prosperity long to live; and finally, after this life, to attain everlasting joy and felicity; through Jesus Christ our Lord. *Amen.*

¶ *The following Prayers are to be omitted here, when the Litany is read.*

A Prayer for the Clergy and People.

ALMIGHTY and everlasting God, from whom cometh every good and perfect gift; Send down upon our Bishops, and other Clergy, and upon the Congregations committed to their charge, the healthful Spirit of thy grace; and, that they may truly please thee, pour upon them the continual dew of thy blessing. Grant this, O Lord, for the honour of our Advocate and Mediator, Jesus Christ. *Amen.*

A Prayer for all Conditions of Men.

O GOD, the Creator and Preserver of all mankind, we humbly beseech thee for all sorts and conditions of men; that thou wouldest be pleased to make thy ways known unto them, thy saving health unto all nations. More especially we pray for thy holy Church universal; that it may be so guided and governed by thy good Spirit, that all who

THE ORDER FOR DAILY MORNING PRAYER. 311

profess and call themselves Christians may be led into the way of truth, and hold the faith in unity of spirit, in the bond of peace, and in righteousness of life. Finally, we commend to thy fatherly goodness all those who are any ways afflicted, or distressed, in mind, body, or estate; that it may please thee to comfort and relieve them, according to their several necessities; giving them patience under their sufferings, and a happy issue out of all their afflictions. And this we beg for Jesus Christ's sake. *Amen.*

A General Thanksgiving.

ALMIGHTY God, Father of all mercies, we, thine unworthy servants, do give thee most humble and hearty thanks for all thy goodness and loving-kindness to us, and to all men. We bless thee for our creation, preservation, and all the blessings of this life; but above all, for thine inestimable love in the redemption of the world by our Lord Jesus Christ; for the means of grace, and for the hope of glory. And, we beseech thee, give us that due sense of all thy mercies, that our hearts may be unfeignedly thankful, and that we show forth thy praise, not only with our lips, but in our lives; by giving up ourselves to thy service, and by walking before thee in holiness and righteousness all our days; through Jesus Christ our Lord, to whom, with thee and the Holy Ghost, be all honour and glory, world without end. *Amen.*

A Prayer of St. Chrysostom.

ALMIGHTY God, who hast given us grace at this time with one accord to make our common supplications unto thee; and dost promise that when two or three are gathered together in thy Name thou wilt grant their requests; Fulfil now, O Lord, the desires and petitions of thy servants, as may be most expedient for them; granting us in this world knowledge of thy truth, and in the world to come life everlasting. *Amen.*

2 *Cor.* xiii., 14.

THE grace of our Lord Jesus Christ, and the love of God, and the fellowship of the Holy Ghost, be with us all evermore. *Amen.*

Here endeth the Order of Morning Prayer.

THE ORDER FOR DAILY EVENING PRAYER.

¶ *The Minister shall begin the* EVENING PRAYER, *by reading one or more of the following Sentences of Scripture.*

THE LORD is in his holy temple; let all the earth keep silence before him.—Hab. ii., 20.

From the rising of the sun even unto the going down of the same, my Name shall be great among the Gentiles; and in every place incense shall be offered unto my Name, and a pure offering: for my Name shall be great among the heathen, saith the LORD of hosts.—Mal. i., 11.

Let the words of my mouth, and the meditation of my heart, be alway acceptable in thy sight, O LORD, my strength and my redeemer.—Psalm xix., 14, 15.

When the wicked man turneth away from his wickedness that he hath committed, and doeth that which is lawful and right, he shall save his soul alive.—Ezek. xviii., 27.

I acknowledge my transgressions; and my sin is ever before me.—Psalm li., 3.

Hide thy face from my sins; and blot out all mine iniquities.—Psalm li., 9.

The sacrifices of God are a broken spirit: a broken and a contrite heart, O God, thou wilt not despise.—Psalm li., 17.

Rend your heart, and not your garments, and turn unto the LORD your God; for he is gracious and merciful, slow to anger, and of great kindness, and repenteth him of the evil.—Joel, ii., 13.

To the Lord our God belong mercies and forgivenesses, though we have rebelled against him; neither have we obeyed the voice of the LORD our God, to walk in his laws which he set before us.—Dan. ix., 9, 10.

O LORD, correct me, but with judgment; not in thine anger, lest thou bring me to nothing.—Jer. x., 24. Psalm vi., 1.

Repent ye; for the Kingdom of Heaven is at hand.— St. Matt. iii., 2.

I will arise, and go to my father, and will say unto him, Father, I have sinned against heaven, and before thee, and am no more worthy to be called thy son.—St. Luke, xv., 18, 19.

Enter not into judgment with thy servant, O LORD; for in thy sight shall no man living be justified.—Psalm cxliii., 2.

If we say that we have no sin, we deceive ourselves, and the truth is not in us; but if we confess our sins, God is faithful and just to forgive us our sins, and to cleanse us from all unrighteousness.—1 John, i., 8, 9.

¶ *Then the Minister shall say,*

DEARLY beloved brethren, the Scripture moveth us, in sundry places, to acknowledge and confess our manifold sins and wickedness; and that we should not dissemble nor cloak them before the face of Almighty God, our heavenly Father; but confess them with an humble, lowly, penitent, and obedient heart; to the end that we may obtain forgiveness of the same, by his infinite goodness and mercy. And although we ought, at all times, humbly to acknowledge our sins before God; yet ought we chiefly so to do, when we assemble and meet together to render thanks for the great benefits that we have received at his hands, to set forth his most worthy praise, to hear his most holy Word, and to ask those things which are requisite and necessary, as well for the body as the soul. Wherefore I pray and beseech you, as many as are here present, to accompany me with a pure heart, and humble voice, unto the throne of the heavenly grace, saying—

A General Confession.

¶ *To be said by the whole Congregation, after the Minister, all kneeling.*

ALMIGHTY and most merciful Father; We have erred, and strayed from thy ways like lost sheep. We have followed too much the devices and desires of our own hearts. We have offended against thy holy laws. We have left undone those things which we ought to have done; And we have done those things which we ought not to have done; And there is no health in us. But thou, O Lord, have mercy upon us, miserable offenders. Spare thou those, O God, who confess their faults. Restore thou those who are penitent; According to thy promises declared unto mankind in Christ Jesus our Lord. And grant, O most merciful Father, for his sake; That we may hereafter live a godly, righteous, and sober life, To the glory of thy holy Name. Amen.

The Declaration of Absolution, or Remission of Sins.

¶ *To be made by the Priest alone, standing; the People still kneeling.*

ALMIGHTY God, the Father of our Lord Jesus Christ, who desireth not the death of a sinner, but rather that he may turn from his wickedness and live, hath given power, and commandment, to his Ministers, to declare and pronounce to his people, being penitent, the Absolution and Remission of their sins. He pardoneth and absolveth all those who truly repent, and unfeignedly believe his holy Gospel. Wherefore let us beseech him to grant us true repentance, and his Holy Spirit, that those things may please him which we do at this present; and that the rest of our life hereafter may be pure and holy; so that at the last we may come to his eternal joy; through Jesus Christ our Lord.

¶ *The People shall answer here, and at the end of every prayer,* Amen.

¶ *Or this.*

ALMIGHTY God, our heavenly Father, who of his great mercy hath promised forgiveness of sins to all those who, with hearty repentance and true faith, turn unto him; Have mercy upon you; pardon and deliver you from all your sins; confirm and strengthen you in all goodness; and bring you to everlasting life; through Jesus Christ our Lord. *Amen.*

¶ *Then the Minister shall kneel, and say the Lord's Prayer; the People still kneeling, and repeating it with him, both here, and wheresoever else it is used in Divine Service.*

OUR Father, who art in heaven, Hallowed be thy Name. Thy kingdom come. Thy will be done on earth, As it is in heaven. Give us this day our daily bread. And forgive us our trespasses, As we forgive those who trespass against us. And lead us not into temptation; But deliver us from evil: For thine is the kingdom, and the power, and the glory, for ever and ever. Amen.

¶ *Then likewise he shall say,*

O Lord, open thou our lips.

Answer. And our mouth shall show forth thy praise.

¶ *Here, all standing up, the Minister shall say,*

Glory be to the Father, and to the Son, and to the Holy Ghost;

Answer. As it was in the beginning, is now, and ever shall be, world without end. Amen.

Minister. Praise ye the Lord.

Answer. The Lord's Name be praised.

¶ *Then shall follow a* Portion *of the Psalms, as they are appointed, or one of the* Selections, *as they are set forth by this Church, with the Doxology, as in the Morning Service.*

THE ORDER FOR DAILY EVENING PRAYER. 317

¶ *Then shall be read the first Lesson, according to the Table or Calendar.*

¶ *After which shall be said or sung the following Psalm, except when it is read in the ordinary course of the Psalms, on the nineteenth day of the month.*

Cantate Domino.   Psalm xcviii.

O SING unto the LORD a new song; for he hath done marvellous things.

With his own right hand, and with his holy arm, hath he gotten himself the victory.

The LORD declared his salvation; his righteousness hath he openly showed in the sight of the heathen.

He hath remembered his mercy and truth toward the house of Israel; and all the ends of the world have seen the salvation of our God.

Show yourselves joyful unto the LORD, all ye lands; sing, rejoice, and give thanks.

Praise the LORD upon the harp; sing to the harp with a psalm of thanksgiving.

With trumpets also and shawms, O show yourselves joyful before the LORD the King.

Let the sea make a noise, and all that therein is; the round world, and they that dwell therein.

Let the floods clap their hands, and let the hills be joyful together before the LORD; for he cometh to judge the earth.

With righteousness shall he judge the world, and the people with equity.

¶ *Or this.*

Bonum est confiteri.   Psalm xcii.

IT is a good thing to give thanks unto the LORD, and to sing praises unto thy Name, O Most Highest;

To tell of thy loving-kindness early in the morning, and of thy truth in the night season;

Upon an instrument of ten strings, and upon the lute; upon a loud instrument, and upon the harp.

318 *THE ORDER FOR DAILY EVENING PRAYER.*

For thou, LORD, hast made me glad through thy works; and I will rejoice in giving praise for the operations of thy hands.

¶ *Then a Lesson of the New Testament, as it is appointed.*

¶ *And after that, shall be sung or said this Psalm, except on the twelfth day of the month.*

Deus misereatur. Psalm lxvii.

GOD be merciful unto us, and bless us, and show us the light of his countenance, and be merciful unto us;

That thy way may be known upon earth, thy saving health among all nations.

Let the people praise thee, O God; yea, let all the people praise thee.

O let the nations rejoice and be glad; for thou shalt judge the folk righteously, and govern the nations upon earth.

Let the people praise thee, O God; yea, let all the people praise thee.

Then shall the earth bring forth her increase; and God, even our own God, shall give us his blessing.

God shall bless us; and all the ends of the world shall fear him.

¶ *Or this.*

Benedic, anima mea. Psalm ciii.

PRAISE the LORD, O my soul; and all that is within me, praise his holy Name.

Praise the LORD, O my soul, and forget not all his benefits;

Who forgiveth all thy sin, and healeth all thine infirmities;

Who saveth thy life from destruction, and crowneth thee with mercy and loving-kindness.

O praise the LORD, ye Angels of his, ye that excel in strength; ye that fulfil his commandment, and hearken unto the voice of his word.

O praise the LORD, all ye his hosts; ye servants of his that do his pleasure.

O speak good of the LORD, all ye works of his, in all places of his dominion; praise thou the LORD, O my soul.

¶ *Then shall be said the Apostles' Creed by the Minister and the People standing. And any Churches may omit the words,* He descended into hell, *or may, instead of them, use the words,* He went into the place of departed spirits, *which are considered as words of the same meaning in the Creed.*

I BELIEVE in God the Father Almighty, Maker of heaven and earth:

And in Jesus Christ, his only Son, our Lord; Who was conceived by the Holy Ghost, Born of the Virgin Mary; Suffered under Pontius Pilate, Was crucified, dead, and buried; He descended into hell, The third day he rose from the dead; He ascended into heaven, And sitteth on the right hand of God the Father Almighty; From thence he shall come to judge the quick and the dead.

I believe in the Holy Ghost; The holy Catholic Church, The Communion of Saints; The Forgiveness of sins; The Resurrection of the body; And the Life everlasting. Amen.

¶ *Or this.*

I BELIEVE in one God the Father Almighty, Maker of heaven and earth, And of all things visible and invisible:

And in one Lord Jesus Christ, the only-begotten Son of God, Begotten of his Father before all worlds; God of God, Light of Light, very God of very God, Begotten, not made, Being of one substance with the Father, By whom all things were made; Who, for us men, and for our salvation came down from heaven, And was incarnate by the Holy Ghost of the Virgin Mary, And was made man, And was crucified also for us under Pontius Pilate. He suffered and was buried, And the third day he rose again, according to the Scriptures, And ascended into heaven, And sitteth on the right hand of the Father; And he shall come again with glory to judge both the quick and the dead: Whose kingdom shall have no end.

And I believe in the Holy Ghost, the Lord and Giver of Life, Who proceedeth from the Father and the Son, Who with the Father and the Son together is worshipped and glorified, Who spake by the Prophets. And I believe one Catholic and Apostolic Church. I acknowledge one Baptism for the remission of sins, And I look for the Resurrection of the dead, And the Life of the world to come. Amen.

¶ *And after that, these Prayers following, all devoutly kneeling; the Minister first pronouncing,*

The Lord be with you.
Answer. And with thy spirit.
Minister. Let us pray.
O Lord, show thy mercy upon us.
Answer. And grant us thy salvation.
Minister. O God, make clean our hearts within us.
Answer. And take not thy Holy Spirit from us.

¶ *Then shall be said the Collect for the day, and after that the Collects and Prayers following.*

A Collect for Peace.

O God, from whom all holy desires, all good counsels, and all just works do proceed; Give unto thy servants that peace, which the world cannot give; that our hearts may be set to obey thy commandments, and also that by thee, we, being defended from the fear of our enemies, may pass our time in rest and quietness; through the merits of Jesus Christ our Saviour. *Amen.*

A Collect for Aid against Perils.

O Lord, our heavenly Father, by whose Almighty power we have been preserved this day; By thy great mercy defend us from all perils and dangers of this night; for the love of thy only Son, our Saviour, Jesus Christ. *Amen.*

THE ORDER FOR DAILY EVENING PRAYER.

A Prayer for the President of the United States, *and all in Civil Authority.*

O LORD, our heavenly Father, the high and mighty Ruler of the universe, who dost from thy throne behold all the dwellers upon earth; Most heartily we beseech thee, with thy favour to behold and bless thy servant THE PRESIDENT OF THE UNITED STATES, and all others in authority; and so replenish them with the grace of thy Holy Spirit, that they may always incline to thy will, and walk in thy way. Endue them plenteously with heavenly gifts; grant them in health and prosperity long to live; and finally, after this life, to attain everlasting joy and felicity; through Jesus Christ our Lord. *Amen.*

A Prayer for the Clergy and People.

ALMIGHTY and everlasting God, from whom cometh every good and perfect gift; Send down upon our Bishops, and other Clergy, and upon the Congregations committed to their charge, the healthful Spirit of thy grace; and, that they may truly please thee, pour upon them the continual dew of thy blessing. Grant this, O Lord, for the honour of our Advocate and Mediator, Jesus Christ. *Amen.*

A Prayer for all Conditions of Men.

O GOD, the Creator and Preserver of all mankind, we humbly beseech thee for all sorts and conditions of men; that thou wouldest be pleased to make thy ways known unto them, thy saving health unto all nations. More especially we pray for thy holy Church universal; that it may be so guided and governed by thy good Spirit, that all who profess and call themselves Christians may be led into the way of truth, and hold the faith in unity of spirit, in the bond of peace, and in righteousness of life. Finally, we commend to thy fatherly goodness all those who are any ways afflicted, or distressed, in mind, body, or estate; that it may please thee to comfort and relieve them, according to their several necessities; giving them patience under their sufferings, and a happy issue out of all their afflictions. And this we beg for Jesus Christ's sake. *Amen.*

A General Thanksgiving.

ALMIGHTY God, Father of all mercies, we, thine unworthy servants, do give thee most humble and hearty thanks for all thy goodness and loving-kindness to us, and to all men. We bless thee for our creation, preservation, and all the blessings of this life; but above all, for thine inestimable love in the redemption of the world by our Lord Jesus Christ; for the means of grace, and for the hope of glory. And, we beseech thee, give us that due sense of all thy mercies, that our hearts may be unfeignedly thankful, and that we may show forth thy praise, not only with our lips, but in our lives; by giving up ourselves to thy service, and by walking before thee in holiness and righteousness all our days; through Jesus Christ our Lord, to whom, with thee and the Holy Ghost, be all honour and glory, world without end. *Amen.*

A Prayer of St. Chrysostom.

ALMIGHTY God, who hast given us grace at this time with one accord to make our common supplications unto thee; and dost promise that when two or three are gathered together in thy Name thou wilt grant their requests; Fulfil now, O Lord, the desires and petitions of thy servants, as may be most expedient for them; granting us in this world knowledge of thy truth, and in the world to come life everlasting. *Amen.*

2 *Cor.* xiii., 14.

THE grace of our Lord Jesus Christ, and the love of God, and the fellowship of the Holy Ghost, be with us all evermore. *Amen.*

Here endeth the Order of Evening Prayer.

THE LITANY,
OR GENERAL SUPPLICATION.

¶ *To be used after Morning Service, on Sundays, Wednesdays, and Fridays.*

O GOD the Father of Heaven ; have mercy upon us miserable sinners.

O God the Father of Heaven ; have mercy upon us miserable sinners.

O God the Son, Redeemer of the world ; have mercy upon us miserable sinners.

O God the Son, Redeemer of the world ; have mercy upon us miserable sinners.

O God the Holy Ghost, proceeding from the Father and the Son ; have mercy upon us miserable sinners.

O God the Holy Ghost, proceeding from the Father and the Son ; have mercy upon us miserable sinners.

O holy, blessed, and glorious Trinity, three Persons and one God ; have mercy upon us miserable sinners.

O holy, blessed, and glorious Trinity, three Persons and one God ; have mercy upon us miserable sinners.

Remember not, Lord, our offences, nor the offences of our fore-fathers ; neither take thou vengeance of our sins : spare us, good Lord, spare thy people, whom thou hast redeemed with thy most precious blood, and be not angry with us for ever.

Spare us, good Lord.

From all evil and mischief; from sin; from the crafts and assaults of the devil; from thy wrath, and from everlasting damnation,
Good Lord, deliver us.

From all blindness of heart; from pride, vain-glory, and hypocrisy; from envy, hatred, and malice, and all uncharitableness,
Good Lord, deliver us.

From all inordinate and sinful affections; and from all the deceits of the world, the flesh, and the devil,
Good Lord, deliver us.

From lightning and tempest; from plague, pestilence, and famine; from battle and murder, and from sudden death,
Good Lord, deliver us.

From all sedition, privy conspiracy, and rebellion; from all false doctrine, heresy, and schism; from hardness of heart, and contempt of thy Word and Commandment,
Good Lord, deliver us.

By the mystery of thy holy Incarnation; by thy holy Nativity and Circumcision; by thy Baptism, Fasting, and Temptation,
Good Lord, deliver us.

By thine Agony and Bloody Sweat; by thy Cross and Passion; by thy precious Death and Burial; by thy glorious Resurrection and Ascension; and by the coming of the Holy Ghost,
Good Lord, deliver us.

In all time of our tribulation; in all time of our prosperity; in the hour of death, and in the day of judgment,
Good Lord, deliver us.

We sinners do beseech thee to hear us, O Lord God; and that it may please thee to rule and govern thy holy Church universal in the right way;
We beseech thee to hear us, good Lord.

That it may please thee to bless and preserve all Chris-

tian Rulers and Magistrates, giving them grace to execute justice, and to maintain truth ;
We beseech thee to hear us, good Lord.

That it may please thee to illuminate all Bishops, Priests, and Deacons, with true knowledge and understanding of thy Word ; and that both by their preaching and living they may set it forth, and show it accordingly ;
We beseech thee to hear us, good Lord.

That it may please thee to bless and keep all thy people ;
We beseech thee to hear us, good Lord.

That it may please thee to give to all nations unity, peace, and concord ;
We beseech thee to hear us, good Lord.

That it may please thee to give us an heart to love and fear thee, and diligently to live after thy commandments ;
We beseech thee to hear us, good Lord.

That it may please thee to give to all thy people increase of grace to hear meekly thy Word, and to receive it with pure affection, and to bring forth the fruits of the Spirit ;
We beseech thee to hear us, good Lord.

That it may please thee to bring into the way of truth all such as have erred, and are deceived ;
We beseech thee to hear us, good Lord.

That it may please thee to strengthen such as do stand ; and to comfort and help the weak-hearted ; and to raise up those who fall ; and finally to beat down Satan under our feet ;
We beseech thee to hear us, good Lord.

That it may please thee to succour, help, and comfort, all who are in danger, necessity, and tribulation ;
We beseech thee to hear us, good Lord.

That it may please thee to preserve all who travel by land or by water, all women in the perils of child-birth, all sick persons, and young children ; and to show thy pity upon all prisoners and captives ;
We beseech thee to hear us, good Lord.

That it may please thee to defend, and provide for, the fatherless children, and widows, and all who are desolate and oppressed ;
We beseech thee to hear us, good Lord.
That it may please thee to have mercy upon all men ;
We beseech thee to hear us, good Lord.
That it may please thee to forgive our enemies, persecutors, and slanderers, and to turn their hearts ;
We beseech thee to hear us, good Lord.
That it may please thee to give and preserve to our use the kindly fruits of the earth, so that in due time we may enjoy them ;
We beseech thee to hear us, good Lord.
That it may please thee to give us true repentance ; to forgive us all our sins, negligences, and ignorances ; and to endue us with the grace of thy Holy Spirit to amend our lives according to thy holy Word ;
We beseech thee to hear us, good Lord.
Son of God, we beseech thee to hear us.
Son of God, we beseech thee to hear us.
O Lamb of God, who takest away the sins of the world ;
Grant us thy peace.
O Lamb of God, who takest away the sins of the world ;
Have mercy upon us.

¶ *The Minister may, at his discretion, omit all that follows, to the Prayer, "We humbly beseech thee, O Father," &c.*

O Christ, hear us.
O Christ, hear us.
Lord, have mercy upon us.
Lord, have mercy upon us.
Christ, have mercy upon us.
Christ, have mercy upon us.
Lord, have mercy upon us.
Lord, have mercy upon us.

¶ *Then shall the Minister, and the People with him, say the Lord's Prayer.*

THE LITANY, OR GENERAL SUPPLICATION.

Our Father, who art in heaven, Hallowed be thy Name. Thy kingdom come. Thy will be done on earth, As it is in heaven. Give us this day our daily bread. And forgive us our trespasses, As we forgive those who trespass against us. And lead us not into temptation; But deliver us from evil. Amen.

Minister. O Lord deal not with us according to our sins.

Answer. Neither reward us according to our iniquities.

Let us pray.

O God, merciful Father, who despisest not the sighing of a contrite heart, nor the desire of such as are sorrowful; Mercifully assist our prayers which we make before thee in all our troubles and adversities, whensoever they oppress us; and graciously hear us, that those evils which the craft and subtilty of the devil or man worketh against us, may, by thy good providence, be brought to nought; that we thy servants, being hurt by no persecutions, may evermore give thanks unto thee in thy holy Church; through Jesus Christ our Lord.

O Lord, arise, help us, and deliver us for thy Name's sake.

O God, we have heard with our ears, and our fathers have declared unto us, the noble works that thou didst in their days, and in the old time before them.

O Lord, arise, help us, and deliver us for thine honour.

Glory be to the Father, and to the Son, and to the Holy Ghost;

Answer. As it was in the beginning, is now, and ever shall be, world without end. Amen.

From our enemies defend us, O Christ.

Graciously look upon our afflictions.

With pity behold the sorrows of our hearts.

Mercifully forgive the sins of thy people.

Favourably with mercy hear our prayers.

O Son of David, have mercy upon us.

Both now and ever vouchsafe to hear us, O Christ.

Graciously hear us, O Christ; graciously hear us, O Lord Christ.

Minister. O Lord, let thy mercy be showed upon us;

Answer. As we do put our trust in thee.

Let us pray.

WE humbly beseech thee, O Father, mercifully to look upon our infirmities; and, for the glory of thy Name, turn from us all those evils that we most justly have deserved; and grant, that in all our troubles we may put our whole trust and confidence in thy mercy, and evermore serve thee in holiness and pureness of living, to thy honour and glory; through our only Mediator and Advocate, Jesus Christ our Lord. *Amen.*

A General Thanksgiving.

ALMIGHTY God, Father of all mercies, we, thine unworthy servants, do give thee most humble and hearty thanks for all thy goodness and loving-kindness to us, and to all men. We bless thee for our creation, preservation, and all the blessings of this life; but, above all, for thine inestimable love in the redemption of the world by our Lord Jesus Christ; for the means of grace, and for the hope of glory. And, we beseech thee, give us that due sense of all thy mercies, that our hearts may be unfeignedly thankful, and that we show forth thy praise, not only with our lips, but in our lives; by giving up ourselves to thy service, and by walking before thee in holiness and righteousness all our days; through Jesus Christ our Lord, to whom, with thee and the Holy Ghost, be all honour and glory, world without end. *Amen.*

A Prayer of St. Chrysostom.

ALMIGHTY God, who hast given us grace at this time with one accord to make our common supplications unto thee; and dost promise that when two or three are gathered

THE LITANY, OR GENERAL SUPPLICATION.

together in thy Name thou wilt grant their requests; Fulfil now, O Lord, the desires and petitions of thy servants, as may be most expedient for them; granting us in this world knowledge of thy truth, and in the world to come life everlasting. *Amen.*

2 *Cor.* xiii., 14.

THE grace of our Lord Jesus Christ, and the love of God, and the fellowship of the Holy Ghost, be with us all evermore. *Amen.*

Here endeth the Litany.

THE ORDER FOR THE
ADMINISTRATION OF THE LORD'S SUPPER,
OR
HOLY COMMUNION.

OUR Father, who art in heaven, Hallowed be thy Name. Thy kingdom come. Thy will be done on earth, As it is in heaven. Give us this day our daily bread. And forgive us our trespasses, As we forgive those who trespass against us. And lead us not into temptation; But deliver us from evil: For thine is the Kingdom, and the Power, and the Glory, for ever and ever. Amen.

The Collect.

ALMIGHTY God, unto whom all hearts are open, all desires known, and from whom no secrets are hid; Cleanse the thoughts of our hearts by the inspiration of thy Holy Spirit, that we may perfectly love thee, and worthily magnify thy holy Name; through Christ our Lord. *Amen.*

¶ *Then shall the Minister, turning to the People, rehearse distinctly the* TEN COMMANDMENTS; *and the People, still kneeling, shall, after every commandment, ask God mercy for their transgressions for the time past, and grace to keep the law for the time to come, as followeth.*

Minister.

GOD spake these words, and said; I am the Lord thy God: Thou shalt have none other gods but me.

People. Lord, have mercy upon us, and incline our hearts to keep this law.

Minister. Thou shalt not make to thyself any graven image, nor the likeness of any thing that is in heaven above, or in the earth beneath, or in the water under the earth. Thou shalt not bow down to them, nor worship them : for I the Lord thy God am a jealous God, and visit the sins of the fathers upon the children, unto the third and fourth generation of them that hate me ; and show mercy unto thousands in them that love me, and keep my commandments.

People. Lord, have mercy upon us, and incline our hearts to keep this law.

Minister. Thou shalt not take the Name of the Lord thy God in vain : for the Lord will not hold him guiltless that taketh his Name in vain.

People. Lord, have mercy upon us, and incline our hearts to keep this law.

Minister. Remember that thou keep holy the Sabbath-day. Six days shalt thou labour, and do all that thou hast to do ; but the seventh day is the Sabbath of the Lord thy God. In it thou shalt do no manner of work ; thou, and thy son, and thy daughter, thy man-servant, and thy maid-servant, thy cattle, and the stranger that is within thy gates. For in six days the Lord made heaven and earth, the sea, and all that in them is, and rested the seventh day : wherefore the Lord blessed the seventh day, and hallowed it.

People. Lord, have mercy upon us, and incline our hearts to keep this law.

Minister. Honour thy father and thy mother ; that thy days may be long in the land which the Lord thy God giveth thee.

People. Lord, have mercy upon us, and incline our hearts to keep this law.

Minister. Thou shalt do no murder.

People. Lord, have mercy upon us, and incline our hearts to keep this law.

Minister. Thou shalt not commit adultery.

People. Lord, have mercy upon us, and incline our hearts to keep this law.

Minister. Thou shalt not steal.

People. Lord, have mercy upon us, and incline our hearts to keep this law.

Minister. Thou shalt not bear false witness against thy neighbour.

People. Lord, have mercy upon us, and incline our hearts to keep this law.

Minister. Thou shalt not covet thy neighbour's house, thou shalt not covet thy neighbour's wife, nor his servant, nor his maid, nor his ox, nor his ass, nor any thing that is his.

People. Lord, have mercy upon us, and write all these thy laws in our hearts, we beseech thee.

¶ *Then the Minister may say,*

Hear also what our Lord Jesus Christ saith:

THOU shalt love the Lord thy God with all thy heart, and with all thy soul, and with all thy mind. This is the first and great commandment. And the second is like unto it; Thou shalt love thy neighbour as thyself. On these two commandments hang all the Law and the Prophets.

Let us pray.

O ALMIGHTY Lord, and everlasting God, vouchsafe, we beseech thee, to direct, sanctify, and govern, both our hearts and bodies, in the ways of thy laws, and in the works of thy commandments; that, through thy most mighty protection, both here and ever, we may be preserved in body and soul; through our Lord and Saviour Jesus Christ. *Amen.*

¶ *Then shall be said the Collect of the Day. And immediately after the Collect the Minister shall read the Epistle, saying,* The Epistle [*or,* The portion of Scripture appointed for the Epistle] is written in the —— Chapter of ——, beginning at the — Verse. *And the Epistle ended, he shall say,* Here endeth the Epistle. *Then shall he read the Gospel (the People all standing up) saying,* The Holy Gospel is written in the —— Chapter of ——, beginning at the — Verse.

¶ *Here the People shall say,*

Glory be to thee, O Lord.

¶ *Then shall be read the Apostles', or Nicene Creed; unless one of them hath been read immediately before in the Morning Service.*

¶ *Then the Minister shall declare unto the People what Holy-days, or Fasting-days, are in the week following to be observed; and (if occasion be) shall Notice be given of the Communion, and of the Bans of Matrimony, and other matters to be published.*

¶ *Then shall follow the Sermon. After which, the Minister, when there is a Communion, shall return to the Lord's Table, and begin the Offertory, saying one or more of these Sentences following, as he thinketh most convenient.*

LET your light so shine before men, that they may see your good works, and glorify your Father which is in heaven.—St. Matt. v., 16.

Lay not up for yourselves treasures upon earth; where moth and rust doth corrupt, and where thieves break through and steal: but lay up for yourselves treasures in heaven; where neither moth nor rust doth corrupt, and where thieves do not break through nor steal.—St. Matt. vi., 19, 20.

Whatsoever ye would that men should do to you, even so do to them: for this is the Law and the Prophets.—St. Matt. vii., 12.

Not every one that saith unto me, Lord, Lord, shall enter into the Kingdom of heaven; but he that doeth the will of my Father which is in heaven.—St. Matt. vii., 21.

Zaccheus stood forth, and said unto the Lord, Behold, Lord, the half of my goods I give to the poor; and if I have done any wrong to any man, I restore fourfold.—St. Luke, xix., 8.

Who goeth a warfare at any time at his own cost? Who planteth a vineyard, and eateth not of the fruit thereof? Or who feedeth a flock, and eateth not of the milk of the flock?—1 Cor. ix., 7.

If we have sown unto you spiritual things, is it a great matter if we shall reap your worldly things?—1 Cor. ix., 11.

Do ye not know, that they who minister about holy things live of the sacrifice; and they who wait at the altar are partakers with the altar? Even so hath the Lord also ordained, that they who preach the Gospel should live of the Gospel.—1 Cor. ix., 13, 14.

He that soweth little shall reap little; and he that soweth plenteously shall reap plenteously. Let every man do according as he is disposed in his heart, not grudgingly, or of necessity; for God loveth a cheerful giver.—2 Cor. ix., 6, 7.

Let him that is taught in the Word minister unto him that teacheth, in all good things. Be not deceived, God is not mocked: for whatsoever a man soweth that shall he reap.—Gal. vi., 6, 7.

While we have time, let us do good unto all men; and especially unto them that are of the household of faith.—Gal. vi., 10.

Godliness is great riches, if a man be content with that he hath: for we brought nothing into this world, neither may we carry any thing out.—1 Tim. vi., 6, 7.

Charge them who are rich in this world, that they be ready to give, and glad to distribute; laying up in store for themselves a good foundation against the time to come, that they may attain eternal life.—1 Tim. vi., 17, 18, 19.

God is not unrighteous, that he will forget your works, and labour that proceedeth of love; which love ye have showed for his Name's sake, who have ministered unto the saints, and yet do minister.—Heb. vi., 10.

To do good, and to distribute, forget not; for with such sacrifices God is well pleased.—Heb. xiii., 16.

Whoso hath this world's good, and seeth his brother have need, and shutteth up his compassion from him, how dwelleth the love of God in him?—1 St. John, iii., 17.

Give alms of thy goods, and never turn thy face from any poor man; and then the face of the Lord shall not be turned away from thee.—Tobit, iv., 7.

Be merciful after thy power. If thou hast much, give plenteously; if thou hast little, do thy diligence gladly to give of that little: for so gatherest thou thyself a good reward in the day of necessity.—Tobit, iv., 8, 9.

He that hath pity upon the poor lendeth unto the LORD: and look, what he layeth out, it shall be paid him again.—Prov. xix., 17.

Blessed be the man that provideth for the sick and needy: the LORD shall deliver him in the time of trouble. —Psalm xli., 1.

¶ *Whilst these Sentences are in reading, the Deacons, Church-wardens, or other fit persons appointed for that purpose, shall receive the Alms for the Poor, and other Devotions of the People, in a decent Basin to be provided by the Parish for that purpose; and reverently bring it to the Priest, who shall humbly present and place it upon the Holy Table.*

¶ *And the Priest shall then place upon the Table so much Bread and Wine as he shall think sufficient. After which done, he shall say,*

Let us pray for the whole state of Christ's Church militant.

ALMIGHTY and everliving God, who by thy holy Apostle hast taught us to make prayers, and supplications, and to give thanks, for all men; We humbly beseech thee most mercifully [* *to accept our alms and oblations, and*] to receive these our prayers, which we offer unto thy Divine Majesty; beseeching thee to inspire continually the Universal Church with the spirit of truth, unity, and concord: And grant that all those who do confess thy holy Name may agree in the truth of thy holy Word, and live in unity,

* *If there be no alms or oblations, then shall the words* [to accept our alms and oblations, and] *be left unsaid.*

and godly love. We beseech thee also, so to direct and dispose the hearts of all Christian Rulers, that they may truly and impartially administer justice, to the punishment of wickedness and vice, and to the maintenance of thy true religion, and virtue. Give grace, O heavenly Father, to all Bishops and other Ministers, that they may, both by their life and doctrine, set forth thy true and lively Word, and rightly and duly administer thy holy Sacraments. And to all thy people give thy heavenly grace; and especially to this congregation here present; that, with meek heart and due reverence, they may hear, and receive thy holy Word; truly serving thee in holiness and righteousness all the days of their life. And we most humbly beseech thee, of thy goodness, O Lord, to comfort and succour all those who, in this transitory life, are in trouble, sorrow, need, sickness, or any other adversity. And we also bless thy holy Name for all thy servants departed this life in thy faith and fear; beseeching thee to give us grace so to follow their good examples, that with them we may be partakers of thy heavenly kingdom. Grant this, O Father, for Jesus Christ's sake, our only Mediator and Advocate. *Amen.*

¶ *When the Minister giveth warning for the Celebration of the Holy Communion, (which he shall always do upon the Sunday, or some Holy Day, immediately preceding,) he shall read this Exhortation following; or so much thereof as, in his discretion, he may think convenient.*

DEARLY beloved, on ——day next I purpose, through God's assistance, to administer to all such as shall be religiously and devoutly disposed the most comfortable Sacrament of the Body and Blood of Christ; to be by them received in remembrance of his meritorious Cross and Passion; whereby alone we obtain remission of our sins, and are made partakers of the Kingdom of heaven. Wherefore it is our duty to render most humble and hearty thanks to Almighty God, our heavenly Father, for that he hath given his Son our Saviour Jesus Christ, not only to die for us, but also to be our spiritual food and sustenance in that holy Sacrament. Which being so divine and comfortable a thing to them who receive it worthily, and so dangerous to those who will presume to receive it unworthily; my duty is to exhort you, in the mean season, to consider the dignity of that holy mystery, and the great peril of the unworthy receiving thereof; and so to search and examine your own consciences, (and that not lightly, and after the manner of dissemblers with God; but so) that ye may come holy and clean to such a heavenly Feast, in the marriage-garment required by God in holy Scripture, and be received as worthy partakers of that holy Table.

The way and means thereto is; First, to examine your lives and conversations by the rule of God's commandments; and whereinsoever ye shall perceive yourselves to have offended, either by will, word, or deed, there to bewail your own sinfulness, and to confess yourselves to Almighty God, with full purpose of amendment of life. And if ye shall perceive your offences to be such as are not only against God, but also against your neighbours; then ye shall reconcile yourselves unto them; being ready to make restitution and satisfaction, according to the uttermost of your powers, for all injuries and wrongs done by you to any other; and being likewise ready to forgive others who have offended you, as ye would have forgiveness of your offences at God's hand: for otherwise the receiving of the holy Communion doth nothing else but increase your condemnation. Therefore, if any of you be a blasphemer of God, an hinderer or slanderer of his Word, an adulterer, or be in malice, or envy, or in any other grievous crime; repent ye of your sins, or else come not to that holy Table.

And because it is requisite that no man should come to the holy Communion, but with a full trust in God's mercy, and with a quiet conscience; therefore, if there be any of you, who by these means cannot quiet his own conscience herein, but requireth further comfort or counsel, let him come to me, or to some other Minister of God's Word, and open his grief; that he may receive such godly counsel and advice, as may tend to the quieting of his conscience, and the removing of all scruple and doubtfulness.

¶ *Or, in case he shall see the People negligent to come to the Holy Communion, instead of the former, he shall use this Exhortation.*

DEARLY beloved brethren, on ——— I intend, by God's grace, to celebrate the Lord's Supper: unto which, in God's behalf, I bid you all who are here present; and beseech you, for the Lord Jesus Christ's sake, that ye will not refuse to come thereto, being so lovingly called and bidden by God himself. Ye know how grievous and unkind a thing it is, when a man hath prepared a rich feast, decked his table with all kind of provision, so that there lacketh nothing but the guests to sit down; and yet they who are called (without any cause) most unthankfully refuse to come. Which of you in such a case would not be moved? Who would not think a great injury and wrong done unto him? Wherefore, most dearly beloved in Christ, take ye good heed, lest ye, withdrawing yourselves from this holy Supper, provoke God's indignation against you. It is an easy matter for a man to say, I will not communicate, because I am otherwise hindered with worldly business. But such excuses are not so easily accepted and allowed before God. If any man say, I am a grievous sinner, and therefore am afraid to come: wherefore then do ye not repent and amend? When God calleth you, are ye not ashamed to say ye will not come? When ye should return to God, will ye excuse yourselves, and say ye are not ready? Consider earnestly with yourselves how little such feigned excuses will avail before God. Those who refused the feast in the Gospel, because they had bought a farm, or would try their yokes of oxen, or because they were married, were not so excused, but counted unworthy of the heavenly feast. Wherefore, according to mine Office, I bid you in the Name of God, I call you in Christ's behalf, I exhort you, as ye love your own salvation, that ye will be partakers of this holy Communion. And as the Son of God did vouchsafe to yield up his soul by death upon the cross for your salvation; so it is your duty to receive the Communion in remembrance of the sacrifice of his death, as he himself hath commanded: which if ye shall neglect to do, consider with yourselves how great is your ingratitude to God, and how sore punishment hangeth over your heads for the same; when ye wilfully abstain from the Lord's Table, and separate from your brethren who come to feed on the banquet of that most heavenly food. These things if ye earnestly consider, ye will by God's grace return to a better mind: for the obtaining whereof we shall not cease to make our humble petitions unto Almighty God, our heavenly Father.

¶ *At the time of the Celebration of the Communion, the Priest shall say this Exhortation.*

DEARLY beloved in the Lord, ye who mind to come to the holy Communion of the Body and Blood of our Saviour Christ, must consider how Saint Paul exhorteth all persons diligently to try and examine themselves, before they presume to eat of that Bread, and drink of that Cup. For as the benefit is great, if with a true penitent heart and lively faith we receive that holy Sacrament; so is the danger great, if we receive the same unworthily. Judge therefore yourselves, brethren, that ye be not judged of the Lord; repent ye truly for your sins past; have a lively and steadfast faith in Christ our Saviour; amend your lives, and be in perfect charity with all men; so shall ye be meet partakers of those holy mysteries. And above all things ye must give most humble and hearty thanks to God, the Father, the Son, and the Holy Ghost, for the redemption of the world by the death and passion of our Saviour Christ, both God and man; who did humble himself, even to the death upon the Cross, for us, miserable sinners, who lay in darkness and the shadow of death ; that he might make us the children of God, and exalt us to everlasting life. And to the end that we should always remember the exceeding great love of our Master, and only Saviour, Jesus Christ, thus dying for us, and the innumerable benefits which by his precious blood-shedding he hath obtained for us; he hath instituted and ordained holy mysteries, as pledges of his love, and for a continual remembrance of his death, to our great and endless comfort. To him therefore, with the Father and the Holy Ghost, let us give (as we are most bounden) continual thanks; submitting ourselves wholly to his holy will and pleasure, and studying to serve him in true holiness and righteousness, all the days of our life. *Amen.*

¶ *Then shall the Priest say to those who come to receive the Holy Communion,*

YE who do truly and earnestly repent you of your sins, and are in love and charity with your neighbours, and intend to lead a new life, following the commandments of God, and walking from henceforth in his holy ways ; Draw near with faith, and take this holy Sacrament to your comfort ; and make your humble confession to Almighty God, devoutly kneeling.

THE MINISTRATION OF
BAPTISM TO SUCH AS ARE OF RIPER YEARS,
AND ARE ABLE TO ANSWER FOR THEMSELVES.

DEARLY beloved, forasmuch as all men are conceived and born in sin, (and that which is born of the flesh is flesh,) and they who are in the flesh cannot please God, but live in sin, committing many actual transgressions; and our Saviour Christ saith, None can enter into the kingdom of God, except he be regenerate and born anew of Water and of the Holy Ghost; I beseech you to call upon God the Father, through our Lord Jesus Christ, that of his bounteous goodness he will grant to *these Persons* that which by nature *they* cannot have; that *they* may be baptized with Water and the Holy Ghost, and received into Christ's holy Church, and be made lively *members* of the same.

¶ *Then shall the Minister say,*

Let us pray.

ALMIGHTY and everlasting God, who of thy great mercy didst save Noah and his family in the ark from perishing by water; and also didst safely lead the children of Israel thy people through the Red Sea, figuring thereby thy holy Baptism; and by the Baptism of thy well-beloved Son Jesus Christ, in the river Jordan, didst sanctify the element of Water to the mystical washing away of sin; We beseech thee, for thine infinite mercies, that thou wilt mercifully look upon *these* thy *Servants*; wash *them* and sanctify *them* with the Holy Ghost; that *they*, being delivered from thy wrath, may be received into the ark of Christ's Church; and being steadfast in faith, joyful through hope, and rooted in charity, may so pass the waves of this troublesome world, that finally *they* may come to the land of everlasting life, there to reign with thee, world without end; through Jesus Christ our Lord. *Amen.*

¶ *Or this.*

ALMIGHTY and immortal God, the aid of all who need, the helper of all who flee to thee for succour, the life of those who believe, and the resurrection of the dead; We call upon thee for *these Persons*, that *they*, coming to thy holy Baptism, may receive remission of *their* sins, by spiritual regeneration. Receive *them*, O Lord, as thou hast promised by thy well-beloved Son, saying, Ask, and ye shall receive; seek, and ye shall find; knock, and it shall be opened unto you. So give now unto us who ask; let us who seek, find; open the gate unto us who knock; that *these Persons* may enjoy the everlasting benediction of thy heavenly washing, and may come to the eternal kingdom which thou hast promised by Christ our Lord. *Amen.*

¶ *Then the Minister shall say,*

Hear the words of the Gospel, written by *St. John*, in the third Chapter, beginning at the first Verse.

THERE was a man of the Pharisees, named Nicodemus, a ruler of the Jews. The same came to Jesus by night, and said unto him, Rabbi, we know that thou art a teacher come from God; for no man can do these miracles that thou doest, except God be with him. Jesus answered and said unto him, Verily, verily, I say unto thee, Except a man be born again, he cannot see the kingdom of God. Nicodemus saith unto him, How can a man be born when

THE MINISTRATION OF BAPTISM. 343

he is old? can he enter the second time into his mother's womb, and be born? Jesus answered, Verily, verily, I say unto thee, Except a man be born of water and of the Spirit, he cannot enter into the kingdom of God. That which is born of the flesh is flesh; and that which is born of the Spirit is spirit. Marvel not that I said unto thee, Ye must be born again. The wind bloweth where it listeth, and thou hearest the sound thereof; but canst not tell whence it cometh, and whither it goeth: so is every one that is born of the Spirit.

¶ *After which he shall say this Exhortation following.*

BELOVED, ye hear in this Gospel the express words of our Saviour Christ, that except a man be born of Water and of the Spirit, he cannot enter into the kingdom of God. Whereby ye may perceive the great necessity of this Sacrament, where it may be had. Likewise, immediately before his ascension into heaven, (as we read in the last Chapter of Saint Mark's Gospel,) he gave command to his disciples, saying, Go ye into all the world, and preach the Gospel to every creature. He that believeth and is baptized shall be saved; but he that believeth not shall be damned. Which also showeth unto us the great benefit we reap thereby. For which cause Saint Peter the Apostle, when upon his first preaching of the Gospel many were pricked at the heart, and said to him and the rest of the Apostles, Men and brethren, what shall we do? replied and said unto them, Repent, and be baptized every one of you for the remission of sins, and ye shall receive the gift of the Holy Ghost. For the promise is to you and your children, and to all that are afar off, even as many as the Lord our God shall call. And with many other words exhorted he them, saying, Save yourselves from this untoward generation. For (as the same Apostle testifieth in another place) even Baptism doth also now save us, (not the putting away of the filth of the flesh, but the answer of a good conscience towards God,) by the resurrection of Jesus Christ. Doubt ye not therefore, but earnestly believe, that he will favourably receive *these* present *Persons*, truly repenting, and coming unto him by faith; that he will grant *them* remission of *their* sins, and bestow upon *them* the Holy Ghost; that he will give *them* the blessing of eternal life, and make *them partakers* of his everlasting kingdom.

Wherefore we being thus persuaded of the good will of our heavenly Father toward *these Persons*, declared by his Son Jesus Christ; let us faithfully and devoutly give thanks to him, and say,

ALMIGHTY and everlasting God, heavenly Father, we give thee humble thanks, for that thou hast vouchsafed to call us to the knowledge of thy grace, and faith in thee: Increase this knowledge, and confirm this faith in us evermore. Give thy Holy Spirit to *these Persons*, that *they* may be born again, and be made *heirs* of everlasting salvation; through our Lord Jesus Christ, who liveth and reigneth with thee and the Holy Spirit, now and for ever. Amen.

¶ *Then the Minister shall speak to the* Persons *to be baptized on this wise:*

WELL-BELOVED, who are come hither desiring to receive holy Baptism, *ye* have heard how the congregation hath prayed, that our Lord Jesus Christ would vouchsafe to receive and bless you, to release you of your sins, to give you the kingdom of heaven, and everlasting life. *Ye* have heard also, that our Lord Jesus Christ hath promised in his holy Word to grant all those things that we have prayed for; which promise he, for his part, will most surely keep and perform.

Wherefore, after this promise made by Christ, *ye* must also faithfully, for your part, in the presence of these your Witnesses, and this whole congregation, promise and answer to the following Questions.

¶ *The Minister shall then demand of the* Persons *to be baptized as follows; the Questions being considered as addressed to them severally, and the answers to be made accordingly.*

Question.

Dost thou renounce the devil and all his works, the vain pomp and glory of the world, with all covetous desires of the same, and the sinful desires of the flesh, so that thou wilt not follow, nor be led by them ?

Answer. I renounce them all ; and, by God's help, will endeavour not to follow, nor be led by them.

Question. Dost thou believe all the Articles of the Christian Faith, as contained in the Apostles' Creed ?

Answer. I do.

Question. Wilt thou be baptized in this Faith ?

Answer. That is my desire.

Question. Wilt thou then obediently keep God's holy will and commandments, and walk in the same all the days of thy life ?

Answer. I will, by God's help.

¶ *Then shall the Minister say,*

O merciful God, grant that the old Adam in *these Persons* may be so buried, that the new man may be raised up in *them.* *Amen.*

Grant that all sinful affections may die in *them*, and that all things belonging to the Spirit may live and grow in *them.* *Amen.*

Grant that *they* may have power and strength to have victory, and to triumph against the devil, the world, and the flesh. *Amen.*

Grant that *they*, being here dedicated to thee by our office and ministry, may also be endued with heavenly virtues, and everlastingly rewarded, through thy mercy, O blessed Lord God, who dost live, and govern all things, world without end. *Amen.*

ALMIGHTY, everliving God, whose most dearly beloved Son Jesus Christ, for the forgiveness of our sins, did shed out of his most precious side both water and blood; and gave commandment to his disciples, that they should go teach all nations, and baptize them In the Name of the Father, and of the Son, and of the Holy Ghost; Regard, we beseech thee, the supplications of thy congregation; sanctify this Water to the mystical washing away of sin; and grant that the *Persons* now to be baptized therein, may receive the fulness of thy grace, and ever remain in the number of thy faithful children; through Jesus Christ our Lord. *Amen.*

¶ *Then shall the Minister take each Person to be baptized by the right hand; and placing him conveniently by the Font, according to his discretion, shall ask the Godfathers and Godmothers the Name; and then shall dip him in the water, or pour water upon him, saying,*

N. I BAPTIZE thee In the Name of the Father, and of the Son, and of the Holy Ghost. Amen.

¶ *Then shall the Minister say,*

WE receive this Person into the congregation of Christ's flock; and do* sign *him* with the sign of the Cross, in token that hereafter *he* shall not be ashamed to confess the faith of Christ crucified, and manfully to fight under his banner, against sin, the world, and the devil; and to continue Christ's faithful soldier and servant unto *his* life's end. Amen.

* *Here the Minister shall make a Cross upon the Person's forehead.*

¶ *The same Rule, as to the Omission of the sign of the Cross, is to be observed here as in the Baptism of Infants.*

¶ *Then shall the Minister say,*

SEEING now, dearly beloved brethren, that *these Persons are* regenerate, and grafted into the body of Christ's Church, let us give thanks unto Almighty God for these benefits; and with one accord make our prayers unto him, that *they* may lead the rest of *their* life according to this beginning.

THE MINISTRATION OF BAPTISM. 347

¶ *Then shall be said the Lord's Prayer, all kneeling.*

OUR Father, who art in heaven, Hallowed be thy Name. Thy kingdom come. Thy will be done on earth, As it is in heaven. Give us this day our daily bread; And forgive us our trespasses, As we forgive those that trespass against us. And lead us not into temptation; But deliver us from evil. Amen.

WE yield thee humble thanks, O heavenly Father, that thou hast vouchsafed to call us to the knowledge of thy grace, and faith in thee: Increase this knowledge, and confirm this faith in us evermore. Give thy Holy Spirit to *these Persons;* that, being now born again, and made *heirs* of everlasting salvation, through our Lord Jesus Christ, *they* may continue thy *Servants,* and attain thy promises; through the same Lord Jesus Christ thy Son, who liveth and reigneth with thee, in the unity of the same Holy Spirit, everlastingly. *Amen.*

¶ *Then, all standing up, the Minister shall use this Exhortation following; speaking to the Godfathers and Godmothers first.*

FORASMUCH as *these Persons have* promised, in your presence, to renounce the devil and all his works, to believe in God, and to serve him; ye must remember, that it is your part and duty to put *them* in mind, what a solemn vow, promise, and profession *they have* now made before this congregation, and especially before you *their* chosen witnesses. And ye are also to call upon *them* to use all diligence to be rightly instructed in God's holy Word; that so *they* may grow in grace, and in the knowledge of our Lord Jesus Christ, and live godly, righteously, and soberly, in this present world.

¶ *And then, speaking to the baptized Persons, he shall proceed and say,*

AND as for you, who have now by Baptism put on Christ, it is your part and duty also, being made the *children* of God and of the light, by faith in Jesus Christ, to walk answerably to your Christian calling, and as becometh the children of light; remembering always that Baptism representeth unto us our profession; which is, to follow the example of our Saviour Christ, and to be made like unto him; that as he died, and rose again for us, so should we, who are baptized, die from sin, and rise again unto righteousness; continually mortifying all our evil and corrupt affections, and daily proceeding in all virtue and godliness of living.

THE END.

www.ingramcontent.com/pod-product-compliance
Lightning Source LLC
Chambersburg PA
CBHW031432230426
43668CB00007B/509